Your Favorite Band
Is Killing Me

Your Favorite Band Is Killing Me

WHAT POP MUSIC RIVALRIES REVEAL
ABOUT THE MEANING OF LIFE

STEVEN HYDEN

BACK BAY BOOKS
Little, Brown and Company
New York Boston London

Back Bay Books / Little, Brown and Company
Hachette Book Group
1290 Avenue of the Americas, New York, NY 10104
littlebrown.com

First Back Bay paperback edition, May 2016

Back Bay Books is an imprint of Little, Brown and Company, a division of Hachette Book Group, Inc. The Back Bay Books name and logo are trademarks of Hachette Book Group, Inc.

The publisher is not responsible for websites (or their content) that are not owned by the publisher.

The Hachette Speakers Bureau provides a wide range of authors for speaking events. To find out more, go to hachettespeakersbureau.com or call (866) 376-6591.

"Don't Believe the Truth" and "The Pope > Robin Thicke" include material from articles that originally ran in *Grantland*. "Bruce Dreams" includes material from an article that originally ran in the *A.V. Club*.

ISBN 978-0-316-25915-6
LCCN 2015952965

10 9 8 7 6 5 4 3 2 1

RRD-C

Book designed by Marie Mundaca

Printed in the United States of America

To Val and Hen

The general fact is that the most effective way of utilizing human energy is through an organized rivalry, which by specialization and social control is, at the same time, organized cooperation.

—Charles Horton Cooley, *Human Nature and the Social Order*, 1902

However unreal it may seem, we are connected, you and I, we are on the same curve…just on opposite ends.

—Supervillain Elijah Price (Samuel L. Jackson) to superhero David Dunn (Bruce Willis) in M. Night Shyamalan's *Unbreakable*, 2000

Well, I hate you with a passion, baby, yeah, you know I do (but call me).

—Monks, "I Hate You," 1966

CONTENTS

CONTENTS

Your Favorite Band Is Killing Me

Preface

WHO YA GOT?

Beatles or Stones? Biggie or Tupac? Prince or Michael Jackson? Pearl Jam or Nirvana? Who ya got and why? More important: What does your choice say about you? Enough about you—what do these endlessly argued-about pop-music rivalries say about *us*?

The media has long stood accused of creating conflict where it didn't previously exist purely for the sake of manufacturing melodrama. This is undoubtedly true, and I angrily denounce any soulless moron who says otherwise. (See what I just did there?) But what about the battles that music fans create on their own? I'm talking about the arguments that take place every day in bars, at parties, and during endless road trips when the radio is broken and the opinions are turned way up.

Some of these debates never seem to die. Was Lynyrd Skynyrd right to go after Neil Young in "Sweet Home Alabama"? Was Kanye West justified in crashing Taylor Swift's speech at the 2009 MTV Video Music Awards? Was Jimi Hendrix a better guitar player than Eric Clapton? Is Toby Keith a better American than the Dixie Chicks? Who would've won a boxing match between Axl Rose and Vince Neil?

Music is not like sports—artists don't have to "defeat" each other in order to gain supremacy. And yet over the course of the sixty or so years that constitute the modern pop era, we as audience members have consistently pitted vaguely similar (though also discernibly *not* similar) artists against each other in order to determine who's best.

I'm not interested in settling these arguments—because I don't think they can be settled and because that wouldn't be any fun. What I am interested in is exploring why music fans are drawn to these dichotomies, how the dynamics of our most heated musical rivalries stem from larger conversations in the culture (then and now), and what we can learn about ourselves by whom we side with.

Also, I want to understand how in the hell anybody could've thought that Mötley Crüe was better than Guns N' Roses. (It can't all be blamed on the blizzard of cocaine blowing through '80s Hollywood.)

Let's be real: musical rivalries are never totally about music. They're about sympathizing with a particular worldview represented by an artist over a different worldview represented by an "opposing" artist. You are what you love—and also what you choose not to love. If you pick Hendrix over Clapton, you probably believe that the "burnout" option for rock stars is ultimately more honorable than the "fade away" option. (Or maybe you prefer LSD to Michelob.) If you like Pavement more than the Smashing Pumpkins, you likely find corporate-fueled '90s "alternative" rock to be highly ridiculous. (Or maybe you prefer California to the Midwest.) If you side with Christina (sorry: Xtina) Aguilera over Britney Spears, you may feel that young girls should emulate a seminaked woman who can sing like Etta James over a seminaked woman who can sing like an oversexed ATM. (Or maybe you're prejudiced against cyborgs.)

This might sound like harmless stuff, but our musical shoot-outs frequently turn into full-on civil wars. (If you don't believe me, see what happens when you play Metallica's "Black Album" for a room full of borderline psychopaths waiting for Megadeth to come onstage.) Musical rivalries don't matter until they matter to you personally. When that happens, it's as vital as protecting your own sense of identity.

It's been said that history is the study of wars and elections—the geography of human dissension, in other words. I think it's time that this paradigm is applied to pop-music history. So pick a side, pump up the volume, and let's dive in.

CHAPTER 1
Don't Believe the Truth

(Oasis vs. Blur)

AROUND THE TIME I started writing this book, I conducted a radical musical experiment: I listened to a Damon Albarn album from front to back.

I realize this won't seem radical to most people. But trust me: in personal terms, it was nothing less than glasnost. For more than twenty years, I consciously avoided the group that Albarn is most famous for, Blur. I also abstained from another high-profile Albarn project, the so-called virtual band Gorillaz. I definitely did not give *another* Albarn side project—the Good, the Bad & the Queen—the time of day, and I suspected that Albarn launched a fourth group, Rocket Juice & the Moon, with Flea from the Red Hot Chili Peppers just to troll me. Sweet Jesus—Damon Albarn and Flea on the same record? Was Anthony Kiedis busy waxing his chest that day?

Avoiding all that music wasn't easy. How many bands was this guy going to force me to hate? I had to admire Albarn's eclecticism, even as I found all the extra spite it produced exhausting.

My resolve to block Damon Albarn out of my life occasionally weakened but never broke. When Albarn wrote the opera *Dr Dee* in 2011, or when he collaborated with Malian musicians in 2013 and released those sessions on the *Maison des Jeunes* LP, I was secretly intrigued but publicly rolled my eyes. Finally, for *Everyday Robots*—Albarn's first official solo album, released in 2014—I demanded change inside my own heart. I roared self-inflicted self-righteousness into the mirror. "Tear down this imaginary Albarn-deflecting wall!" I declared.

Now, you're probably wondering why I put so much effort into loathing an artist who is probably one of the most accomplished rock musicians of his generation. The reasoning behind my Albarn boycott is predictable and admittedly sort of dumb: Oasis was my favorite Britpop band in high school. And back then, hating Blur, Oasis's biggest rival, was a requirement for "true" Oasis fans. This perception was due in large part to Oasis's primary songwriter and guitarist, Noel Gallagher, who once publicly declared his wish that Albarn and his Blur bandmate Alex James catch AIDS and die. (Incredibly, I chose to hate the person who *didn't* say that.) So I've loathed Damon Albarn for all this time because I've stubbornly refused to relinquish an opinion I formed when I was seventeen.

What was interesting about Oasis vs. Blur (if you were an American rock fan in the mid-'90s) is that the rivalry absolutely did not translate in the States. Oasis was way more famous in America—"Wonderwall" was a genuine stateside alterna-era hit and remains a rock radio standard. If the average American knows Blur at all, it's for the sports-stadium anthem "Song 2," or, as we Yankees refer to it, "the woo-hoo song." In Britain, however, it was different. Over there, Blur was more popular, at least for a while.

The animus between the bands originally started in August of 1995 because Blur decided to bump up the release of its single "Country House" to coincide with the release of Oasis's single "Roll with It." This was a direct challenge by a big shot to an upstart: Blur was the biggest band in England at the time, but Oasis was on the rise. It set up a highly publicized, head-to-head war for the top of the British pop charts, which Blur won in the short term ("Country House" outsold "Roll with It" by fifty thousand units) but Oasis crushed in the long run (by the following summer, Oasis had played two consecutive nights at Knebworth for more than three hundred thousand people).

As an American, deciding to care about this was akin to suddenly getting really worked up about the minutiae of local government bureaucracy in Kingston upon Hull. Personal relevance had to be constructed. So that's what I did: I transformed Oasis vs. Blur into a vast cathedral of made-up meaning.

Loving Oasis and hating Blur was a way for me to work out my aesthetic preferences at a formative age. In my mind, Oasis was associated with words such as *rock, intoxicated, testicles,* and *cool,* whereas Blur was *pop, academic, elitist, narrow,* and *clever.* Again, I'm not defending these reductive descriptions but rather asking how musical biases become ingrained at any early age and over time become "truth." What mattered to me is that I perceived these bands as having a binary relationship that had great symbolic meaning to me (and likely to other people who cared about this tête-à-tête). I was using these bands to help me figure out who I was and what I stood for (and also who I wasn't and what I didn't stand for). To this day, whenever I hear a Blur fan talk about why Blur is great, I understand it only as a critique of Oasis and, by extension, a particular way of looking at the world. It's like when a cat person tries to explain why cats are superior pets—in some way, it's really about why dogs are inferior. And sorry, but I can't hear that, *because dogs are and always will be better*. Yes, Blur is cleaner and doesn't drink out of the toilet. But I'll always have a weakness for shaggy, sloppy, and lovably aggressive creatures who craft spectacular songs about smoking cigarettes and living forever.

I tend to do this with pop rivalries. It's just how my brain works. I have pop-rivalry OCD—every Oasis I see must be paired with a Blur or else I claw my face off.

Over time, I took my pro-Oasis/anti-Blur stance to its logical extreme by not even listening to the music I'd dedicated my life to despising and, paradoxically, I allowed this know-nothingness to form the basis of my opinion of that (unheard) music. When Blur's catalog was reissued in 2012 and music critics lined up to declare the greatness of records such as *The Great Escape* and *Parklife*, I was intensely annoyed that albums I had never played in their entirety were being so grossly overrated. Not that I actually *read* those reviews, mind you, as this would have also violated my draconian anti-Albarn ordinance. But I could only imagine what those writers were probably saying.

Those albums must be terrible, I thought. Because Oasis's 1994 debut, *Definitely Maybe*, is on my personal top five greatest albums of all time list and my love of that record requires believing that anything related to Blur unequivocally sucks. My logic makes as much sense as the lyrics to Oasis's "Shakermaker" ("I've been driving in my car / With my friend Mr. Soft / Mr. Clean and Mr. Ben / Are living in my loft"), but it speaks to me with equal clarity and persuasiveness.

This is where I need to state explicitly that, intellectually speaking, I know I'm being unreasonable. I'll go even further and acknowledge my indefensible lunacy.

Enough is enough, I decided. Even if after sampling *Everyday Robots* I still found that Albarn wasn't my thing, surely informed indifference is better than benign neglect. Right?

In 1902, a sociologist named Charles Horton Cooley devised a concept called the looking-glass self, which posits that a person's sense of identity is shaped by interaction with social groups and the ways in which the individual thinks he or she is perceived by others. Cooley believed this process involved three steps:

• You imagine how you appear to other people.
• You imagine the judgment of other people.
• You base your feelings about yourself on how you think you appear to other people.

This might seem intuitive in the twenty-first century, but at the time it broke people's brains. Cooley's theory challenged the idea that the self is innate, arguing instead that we are who we think other people think we are. Cooley separated those "other people" into primary and secondary social groups. The primary group is composed of people with whom you are intimately involved, including your immediate family and close friends. This is the most important group in terms of influencing the person you are and will become. The secondary group is broader, and, unlike the primary group, it's something you belong to on a voluntary and often transient basis. Secondary groups might include people at your school or your place of work.

Cooley's book predates the emergence of modern pop music as a cultural phenomenon. Unless Mr. Cooley comes back from the grave to inform me otherwise, I'm going to suggest that Oasis fans and Blur fans (and punks and metalheads and Deadheads and Parrotheads and Juggalos) are examples of secondary groups.

Rivalries certainly occur among primary groups, such as the nineteenth-century blood feud between the Hatfields and McCoys and the seemingly endless battle for the White House between the Bush and Clinton dynasties. (Rivalries are also common within families, but that's a topic for another book, or perhaps for therapy.) But more often rivalries are seen among secondary groups—the participants have chosen to identify with an institution or group, and in some way they are measuring themselves against an alternative that represents an opposing viewpoint.

In terms of national identity, this goes back at least as far as Athens (enlightened democracy) vs. Sparta (militaristic fascism), though it likely began the moment one group of prehistoric ape-men splintered off from the main group of prehistoric ape-men in order to secure superior cave lodging.

For Americans, the sexiest geopolitical rivalry was the twentieth-century battle between the United States and the USSR, which inspired a series of lousy but watchable Sylvester Stallone films in the '80s and a few truly terrifying TV movies about nuclear apocalypse (such as 1983's *The Day After*, which was viewed by more than one hundred million people—it's still the highest-rated TV movie ever). But the most lasting rivalry between American landmasses is the one between the northern United States (really the northeastern United States) and the southern United States (really Texas, Alabama, Georgia, Mississippi, South Carolina, all of Louisiana except New Orleans, and the whitest, most strip-mally regions of Florida). Although the North and South fought a war 150 years ago in order to determine which region's values were going to wind up guiding this nation forward, North vs. South has subsequently played out largely in our elections and pop culture. Just as it seems that this country will never elect a president who doesn't pay lip service to protecting the sanctity of church on Sunday and guns in every suburban home, we will likely never reach a point where media isn't consolidated in Manhattan and Los Angeles and run by intensely myopic people who won't stop producing programs about annoying twentysomethings trying to make it in Manhattan and Los Angeles.

The conversation around sports routinely (some might say excessively) involves investing rivalries between athletes and teams with a cultural significance that goes beyond wins and losses. Sometimes this significance is indisputable. Jesse Owens traveling to Berlin in 1936 and winning four gold medals as Adolf Hitler looked on was not only the ultimate "in your face" moment against the most detestable opponent imaginable, it also resoundingly disproved the myth of white supremacy. A matchup between Loyola University Chicago and Mississippi State in the second round of the 1963 NCAA college basketball tournament was later dubbed the Game of Change because Loyola won with a lineup that included four black starters, which was instrumental in desegregating the sport. In the early '70s, the historic first boxing match between Muhammad Ali and Joe Frazier was widely viewed as a battle between liberal and conservative ideologies. The antiwar side cheered for Ali, and supporters of US involvement in Vietnam backed Frazier. It didn't matter that Frazier was apolitical—Ali's detractors turned Frazier into a right-wing hero because he was the guy who was supposed to dismantle Ali's face on their behalf.

Most sports rivalries are regional and therefore don't bear that kind of political weight, but in their own way they matter just as much because they fester for decades and get passed down from generation to generation. When I first started caring about sports, in the '80s, the preeminent rivalry was Lakers vs. Celtics, which was practically a national rivalry because the teams are separated by a whole country. I loved the Lakers—I was in grade school, and grade-schoolers like bright, shiny things that move very fast.

Growing up in Wisconsin, I also cared about the Green Bay Packers vs. the Chicago Bears, the NFL's oldest rivalry. As I write this, the Bears somehow hold a narrow edge in victories over the Packers, despite the Packers' general dominance over the Bears for the past few decades. The matchup has been so lopsided during my lifetime that I barely dislike the Bears now—they are rarely good at the same time that the Packers are good. (The Minnesota Vikings have generally been the strongest, most hateable foe in the NFC North, especially during the Dennis Green era, in the '90s.)

But Packers vs. Bears will always be the most significant rivalry for Wisconsinites because no matter how ineffectual the Bears are, our loathing of Chicagoans will remain undiluted. In Wisconsin we call them FIBs—short for "fucking Illinois bastards"—and they are distinguished by their pushiness on our roadways and overall unpleasantness in our stores and gas stations as they venture up north to wash off their Chicago grime in our beautiful lakes. The only way to get revenge on these rude visitors is by proxy. We can't physically assault the FIBs, because we've been bred to be passive middle-American folk. But the Packers can demolish the Bears at Lambeau Field every year.

Please note that I'm not talking about any actual, real-life citizens of Chicago here. I know numerous residents of the Windy City, and they're all kind, lovely people. I would be disturbed and outraged if any of them suffered a beatdown, and I don't know any of them to be grimy. I am referring to Chicagoans strictly in terms of an archetype that exists in tandem with my regional identity as a native upper midwesterner. Hating the Bears keeps me from becoming spiritually unmoored. It forms the very fabric of who I am.

The subtext of the Packers vs. Bears rivalry is that one of this country's great metropolitan areas is frequently humiliated on national television by a community that has one twenty-sixth of its population. It's the same dynamic as North vs. South—it's city vs. country, powerful vs. marginalized, "normal" fat people vs. the morbidly obese. I ride with the morbidly obese until the end of time.

The difference between rivalries in sports and rivalries in music is that there are no winners in music. Not that people haven't tried to determine winners—sales charts and awards shows and rock-critic polls exist to "prove" such things. In hip-hop, the battle has long been a vital tradition distinguishing the true MC from a field of suckers. But even the most hardcore MC battle is essentially a figure-skating competition—it's never decided primarily by the players themselves. An outside judge or the audience must decide who is best.

When Loyola beat Mississippi State with a mostly black lineup, even the most ardent redneck could see the fallacy of suggesting that black players shouldn't be allowed on the same court as white players. But there is no arena in which Oasis definitively "defeated" Blur or vice versa. Music rivalries are almost all projection, and what's being projected are our own desires, hopes, ideologies, and shortcomings. Sports have guided our society toward answers to questions we couldn't or wouldn't address elsewhere; music and art put us on a more personal journey, allowing us to work through issues that can only be resolved in our own hearts.

If I had to pinpoint the moment when I went from being an Oasis fan to absorbing the band into my psyche, it was probably when I saw the cover of 1994's "Cigarettes and Alcohol" single. My favorite part of following Oasis in high school was tracking down imports, which would arrive at my local store every couple of months. I had to be patient and occasionally pay exorbitant prices, but my loyalty was always rewarded. Between 1994 and '96, Oasis turned out a steady stream of nonalbum tracks that were often better than what ended up on the records. If you liked Oasis as much as I did, you probably spent a similar amount of time ranking your personal favorites. (The number one Oasis B side has to be "Acquiesce," though if I wrote this on a different day I might say "Fade Away.")

People who only knew the Oasis songs that were played on MTV were missing something important. Not only was the music on those singles phenomenal, but the iconography was indelible. With the possible exception of the image of Marc Bolan blasting out a glammed-up Chuck Berry riff on the cover of T. Rex's *Electric Warrior*, nothing comes close to personifying what I love about music better than the sleeve of "Cigarettes and Alcohol." We see Noel and Liam Gallagher slugging Champagne and smoking cigarettes on a bed flanked by two beautiful women in a resplendent London hotel room. Are they about to have sex? Are they already too wasted to have sex? As a kid who had never been wasted or had sex, I had no idea. But I stared at that cover endlessly and fantasized about the possibilities.

DON'T BELIEVE THE TRUTH

Oasis came into my life just a few months after my heart was broken by Kurt Cobain's suicide. I was being raised on bands that looked upon rock stardom as a burden and pleasure as an empty alternative to the reality of pain. Oasis had a different idea. They were reveling in the glory of rock-and-roll stupidity. They were making a persuasive case for life. I wanted that, and Oasis made me think it could be mine. What Oasis promised was self-actualization. When Liam Gallagher sang, "Tonight I'm a rock-and-roll star," he subsequently became an actual rock-and-roll star. How could I not hang on Oasis's every word after that?

I didn't have to listen to Blur or read Blur's record reviews, because any defense of Blur was already countered perfectly by Noel Gallagher, one of the best interview subjects in rock history. Two hundred years from now, high school students will study Noel Gallagher interviews for their rhetorical brilliance the way kids today look at the Lincoln-Douglas debates from the 1850s. Noel is, was, and always will be my guy, and I've trusted in him to show me the way.

Based on the Noel Gallagher interviews I've read or watched on video, people who prefer Blur to Oasis feel that way for two reasons:

(1) BLUR MADE MORE GOOD ALBUMS THAN OASIS DID

Again, I'm in no position to judge the quality of Blur's discography, but I suspect this is correct. Blur seems like the more consistent band. I just don't think it matters.

Whenever Noel Gallagher talks about Oasis albums, he always sets the first two LPs, *Definitely Maybe* and *(What's the Story)*

Morning Glory, apart from the other records as obvious high-lights. (Oasis famously went off the rails with its coke- and hubris-fueled third album, *Be Here Now*, which is remembered as "the Aristocrats" joke of '90s rock—it's really long, it's really tedious, and the payoff is underwhelming.) Gallagher never pretends that whatever he's currently promoting will ever touch "Live Forever" or "Champagne Supernova." And he seems perfectly comfortable in his own skin when he does this. Gallagher knows Oasis had its moment, and nobody can take it away from him.

Damon Albarn, on the other hand, seems like a guy who's deeply invested in his own continued relevance. He is constantly seeking out new collaborators and attempting new music styles. Albarn probably believes that whatever record he's presently making will be his best. Gallagher, meanwhile, reminds me of an observation that rock critic Greil Marcus once made about Rod Stewart: "If it was necessary to become a great artist in order to get the money to spend and the star to fuck, well, Rod was willing." Noel was willing, too. Once he achieved success, he didn't seem especially motivated to keep on achieving it. He was content to lounge comfortably on his laurels.

I suppose that this attitude should diminish Gallagher (and that Albarn's contrary point of view should make him the superior artist). But to me Gallagher's approach is weirdly refreshing, because it seems more honest about the motivations and abilities of artists of his age and stature. Gallagher believes that the first two Oasis records (and the accompanying singles) are his true legacy, and he is absolutely right. Anything that came after is beside the point.

Let's say Oasis and Blur traded discographies. Instead of peaking early with two enormous triumphs, then following up with a series of inconsistent LPs that even many Oasis fans dismiss as recycled versions of the band's glory years, Oasis had a more varied, adventurous, and altogether stronger overall body of work than that of Blur. Is there any part of Noel Gallagher's brain that would be happy with that swap? I *know* he wouldn't be happy, because he's talked about this very subject.

"At the end of the cycle of *Morning Glory*, I was hailed as the greatest songwriter since Lennon and McCartney," Gallagher told *Grantland*'s Chuck Klosterman in 2011. (I don't think anyone ever actually said, "Noel Gallagher is the greatest songwriter since Lennon and McCartney." But let's just assume somebody did for argument's sake.) "Let's say my career had gone backwards. Let's say this new solo album had been my debut, and it was my *last two* records that sold twenty million copies instead of the first two records. Had this been the case, all the other albums leading up to those last two would be considered a fucking journey. They would be perceived as albums that represent the road to greatness. But just because it started off great doesn't make those other albums any less of a journey. I'll use an American football analogy, since we're in America: let's say you're behind with two minutes to go and you come back to tie the game. It almost feels like you've won. Right? But let's say you've been ahead the whole game and you allow the opponent to tie things up in the final two minutes. Then it feels like you've lost. But the fact of the matter is it's still a fucking tie. The only difference is perception. And the fact of the matter is that Oasis sold fifty-five million records. If people think we were never good after the nineties, that's irrelevant."

I'm not sure I totally buy Gallagher's argument here. He seems to believe that the journey *toward* greatness is no different from the journey *away* from greatness. Regardless: when

Oasis was great, it was the best. It doesn't matter where on Oasis's career arc that greatness occurred—it still far outstrips the accomplishments of the competition. So, you know, fuck Blur.

(2) BLUR IS SMARTER THAN OASIS

Again, no dispute from the pro-Oasis camp on the question of the bands' relative intelligence. In fact, Oasis's supposed lack of smarts arguably worked in its favor. Oasis was perceived in Britain as the working-class alternative to Blur's brainier, more collegiate brand of indie music. Even in America, where anyone with a British accent is instantly viewed as a snooty fussbudget magically transported from the nineteenth century, Oasis's music translated better because it never bothered with the pointed, Kinks-inspired satire that Blur's did. In the mid-'90s, Albarn presented himself as a critic of American corporate imperialism encroaching upon European culture, which was obviously not going to translate terribly well in the States. Gallagher's songwriting MO, by contrast, had nothing to do with raising his audience's consciousness and sense of British nationalism. He just wrote anthems that prompted throngs of drunken people to raise their pints.

Was the dichotomy between "Blur is the uptight university band" and "Oasis is the blue-collar hero band" unfairly reductive? Sure. Even Noel Gallagher acknowledged as much. In the 2003 Britpop documentary *Live Forever*, Gallagher talks about Blur while seated in a high-backed chair that looks like a fucking throne, for crying out loud.

"They've never been on a building site. Which is not to say the dirt under your fingernails is a badge of honor—it's not.

It's just a fact," Gallagher says in the film, then with a sardonic glimmer he adds: "I worked on building sites. That fundamentally makes my soul more pure than theirs."

Gallagher lets the audience know that he's not being totally serious, but he's not totally joking, either. If Gallagher was self-aware enough to playfully undermine his own band's hardscrabble image, he really relished taking the piss out of his rival's pretensions. Whether Oasis was the more "authentic" band because it had a broader appeal is a tired question probably not worth asking. But Oasis was unquestionably taken less seriously than Blur by rock critics, then and now, which allowed Gallagher to bludgeon Albarn with all the intellectual baggage that music writers affixed to Blur's music.

"If you've got the time to worry about American culture creeping into British society, then I would get a proper fucking job," Gallagher says in one of the DVD extras for *Live Forever*. "Other people are too busy trying to make a living. Such a condescending cock—*I wrote this album so I could stop American culture coming to Britain*. Fucking wanker. What does he know about British culture? He's a fookin' student."

Blur might be smarter than Oasis, but Oasis is definitely wiser than Blur.

Nobody wins a music rivalry, but the primary actors can decide to grow up and call a truce. That's what happened by the early '10s—Oasis vs. Blur, one of the longest and most entertaining rivalries in rock history, petered out. Noel was telling fans via his interviews to forgive Damon Albarn. I was beside myself. It was as if my Packers decided to shut down Lambeau.

"Funnily enough, when I was out last night, I bumped into him," Gallagher told *ShortList* magazine in 2011. "I literally haven't seen the guy for fifteen fucking years and I bump into him in some club. We both went, 'Hey! Fucking hell!' and then he said, 'Come on, let's go for a beer.' So we're sitting there, having a beer, just going, 'What the fuck was all that about fifteen years ago? That was mental.' Then he said, 'It was a great time, though,' and I was like, 'Yeah, it was a fucking good laugh.' It was cool, man."

Just like that, a man whom Noel Gallagher once publicly wished would catch AIDS and die was now a-okay in his book. All the mental energy I had put into making that rivalry meaningful in my mind was being chalked up as "mental." It was time to start over.

So I listened to *Everyday Robots*. More than once, even. And I liked it. It's like one of those Beck albums on which Beck decides to be a sad bastard (except smarter) or Thom Yorke's *The Eraser* (except not as frigid). It reminds me of Bobby Womack's fine 2012 comeback record, *The Bravest Man in the Universe*, which Albarn oversaw. (My ban did not extend to Albarn-produced records by musical geniuses.) All the songs on *Robots* are similarly constructed, with spare piano chords or delicate guitar picking set against an austere tapestry of synths, samples, and contemplative, purposeful beats. It is casually cosmopolitan music. At this point, Albarn can apply African and Caribbean accents to his own distinctively British sensibility without a trace of strain. He makes highly conceptual records that feel natural, always an impressive maneuver.

While occasionally playful (see, for example, "Mr. Tembo," which is supposedly about a baby elephant, because that's what you write about if you survive your "writing songs about heroin" period), *Everyday Robots* is mostly a "mortality" record—a record on which all the songs are about aging and death and the singer tries to sound like he's ninety years old. (Rick Rubin invented it when he hooked up with Johnny Cash.) This is the only kind of record that an aging but still engaged artist such as Albarn is seemingly allowed to make anymore, and Albarn works hard to make the most of it. It's often hard to tell exactly what the songs are about, given the vagueness of the lyrics. (In spite of his reputation for social commentary, Albarn appears to be no more of a wordsmith than Gallagher—but again, my experience is limited.) When he softly coos, "Some days I look at the morning, trying to work out how I got here" in "You and Me," it's not immediately apparent what specifically he's working out. (My best guess: "Why did I make a record with Flea? And why did Thom Yorke also make a record with Flea? Is Flea a fucking hypnotist?") But it's pretty obvious what Albarn's vocals and the restrained, tastefully assembled, endlessly downbeat music are communicating: the '90s were a *loooong* time ago. And now my audience and I are very, very old.

Everyday Robots is inherently nostalgic, yet it seems forward-thinking. This is a clear victory for Albarn, who gets called a sonic explorer by the *New York Times* while making a middle-of-the-road record that will alienate exactly no one. (Sorry: that's the strident anti-Blur fundamentalist in me talking.) I guess it's a victory for me, too. I'm done depriving myself of Albarn's intelligent and engaging musical and cultural synthesis, and this is good if also slightly hollow. His music is more amenable and less important to me now. My hate has been replaced by dutiful dispassion. I've traded made-up meaning for boring old grudging respect.

Clearly it's time for me to rethink my feelings about other pop rivalries.

CHAPTER 2

Bruce Dreams

(Nirvana vs. Pearl Jam)

THE FIRST MUSIC rivalry I ever cared about as it unfolded in real time was Nirvana vs. Pearl Jam. Oasis vs. Blur was a mid-'90s thing, whereas Nirvana vs. Pearl Jam was strictly early '90s. This might seem like a minor difference, but two or three years is a lifetime when you're a kid, especially if we're talking about the time between ages fourteen and seventeen, the "Vietnam" era of adolescence.

Considering that I was a painfully serious middle schooler when Nirvana vs. Pearl Jam was at its height, my position was entirely predictable: I loved Nirvana, and I hated Pearl Jam. Nirvana's 1991 major-label debut, *Nevermind*, was, in my mind, the pinnacle of "honest" and "authentic" music, while Pearl Jam's Epic Records–distributed first LP, also released in '91, *Ten,* was the epitome of what people who loved *Nevermind*—people like me—were supposed to be against. *Ten* was corporate. *Ten* was stadium rock. *Ten* was for jocks and frat boys.

In retrospect I'm not sure why exactly I was against those

things. I don't think I even knew what those things really were. For instance, I still played sports on a daily basis—in eighth grade, I was the Paul Mokeski-esque backup center for my junior high basketball team. After reading my yearbooks from this period, I discovered that I also ran cross-country, though for the life of me I don't remember this or comprehend how it happened. Even in junior high, I was blessed with the pure athleticism of Jeffrey Tambor. (Back then, I was *Mr. Mom*–era Tambor. Today I'm solidly third-season-of-*Arrested Development*–era Tambor.) But technically, I was still a jock. As for frat boys, my experience with fraternities consisted solely of viewings of the edited version of *Animal House* on basic cable. I was aware that frat boys were big fat party animals. But my knowledge was otherwise very limited in this regard. If I had seen the unedited *Animal House*, at least I would've known that frat boys said "fuck" and not "freak" or "fudge."

Basically, I understood what "jocks" and "frat boys" meant as signifiers, and in spite of the evidence, I believed that I belonged to a different species. After all, jocks were not as sensitive, smart, or soulful as I was—therefore, how could I be a jock? My argument was circular but convincing: jocks would never "get" alternative music on a deep level because they were not sufficiently alienated to grasp the nuances. They only heard distorted guitars and bellowing vocals, whereas I discerned the *meaning* of those distorted guitars and bellowing vocals. For everybody else in my grade, the video for "In Bloom" was merely a grainy black-and-white clip starring the host of *The People's Court* that accompanied the fourth-best single off *Nevermind*. They couldn't possibly understand that this video was actually an incisive satire of mindless mainstream media, which individuals like Kurt Cobain and myself could totally see as the soul-deadening circus it truly was. No way: *those* people were sheep, and they lapped up whatever was served to them.

This was why, I reasoned, Pearl Jam was so much more popular than Nirvana at my school. There were no deep layers of ironic subtext in the video for Pearl Jam's "Even Flow." The "Even Flow" video, if you'll recall, is a straightforward performance clip culled from a concert filmed in early 1992. The video opens with Eddie Vedder screaming at director Josh Taft to turn down the lights for his cameras. "This is not a TV studio, Josh," Vedder yells, sounding somewhat petulant but nevertheless making an accurate observation. (It wasn't a TV studio; it was Seattle's Moore Theatre.)

In spite of Eddie's public hectoring, Taft wound up doing wonders for Pearl Jam's career, spotlighting the band (particularly Vedder) at its energetic, sweat-stained best. The clip culminates ingeniously with Vedder climbing the theater's balcony and falling back into the crowd. For those who weren't into rock music at the time, let me explain: audiences in the '90s paid good money for musical artists to jump on top of them. It was considered the pinnacle of a live rock experience for some reason. So the "Even Flow" video only made Pearl Jam's music seem more attractive.

If memory serves, "Even Flow" played approximately 379 times per day on MTV in the summer of '92. Few at the network would've acknowledged it at the time, but "Even Flow" was essentially the same clip as another video that dominated the channel's playlist just four years earlier—Def Leppard's "Pour Some Sugar on Me." In that video, Def Leppard singer Joe Elliott and his exquisitely ripped jeans are prominently featured in a live performance filmed at Denver's McNichols Sports Arena in front of an audience composed exclusively of pretty, blond, nymphomaniac Coloradoans. The idea with both the "Even Flow" and "Pour Some Sugar on Me" clips was to make attending a concert by the band in question seem massively appealing to music consumers between the ages of fourteen and twenty-three. And it worked: Pearl Jam went from a second-tier act on that summer's Lollapalooza tour to the biggest band in the world by the fall.

This development gave me all the more reason to despise Pearl Jam.

I should point out that I don't feel this way about Pearl Jam anymore. In fact, I got over my anti–Pearl Jam stance pretty early. By 1993, it just seemed stupid to dislike Pearl Jam for supposedly being a sellout band, particularly in light of my discovery that Pearl Jam's music was fucking awesome. The turning point occurred when Pearl Jam appeared on the 1993 MTV Video Music Awards and played an incredible new song ("Animal," which came out soon thereafter on Pearl Jam's second record, *Vs.*). Then Neil Young came out and joined Pearl Jam for an even more incredible rendition of "Rockin' in the Free World." A rock band inviting a rock legend to play guitar-based music for more than ten minutes at the VMAs seems like something that might've occurred in the 1890s, not the 1990s. But YouTube confirms that my timeline is accurate.

At this point I was actively pretending to not like Pearl Jam while secretly watching the VMA performance over and over again on my VCR. Which is clearly insane, not only because nobody in my life cared about my opinion regarding Pearl Jam's legitimacy but also because my reason for pretending to dislike a band that I actually liked was based on my belief that another band better represented the "real" me. In the parlance of the time, Nirvana was the "legitimate" band, while the members of Pearl Jam were just a bunch of poseurs. I was so invested in my contrived relationship with Nirvana's music that it forced me to obfuscate a genuine connection I had to Pearl Jam.

This sort of thinking seems silly now, but it certainly existed in the minds of other grunge-era rock fans. Nirvana and Pearl Jam were far more similar than they were dissimilar—their songs were played on the same radio stations, their videos were played on the same *Alternative Nation* shows on MTV, and the same people generally liked both bands. And yet many impressionable listeners felt compelled to pick a side. Regardless of how illogical the reasoning was, Nirvana vs. Pearl Jam was a real rivalry. It's important to remember this, because there's been a concerted effort to revise history in the years since the rivalry cooled.

To pick one example: I just read a 2013 *Esquire* interview with Pearl Jam guitarist Mike McCready in which he refers to the Nirvana–Pearl Jam rivalry as a "press-created thing." He then says:

> I think [Cobain] and Ed had talked. I remember we were at the MTV VMAs, and I just jumped over the seats, and I said [to Cobain], "Hey, I heard you and Ed might be doing a record someday. I'd love to play a lead on it." And he goes, "Oh, we'll talk about it some other time." I just felt like I had to reach out, because there was this weird wall between us, us versus them or them versus us.

McCready's comments are typical of how the members of Pearl Jam have talked about Cobain in the years since his untimely death. First McCready frames the Nirvana–Pearl Jam rivalry as a media-driven creation. Then he relates an anecdote that suggests that Nirvana and Pearl Jam were friendly (if not friends) and that Cobain saw Eddie Vedder as an artistic equal and possible collaborator.

I'm sure McCready wasn't lying in that interview, but I suspect that what he said isn't *exactly* true. Let me concede at the start that I don't know any of these people personally. What I do know intimately are Cobain's public statements about Pearl Jam. I have studied the written record closely—first as an amateur rock obsessive, then as a paid rock obsessive—for more than twenty years. I can't play "Serve the Servants" on guitar, but I could perform decent covers of Cobain's *Rolling Stone* interviews. If Kurt and Eddie really were pals in their private lives, I *know* this directly contradicts what's in the public record.

For starters, the Nirvana–Pearl Jam rivalry was press-driven only in the sense that Cobain relished trashing Pearl Jam publicly right up until the end of his life. It commenced after Nirvana topped the charts with *Nevermind* and Pearl Jam swiftly appeared in Cobain's rearview. "I find it offensive to be lumped in with bands like Pearl Jam," Cobain told the *Chicago Tribune* in 1992. Soon after, in *Musician,* Cobain dismissed Pearl Jam as a "corporate, alternative, and cock-rock fusion." Then, in *Rolling Stone,* he accused Pearl Jam of "jumping on the alternative bandwagon." Cobain even dissed Pearl Jam in his private journals (which were later posthumously published), wishing he could "be erased from [Nirvana's] association" with the band.

This is all familiar territory for grunge fans, and it's been rehashed many times in magazine articles and books about '90s rock. But what's often forgotten (or straight-up whitewashed) is that even after Cobain met Vedder and came to like Vedder personally, he never warmed to Pearl Jam's melodramatic, fist-pumping anthems. This inconvenient fact was carefully massaged by Cameron Crowe in his otherwise entertaining 2011 documentary, *Pearl Jam Twenty.*

When Crowe and the members of Pearl Jam promoted the film, the most frequently used clip was of Vedder slow-dancing with Cobain to Eric Clapton's "Tears in Heaven" backstage at the 1992 MTV Video Music Awards. (This is the first of many references to the 1992 VMAs in this book.) It was a tacit acknowledgment of Cobain's importance to Pearl Jam's story: while Vedder and Pearl Jam warrant only a handful of mentions in major Nirvana books, including Michael Azerrad's *Come as You Are* and Charles R. Cross's *Heavier Than Heaven,* Cobain is always a significant character in retellings of Pearl Jam's early years. Nirvana's career arc would likely remain unchanged with or without Pearl Jam's presence. But Pearl Jam's early years were greatly informed by Nirvana, who represented the greatest hurdle Pearl Jam had to overcome in terms of establishing long-term credibility.

While Vedder has declined to divulge specifics about his VMA conversation with Cobain—in *Pearl Jam Twenty,* he claims he doesn't remember what Cobain said—Cobain repeated verbatim what he told Vedder to Azerrad:

> I stared into his eyes and told him that I thought he was a respectable human. And I did tell him straight out that I still think his band sucks. I said, "After watching you perform, I realized that you are a person that does have some passion." It's not a fully contrived thing. There are plenty of other more evil people out in the world than him and he doesn't deserve to be scapegoated like that.

It's reasonable to conclude after reading this quote that Kurt Cobain might've liked Eddie Vedder as a guy but was also unapologetic about sticking to his low opinion of Vedder's music. Even Cobain's apparent capitulations to Vedder are carefully qualified—Pearl Jam has *some* passion; it isn't *fully* contrived; there are *more* evil people out there. However, in *Pearl Jam Twenty*, the part where Cobain thinks Pearl Jam sucks is gently set aside, so that the "respectable human" part can be emphasized.

While Cobain did eventually express remorse about slagging Pearl Jam in the press, he never actually stopped doing it, even as he acknowledged that smack-talking Nirvana's increasingly more successful rival was bad PR. "One of the things I've learned is that slagging off people just doesn't do me any good," Cobain told David Fricke in a *Rolling Stone* cover story that ran three months before his suicide. "I hadn't met Eddie at the time. It was my fault; I should have been slagging off the record company instead of them. They were marketed—not probably against their will—but without them realizing they were being pushed into the grunge bandwagon."

When Fricke asked a follow-up question about whether Cobain "felt any empathy" for Pearl Jam, Cobain couldn't resist getting one last jab in. "Yeah, I do," he said, answering Fricke's initial question but deciding to keep talking anyway. "Except I'm pretty sure that they didn't go out of their way to challenge their audience as much as we did with this record. They're a safe rock band. They're a pleasant rock band that everyone likes. God, I've had much better quotes in my head about this."

It was only after Cobain was no longer able to speak for himself that his feelings about Pearl Jam magically improved.

And a lot of that had to do with Vedder, who never lashed back at Cobain when Cobain was alive and in fact seemed to hold his most vocal critic in high regard. Cobain might've despised Pearl Jam's records, but Vedder remained a Nirvana fan who felt indebted to Cobain. Perhaps it was this fandom that provoked Vedder to imagine how his relationship with Cobain might've been different had his erstwhile adversary not killed himself.

"Sometimes—I don't sit around and think about it all the time by any means—I wish that Kurt and I had been able to, like, sit in the basement a few nights and just play stupid songs together, and relate to some of this," Vedder told *Spin*'s Craig Marks in 1994, several months after Cobain's death. "That might've helped us to understand each other, that he wasn't the only one, or that I wasn't the only one. We kind of knew that in the back of our heads, but we certainly never...I mean, we had a conversation on the phone, but we didn't really address that."

Many years later, in a 2009 interview, Vedder once again speculated on what Cobain's opinion would be of him had Cobain lived. "I don't talk too much about him in respect to Krist [Novoselic] and Dave [Grohl] and I know he said that early stuff about not liking us," he told Britain's *Sun* newspaper. "But if Kurt were around today, I know he'd say to me, 'Well, you turned out OK.'" Then, in *Pearl Jam Twenty*, Vedder talks again about theoretically hanging out with Cobain: "It always comes up around a campfire or playing music with a few guys in a garage for no particular reason. I always think, 'He would've liked this.'"

Am I saying that Eddie Vedder is wrong to imagine a postdeath friendship with Cobain? No, it's not wrong. But it feels inaccurate. Again, based on the public record, Kurt Cobain never chose to hang out with Eddie Vedder when such a thing was physically possible. Aside from the occasional phone conversation or an impromptu backstage dance, they didn't appear to have much of a personal relationship. While I can imagine an undead Kurt Cobain accepting an invitation to enjoy a campfire with Eddie Vedder, I can just as easily envision Kurt sneaking away and calling Kurt Loder in order to complain about how *Lightning Bolt* sucks.

It's a real bummer when your hero doesn't love you back.

I dream about Bruce Springsteen sometimes.

By "sometimes," I mean maybe once or twice per year. But whenever it happens, I remember it, and I'm not a person who normally remembers his dreams. My Bruce Springsteen dreams unfold the same way each time: usually Bruce and I are sitting in close proximity to a concert stage, maybe in a tour bus or a backstage lounge area. The particulars of our conversations are never all that important—we might talk about records, we might talk about our kids, we might talk about the contents of our refrigerators. The point is that I'm sitting with the Boss, and we're sharing a moment the way two old friends would. What I'm left with when I wake up is that glow you feel after spending several hours with a pal you haven't seen in years but are still able to instantly connect with. It's a vividly real sensation about a patently fake encounter.

I feel embarrassed admitting this, because I can already sense the massive eye rolls that a sentence like "I dream about Bruce Springsteen sometimes" will prompt. I'm sure dreaming about Bruce Springsteen is an utterly common occurrence among white men between the ages of thirty-five and fifty-five who sneak away once the wife goes to bed to drink bourbon in the dark and play side 2 of *Darkness on the Edge of Town*. The character played by John Cusack in *High Fidelity* daydreams about confiding in Springsteen, so not only is "I dream about Bruce Springsteen sometimes" banal, it's also a cliché. I understand if you've already fucking heard fucking enough about Bruce fucking Springsteen dreams. The only reason I brought it up is because "I dream about Bruce Springsteen sometimes" is a manifestation of a prevalent form of delusion experienced by millions of individuals—including me, possibly Eddie Vedder, and (I'm willing to bet) you.

If you're reading this book, there is probably an artist or band whose music you have an intense personal relationship with. (This band may very well be one of the bands covered in this chapter, in which case I apologize if I have already inadvertently pissed you off.) I would also guess that this artist or band came into your life during a time when you were highly vulnerable. If this is the case, this artist or band might've been the closest thing you had to a confidant. In fact, he, she, or it was better than a confidant, because his/her/its music articulated your own thoughts and feelings better than you ever could. This music elevated the raw materials of your life to the heights of art and poetry. It made you feel as if your personal experience was grander and more meaningful than it might otherwise have been. And, naturally, you attributed whatever that music was doing to your heart and brain to the people who made the music, and you came to believe that the qualities of the music were also true of the music's creators. "If this music understands me, then the people behind the music must also understand me," goes this line of thought.

The reality of music fandom is that it's a one-way street. Music can't love you back; getting overly wrapped up in an album is basically a socially acceptable version of having an imaginary friend. Listeners project meaning onto records and come to believe that meaning is universal when in fact it might exist only inside their own heads. If you're lucky, this will only lead to bawling your eyes out whenever you put on *Blood on the Tracks* or *Sea Change* because that record is "about" the worst heartbreak of your life. If you're Charles Manson or Mark David Chapman, the consequences are a little direr.

And yet here we are. I can offer a diagnosis of music fandom but no cure. Even after working as a music journalist for more than fifteen years and interviewing hundreds of musicians, I still have romantic notions of what my heroes are "really" like and steadfastly believe that if we ever had a chance to meet, they would like me. If I step outside myself, I can see how arrogant this is. Given the right social situation and correct number of drinks, I can be adequately charming. But my charm is not transcendent. (I am not Barbra Streisand in *What's Up, Doc?*) Getting genuinely magnetic people to like me is hardly a lock. But I also understand that wanting to be liked by my favorite artists has nothing to do with the artists. It's not that I believe that I would be good for them, it's that for some weird reason I'm looking for them to validate all the thoughts and feelings I've put into my *version* of them.

My saving grace is that I'm probably never going to meet Springsteen or Bob Dylan or Axl Rose or Kanye West in the flesh. It's possible that these guys might like me if we were to meet. They might also hate me. Most likely, they wouldn't care about me enough to have an opinion either way. But I'll never know what they think of me, and for that I'm glad. I can't imagine what it would be like to put someone on a pedestal only to have that person look down on me in disgust.

Actually, I don't have to imagine it, because I just have to look at New Jersey governor Chris Christie and his one-way love affair with the Boss.

As Christie went from being a prominent figure in Jersey politics to a nationally known fixture of the Republican Party, his love of Springsteen became an oft-referenced item from his personal history. The *New York Times* and *The Atlantic* were among the media outlets that ran lengthy profiles (in 2009 and 2012 respectively) focused exclusively on Christie's passionate appreciation of Springsteen's music. In 2014, when Christie was facing the worst political crisis of his career, his love for Springsteen was once again national news. Springsteen appeared on *Late Night with Jimmy Fallon* and satirized Christie's "Bridgegate" scandal with a "Born to Run" parody called "Governor Christie Traffic Jam."

If you were on Facebook or Twitter at the time, somebody likely shared this clip with you. It's fairly amusing for a late-night talk-show bit — Fallon's Springsteen impression is pretty great, and Springsteen does a decent job of approximating his younger, less haggard self. But I couldn't help feeling a smidge of sympathy for Christie when I watched it. Yes, Christie is a public figure. And his beliefs exist on the opposite end of the political spectrum from my beliefs. But he was mocked by his idol in front of millions on national television. On the scale of publicly humiliating experiences, where an extramarital sex scandal is a 10 and being photographed while napping in a non-nap-friendly setting is a 1, this ranks at least a 6.5.

When Christie was asked about the sketch during a public forum not long afterward, he resorted to his only available

move—retreating to the comfort of imagining a better relationship with Springsteen at some point in the future. "I still
live in hope that someday, even as he gets older and older,
he's going to wake up and go, 'Yeah, maybe he's a good guy.
He's alright, you know,'" Christie was quoted as saying by the
Newark Star-Ledger.

According to various media reports that I've read, Christie
has met Springsteen at least three times—once during a flight
to Minneapolis in 1999, once during a ceremony inducting
Danny DeVito into the New Jersey Hall of Fame in 2010, and
once during a telethon for Hurricane Sandy victims in 2012.
Meanwhile, by his own count, Christie has attended more than
130 Springsteen shows dating back to the 1970s. Given his position of authority in New Jersey, you'd think Christie would
have more opportunities to get some Springsteen face time. But
Springsteen has brushed him off consistently. *The Atlantic* described one snubbing in such pathetic terms that even Rachel
Maddow might weep for Christie:

> At concerts, even concerts in club-size venues—the Stone
> Pony, in Asbury Park, most recently—Springsteen won't
> acknowledge the governor. When Christie leaves a
> Springsteen concert in a large arena, his state troopers
> move him to his motorcade through loading docks. He
> walks within feet of the stage, and of the dressing rooms.
> He's never been invited to say hello. On occasion, he'll
> make a public plea to Springsteen, as he did earlier this
> spring, when Christie asked him to play at a new casino
> in Atlantic City. "He says he's for the revitalization of the
> Jersey Shore, so this seems obvious," Christie told me. I
> asked him if he's received a response to his request. "No,

we got nothing back from them," he said unhappily, "not even a 'Fuck you.'"

The reason for Springsteen giving Christie the cold shoulder is pretty obvious: Springsteen is classic rock's most celebrated populist and old-school liberal. In 1984, the year Springsteen's bestselling album *Born in the U.S.A.* made him the biggest bar-band rocker on the planet, Ronald Reagan appropriated the album's title track and deliberately misconstrued its strident protest sentiment as a simplistic celebration of American might. Nearly thirty years later, Springsteen still suffered from the consequences of this. When Springsteen made "We Take Care of Our Own," an outraged call to arms partly inspired by the Bush administration's apathetic response to Hurricane Katrina, the lead single from his 2012 album, *Wrecking Ball*, *New York Times* music critic Jon Caramanica took the chorus ("We take care of our own / Wherever this flag's flown") at face value and accused Springsteen of jingoism. So if Springsteen is sensitive about political associations with his art and how they affect the way that art is perceived, it's not without cause.

"There is some of his work that is dour and down," Christie acknowledged in *The Atlantic*, "but the thing that attracted me to his music is how aspirational it is—aspirational to success, to fun, to being a better person, to figuring out how to make your life better—and you can't say that about most people's music.... What's funny is that his progression is what Republicans believe can happen. That's what Republicans believe—hard work, talent, ambition. We all know he's the hardest-working man in show business. It's a meritocracy."

Now, this might seem like as gross a perversion of Springsteen's life and art as what Reagan did in order to wallop

Walter Mondale. But if you disregard the politics for a moment, what Christie is doing here is what all fans do with their favorite music. We take whichever portion seems to apply most directly to our own lives, and we make the whole thing about that. It's why married couples swoon over R.E.M.'s misanthropic anthem "The One I Love" and sports fans pretend that Gary Glitter wasn't thinking about molesting eight-year-olds when he wrote the deathless jock jam "Rock and Roll Part 2." I suspect Christie's belief that Springsteen represents the supposed Republican ideals of hard work and self-sufficiency is pretty common; at this point, given the demographic makeup of Springsteen's audience, it might even be the predominant view. But Christie isn't totally deluded. He knows that his politics will probably always alienate him from Springsteen—though that doesn't mean a guy can't wish for a different outcome.

"My view on it is that I'm not a priority of his right now," Christie said to *The Atlantic*. "At some point maybe I will be. If Bruce and I sat down and talked, he would reluctantly come to the conclusion that we disagree on a lot less than he thinks."

The sad part for Christie (or maybe it's just inconvenient) is that Springsteen will almost certainly outlive him, even though Springsteen is thirteen years older. Springsteen is in incredible physical shape, while the relative fitness of Chris Christie has been a constant source of humor for hack comedians. As long as Bruce Springsteen can speak for himself, no fantasy will be able to overshadow the reality of his true feelings for Chris Christie.

One of my favorite movies about '90s pop culture is Nick Broomfield's 1998 documentary, *Kurt & Courtney*. People who haven't seen *Kurt & Courtney* (and even many of those who have seen it) refer to it as the "Courtney Love had Kurt Cobain killed conspiracy movie." But that's really just another instance of misinterpreting a given piece of art as endorsing what it's about. I think it's clear from Broomfield's authorial voice that, at best, he's suspicious of the assorted freaks and sycophants who orbited Cobain in his final years and later agreed to look ridiculous in his film. At times, Broomfield is downright contemptuous of those people.

When Broomfield (who appears on camera as the film's narrator and de facto protagonist) encounters individuals outright accusing Love of murder—most notably a crazy-ass punk singer named El Duce and Love's estranged crazy-ass father, Hank Harrison—he edits the interviews in such a way as to encourage the audience's incredulity. At no point does *Kurt & Courtney* make the conspiracy charges seem credible, and unless Broomfield is a completely inept filmmaker (which, judging by his other films, I don't think he is), this must be intentional.

What Broomfield does instead is depict the ways in which marginal figures in the life of an icon use that association, no matter how tangential, to make themselves appear more significant. If Cobain hadn't died, none of the people Broomfield interviews in *Kurt & Courtney* would be considered the least bit noteworthy. But because Cobain *did* die, being a person who once copped heroin with the lead singer of Nirvana is almost enviable in the minds of celebrity rubberneckers and the least intelligent Nirvana fans. Cobain supposedly hated stardom so much that he killed himself to escape it. But for dozens, if not hundreds, of people Cobain barely knew but casually associated with, his celebrity facilitated their own micro-size slice of fame after his death.

Art is frequently dismissed by those who might be threatened by what it suggests about them. Love, unsurprisingly, attempted to bury *Kurt & Courtney*. Even if Broomfield didn't convincingly implicate Love as her husband's killer, the film's suggestion that she was the primary exploiter of Cobain's tragic death must've been infuriating (though it rings true). But taking a broader view of *Kurt & Courtney*, I think Broomfield makes a profound point: anyone faintly connected to an iconic figure's demise (even casual fans) in some way takes advantage of that event for his or her own ends. This might seem like a cynical observation, but this process doesn't have to always produce a cynical outcome.

Pearl Jam can hardly be equated with the cast of bottom-feeders whom Broomfield rounds up in *Kurt & Courtney*. But Pearl Jam nonetheless has integrated Cobain's death into its mythos and subsequently held itself up against what Cobain's suicide represents in the culture. This has been largely implicit, but occasionally the members of Pearl Jam have stated it outright. In *Pearl Jam Twenty*, Stone Gossard observes that Cobain "made us think about everything we did.... If we're good today it's partly because of him."

One way to interpret this is to say that Pearl Jam's music was superficially "less safe" in the immediate aftermath of Cobain's death. In the late fall of 1994, Pearl Jam released its third record, *Vitalogy*, regarded by many as Pearl Jam's best LP in part because it's considerably less consistent than the band's first two, "straighter" albums. *Vitalogy* includes several tracks that seem like they were intended to alienate the same sort of hypothetical milquetoast listener that Nirvana wanted to shoo away with *In Utero*. In fact, *Vitalogy* is more abrasive than *In Utero*—Cobain didn't attempt anything as singularly weird or off-putting as the accordion-based doodle "Bugs" or the seven-minute sound collage "Hey, Foxymophandlemama, That's Me."

Pearl Jam's next record, 1996's muted *No Code*, is a fan favorite, but it effectively ended Pearl Jam's tenure as a platinum-selling band. By the early aughts Pearl Jam was actively subsuming the operatic emotionalism of their more popular early records in order to cater to hard-core loyalists who had the time and interest to get something out of the murk of *Binaural* and *Riot Act*. In less than a decade, Pearl Jam went from selling one million albums per week to barely going gold during an entire record cycle (back when a band of Pearl Jam's stature could still be expected to sell a lot of units).

The way Vedder purposely piloted Pearl Jam toward a significantly smaller audience is still remarkable. Other than Radiohead, no rock band has ever been more deliberate about ferreting out precisely the people it wanted to care about its music. This can probably be attributed to Cobain's influence. That seems like the narrative that Pearl Jam would prefer, anyway. But I think this characterization overlooks an important truth about Pearl Jam's relationship with Nirvana, which can be viewed more clearly if you are conversant with Pearl Jam's voluminous concert bootlegs.

Eddie Vedder's favorite band is the Who, and the most vital (though no doubt accidental) similarity between the Who and Pearl Jam is that neither band has ever been as good on record as they are onstage. Nearly every Who and Pearl Jam song is better when heard on a live album or bootleg. Therefore, Pearl Jam's official discography leaves out a crucial part of the band's story. (I realize that music geeks have mounted similar arguments for every significant rock group ever, but in the case of Pearl Jam it happens to be true.)

Some of my favorite Pearl Jam bootlegs originate from shows the band played in early April of 1994, right before and immediately after Cobain's death. Pearl Jam performed two concerts in Atlanta a few days before authorities discovered Cobain's body at his Seattle-area home, on April 8. At that point Cobain had already been reported missing, which naturally caused alarm in the Seattle music community, given that it was not long after his unsuccessful suicide attempt in Rome and an aborted stint at an LA-area rehab facility. At the April 3 concert, Vedder dedicated "Go" to Cobain—no doubt he directed the chorus ("Please / Don't go on me") to his troubled peer.

Pearl Jam played a concert in Fairfax, Virginia, the night Cobain's death was confirmed. Vedder later told a *Los Angeles Times* reporter that he trashed his hotel room after he heard the news. He added, "Then I just kind of sat in the rubble, which somehow felt right.... [It felt] like my world at the moment." But Pearl Jam's performance is remarkably controlled given the circumstances—Vedder occasionally makes oblique references to the tragedy during the first half of the show, but otherwise the band carries on in a professional (if emotionally exhausted) manner. If you didn't know the context of the concert, the bootleg wouldn't seem all that different from other live recordings of this period.

Later in the set, Vedder launches into a brief monologue—sometimes referred to by Pearl Jam fans as "the elevation speech"—that pays heartfelt (if also surprisingly restrained) tribute to Cobain.

There's a lot of space between us tonight.... We're not only kind of far, you know, we're kind of elevated, I noticed, a little more than usual. Either that or I've gotten taller. But I don't think it's very good to elevate yourself. That can be very dangerous. Sometimes whether you like it or not people elevate you, you know, whether you like it or not. It's real easy to fall…but I don't think any of us would be in this room tonight if it weren't for Kurt Cobain.

Nirvana vs. Pearl Jam became a rivalry initially because Kurt Cobain sought to set Nirvana apart as a "not-safe" rock band. But when Cobain died, the rivalry didn't die so much as evolve into a benign contrast between two ways of navigating success. Cobain will always be a romantic figure because he was cut down in his prime. But Vedder found a way to survive. Pearl Jam's story of long-term endurance is more poignant precisely because Nirvana exists as an alternative path to early destruction. The rivalry doesn't diminish Pearl Jam; rather, it helps to explain why living can be just as meaningful as dying. In this way, I suppose Vedder is right to invoke Cobain as an important character in his own story, no matter the particulars of their personal relationship. Cobain and Vedder will always be connected—not as friends but as signifiers of diverging paths that split at a fork in the road.

CHAPTER 3

A Quirky Theory About Quirk Theory

(Prince vs. Michael Jackson)

I DECIDED TO become a writer not long after I turned thirteen. I came to this decision after noticing that I was consciously taking mental notes on the worst night of my life as it was happening.

It was the night of my first junior high school dance. I had been in seventh grade for a week, and I was flush with sixth-grade arrogance. Misconstruing alpha-dog status in elementary school as meaningful in a junior high context was a foolish mistake. But I did not know this until the dance. I talked a big game heading into the soiree. I bragged to friends about all the girls I was going to dance with. (My slow songs of choice included Mariah Carey's "Vision of Love" and Queensrÿche's "Silent Lucidity.") I confidently assumed that at least one of the lovely ladies at my school would totally be into "going with me" after a romantic spin on the dance floor. I pictured myself as John Travolta in *Saturday Night Fever* or Patrick Swayze in *Dirty Dancing*—a guy with all the moves, a handsome lothario whose hips could sexually enchant any female.

Honestly, I don't know what in the hell I was thinking. My bravado was shockingly ill-advised. I had bad acne. I had braces. My glasses were so bulky I'm surprised I wasn't arrested on suspicion of mugging a shortsighted grandmother and stealing them off her face. My hair resembled a wig left over from a Broadway revival of *Heavy Metal Parking Lot.*

I was not a good-looking young man is what I'm saying.

But even if I had resembled 1978-era Scott Baio, my lack of smooth talk would've crippled me. I was painfully shy and awkward around the opposite sex. Putting my hand in a garbage disposal was less frightening to me than chatting up some adolescent minx. Oh, and have I mentioned that I was (and always will be) a terrible dancer? Thank God my wife finds my pitiful attempts at rhythmic movement adorable. Otherwise I'd be sentenced to a life of living like Travolta in *Battlefield Earth.*

I was basically set up to fail horribly at this dance. And fail horribly is precisely what I did. Here's what I did not anticipate during my initial attempts to charm women into liking me: flirting is a competitive sport when you're in the seventh grade. Boys and girls travel in packs, so four or five guys are always trying to hit on the same two or three girls simultaneously. This was not an environment conducive to being witty. My quips kept pulling a hammy. I froze as my friends swept up all the available women. When I finally did summon enough courage to ask a girl to dance, it did not go well, to put it mildly.

Here's a transcript of our conversation, which was instantly burned into my memory for the eventual enjoyment of the people reading this book:

Me: Would you like to dance?
Her: [Disgusted face]

Me: Oh come on, I'm not that bad.

Her: Are you sure?

Are you sure?!

Let me make a confession: if this anecdote seems a little precious or overly rehearsed, it's probably because it is. I have told this story many times. I have used it as an adult to endear myself to countless women. And it almost always works. I'm a very sympathetic character in this story. But while everything I've told you is true, I feel like a phony.

Did you notice that pointing out how not great I used to be illustrates how great I've become? Look at where I was and where I am now! I'm trying to be funny in a self-deprecating way, but I suspect my constant retellings of this story really represent the height of vanity. I can see this more clearly when I hear pathetic geek stories told by other people. There are a lot of these stories, and everybody tells them, even celebrities. God, *especially* celebrities.

If you do an Internet search for "nerdy celebrity childhood," a plethora of click bait instantly unfolds before you like a bountiful garden of flowers made out of fast-food wrappers. At random I pulled out a *BuzzFeed* article with the headline 20 CELEBRITIES THAT WEREN'T COOL IN SCHOOL. This fascinating and culturally vital work of journalism informed me that supernaturally sexy *Mad Men* star Christina Hendricks "had the worst high school experience ever" because her friends were "all weird theatre people and everyone just hated us." Also, perfect Aryan goddess Charlize Theron "didn't have any boyfriends in high school," *l'ange de Charlie* Cameron Diaz was "a total goon," and Batman himself, Christian Bale, "took a beating from several boys for years."

Why stop at twenty celebrities? Having a nerdy childhood is an essential part of any celebrity's origin story. If you want to be a superhero, your parents need to be murdered when you are at a young, impressionable age; if you want to be a celebrity, your parents merely need to dress you in unfashionable, ill-fitting clothes during your teen years.

Nobody wants to believe that rich, famous, and fabulously attractive people have always had it all. You must demonstrate that you earned your privileged status by enduring constant humiliation and heartbreak as a kid. Otherwise you barely register as human.

I think we can all agree that Prince is one of the five coolest people on the planet. (The others are LeBron James, Beyoncé, Bill Clinton, and Jennifer Lawrence. If you don't like this list, I'm sorry, but these are the people that everybody else on earth signed off on.) And yet even Prince isn't immune to mythologizing his pathetic geek heritage.

"He was the obnoxious, nerdy guy in school," former Prince associate Alan Leeds tells Touré, author of *I Would Die 4 U: Why Prince Became an Icon*. "Nobody liked him. He was ostracized. Guys picked on him because his mama left him and his dad wasn't capable of being a serious father. He was an excellent basketball player but nobody took him seriously because he was too short. He was constantly in the shadow of everybody and everything."

Leeds's point isn't just that Prince was driven to be great by his childhood hardships, it's also that he was *already* great in high school: other people just wouldn't give him the proper respect. And this is what drove him. Prince had to make *Purple Rain* because the world failed to recognize his superior baller skills.

In the early part of his career, back when he would still grant interviews on a semiregular basis, Prince cultivated the impression that he had a hard, lonely upbringing. Speaking to *Rolling Stone* in 1981, he claimed that he ran away from home at age twelve and that he had lived at thirty-two different addresses in Minneapolis by the time he was in his early twenties. In a cover story for the same magazine in 1985, Prince pointed out a phone booth where as a teenager he had tearfully called his father and asked to move back home, only to have his father refuse. Prince told the *Rolling Stone* reporter that he never cried again after that day. A less believable (but more famous) story involves Prince's stepfather, who allegedly locked Prince up in his room for six weeks, during which time he learned to play piano. In his book, Touré concludes that Prince was "a functional orphan."

What these stories did was help set Prince apart from his chief competition on the pop charts in the '80s, Michael Jackson. There are some superficial similarities between the two superstars: They were born two months apart in the summer of 1958. They were both ambitious enough to create a bridge between black R & B and white rock-and-roll audiences. They were both criticized by critic Nelson George in his book *The Death of Rhythm and Blues* for "[running] fast and far from both blackness and conventional images of male sexuality." Where they diverged was their backgrounds, which seemed to inform their art and their respective approaches to their careers.

"Prince was totally a self-made man and the Jacksons, especially Michael, [were] born, bred, groomed, prepared, honed, shaped and molded to become what [they] became," Susan Rogers, another Prince associate, told Touré. "Prince did his by a singular force of will coupled with his talent."

This is a reductive but otherwise illustrative summation of the Michael Jackson–Prince dynamic, which was at its peak in the '80s. By any other measure, Prince is a pop institution who takes a backseat to nobody in terms of popularity, talent, and ego. Only when compared with Michael Jackson—particularly '80s Michael Jackson—can Prince be credibly cast as a scrappy upstart. That's what he was back when *Thriller* and *Purple Rain* were dueling on the *Billboard* album charts and the videos for "Beat It" and "Little Red Corvette" were vying for airtime on MTV. Michael Jackson was the mainstream behemoth; Prince was the hardworking middle-American alternative.

Our collective perception of Michael Jackson was thrown out of whack after he died at the age of fifty in 2009. History was rewritten to indicate that Jackson was always a beloved figure. But even in his '80s prime, MJ was hated by millions because of his merciless cultural dominance. Anyone who felt alienated from the mainstream could curse Jackson as the mainstream's most overbearing figurehead. Few pop stars have ever been ubiquitous the way Michael Jackson was in the mid-'80s, and cultural commentators lined up to take him down like film critics at an Adam Sandler screening.

One of MJ's most virulent critics was *Village Voice* writer Greg Tate, who, in his review of 1987's *Bad,* accused Jackson of achieving "a singular infamy in the annals of tomming." That's an incredibly unfair and vicious criticism, but it wasn't exactly uncommon to argue that Jackson shamelessly pandered his way to the top. In terms of targets, Michael Jackson was so big he was amorphous. Complaining about MJ was like bitching about the media or "those politicians in Washington."

Prince only briefly achieved the level of fame that triggers that sort of abuse. After the massive success of the *Purple Rain* film and sound track, Prince was popular enough to be put in the same sentence as Jackson—though in the case of LL Cool J's 1985 track "Rock the Bells," it wasn't meant as a compliment. ("You hated Michael and Prince all the way, ever sense / If their beats were made of meat, then they would have to be mince.") But on his next two albums, *Around the World in a Day* and *Parade,* Prince subsequently seemed determined to confound the public.

I love *Around the World in a Day* and *Parade.* My favorite Prince music is puckish and psychedelic and derives from unwatchable screwball comedies. But there's no question that those albums fucked up the trajectory of Prince's career. Even if there was nowhere to go but down after the stratospheric high of *Purple Rain*—not even Michael Jackson could pull off a movie that required so much motorcycle riding and finger licking—*Around the World in a Day* and *Parade* represented a nosedive into the side of a mountain commercially. Not even *Sign o' the Times,* arguably Prince's most brilliant album, could fully pull him out of the wreckage.

(Carrying over the metaphor, I suppose *Lovesexy* is Prince's "resorting to cannibalism by dining on his naked travel companions" record, while the *Batman* sound track is his "unexpectedly airlifted out of hell by a coked-out Jack Nicholson" album.)

While Prince produced some of his best-ever singles during this period—"Raspberry Beret," "Pop Life," "Kiss"—his albums were perceived as perverse at best and willfully self-destructive at worst. Instead of trying to replicate the blockbuster example of *Purple Rain,* as Jackson followed *Thriller* with *Bad,* Prince responded to superstardom by making the least commercial music of his career up to that point. Right when he had finally grabbed the world's attention, Prince reverted back to his odd, alienated, nerdy self. *Bad,* meanwhile, became the first album ever to spin off five consecutive number one singles. The proper order—MJ as unstoppable capitalist, Prince as mercurial artiste—had been restored.

Michael Jackson and Prince always denied being rivals, but there are four instances in which they clashed.

(1) MICHAEL JACKSON ATTEMPTS TO SHOW UP PRINCE AT A JAMES BROWN CONCERT

On the Internet you can easily track down video of a James Brown concert from 1983 at the Beverly Theater in Los Angeles. The video is noteworthy because Brown invites Jackson to appear onstage and blow Brown's crazy-ass mind with his perfectly executed James Brown dance moves. After that, MJ whispers in JB's ear, and all of a sudden Prince magically materializes onstage and does *his* James Brown moves and shreds a little on a guitar. The footage is fuzzy, but its awesomeness can't be denied: it's like watching three faces on America's funky Mount Rushmore come to life and duel it out.

What's interesting about the video is that members of Prince's entourage were convinced that MJ intended to humiliate Prince, and (in their view) he succeeded. "He played a few licks, did some dancing and knocked over a prop by accident," Alan Leeds told *Vibe.* "[Prince's drummer] Bobby Z called and said, 'Oh boy…he made an ass of himself tonight.'" But as a mortal watching the video, I don't think Prince looks like an ass; he looks like a god showing off for two other gods. (Advantage: tie.)

(2) PRINCE BAILS ON THE RECORDING SESSION FOR "WE ARE THE WORLD"

In retrospect, backing out of recording "We Are the World," a maudlin exercise in instantly dated limousine liberalism, seems like a wise decision. When Prince dies, at least there will be no embarrassing footage of him singing between Kenny Rogers and Kim Carnes. But at the time, not doing "We Are the World" was a major PR disaster. Prince was viewed as a conceited jerk, whereas Michael Jackson was depicted as selfless for spearheading the project. Reports that Prince didn't show up because he was waylaid by an altercation between a photographer and his bodyguards outside a Mexican restaurant on the Sunset Strip led to the bizarre, only-in-'85 indignity of Billy Crystal impersonating Prince on a *Saturday Night Live* parody called "I Am the World." That's right: Prince was so reviled over "We Are the World" that Billy Crystal in blackface was considered an appropriate corrective. (Advantage: MJ.)

(3) PRINCE BEATS MICHAEL JACKSON AT PING-PONG

Jackson famously paid Prince a visit while Prince worked on *Under the Cherry Moon,* his ill-fated cinematic follow-up to *Purple Rain.* Always a hospitable host, Prince invited Jackson to play Ping-Pong. "I don't know how to play but I'll try," Jackson replied.

Naturally, all the bystanders stopped what they were doing and watched the game, as this surely was the single most electrifying Ping-Pong match ever. As eyewitnesses later recounted, it started with some soft hits back and forth. Then Prince said, "Come on, Michael, get into it." Then Prince taunted MJ again: "You want me to slam it?"

What happened next represents the most iconic moment in

the history of sporting events between '80s musical icons: Jackson dropped his paddle, and Prince slammed the Ping-Pong ball into MJ's crotch. After Jackson left, Prince was justifiably feeling himself. "Did you see that?" he declared, according to Ronin Ro's *Prince: Inside the Music and the Masks.* "He played like Helen Keller!" (Advantage: Prince.)

(4) PRINCE DECLINES TO DUET WITH JACKSON ON "BAD"

MJ envisioned it as a can't-miss publicity stunt, with both singers' camps hurling fake insults at each other in the media until the single dropped. Prince supposedly considered going along with it, but he balked at the song itself: he didn't want to be the one who says "Your butt is mine" to Michael Jackson, and he didn't want Michael Jackson singing the lyric to him. I'm very upset that this duet didn't happen, but I can't argue with Prince's reasoning. (Advantage: tie.)

Something unexpected happened to Michael Jackson and Prince by the dawn of the twenty-first century: Jackson was so weird that he was only barely a pop star, whereas Prince was relatively less weird, which allowed him to stage a comeback. In the familiar "pathetic geek" celebrity narrative, it was as if Prince had finally matured into "normal" adulthood. On his 2004 *Musicology* tour, his first tour in six years, Prince satisfied millions of fans by playing his hits relatively straight, save for a misplaced curse word or two. (Prince's religious beliefs prompted him to tone down the songs.) Meanwhile, on *Chappelle's Show,* Dave Chappelle made Prince's '80s weirdness appear cuddly and endearing, a full 180 from the way those attributes were perceived two decades earlier, when Prince was in his mocked-by-blackface-Billy-Crystal doldrums.

Now Jackson was the one who suffered in comparison. His story was the flip side of the pathetic geek narrative—the former prom king who grows up to be a weirdo loser. For the average popular kid, this process typically involves getting fat, bald, and working a dead-end job; for an extraordinarily popular person like Jackson, it was manifested by the media depicting him as a Kabuki pederast. Even Prince took shots at MJ in the mid-aughts: "My voice is gettin' higher / And I ain't never had my nose done / That's the other guy," he sings on "Life o' the Party" from *Musicology*.

Again, Jackson's marginalization in our culture has been obscured by his death, but Jackson's status was diminished significantly before he passed. "I was a fan my whole life. [But] I'm fucking done," Chris Rock said in his 2004 stand-up special, *Never Scared*. I almost typed "joked," but Rock seemed honestly pissed. "Another kid? That's like another dead white girl showing up at O.J.'s house," he says. Then Rock *really* goes for the jugular: "Remember when everybody used to have those arguments about who's better, Michael Jackson or Prince? Prince won."

But why exactly did Prince win?

As a commonly held belief, "Individuals who were unpopular as children will grow up to be successful, while people who were popular as children will grow up to have disappointing lives" is practically intuitive. Like everything else that seems intuitive, this idea has been codified and perpetuated by a bestselling author. For her 2011 book, *The Geeks Shall Inherit the Earth*, Alexandra Robbins followed seven real-life students whom she pigeonholed into convenient archetypes: the Loner, the Popular Bitch, the Nerd, the New Girl, the Gamer, the Weird Girl, and the Band Geek. Robbins's intention was to "explain the fascinating psychology and science behind popularity and 'outcasthood.'" At the core of this explanation is "quirk theory," which posits that characteristics that cause young people to feel rejected in school will later help them in adulthood.

"Many of the successful and appreciated adults I know were not part of the mainstream popular crowd at school," Robbins writes. "The artsy girl is now a beloved art teacher who has made additional money and a wide circle of friends with her creative freelance ventures. The Goth, whom Midwestern classmates picked on because her intense curiosity diverted her interests from parties and sports to museums, classical music, and books, now prospers in Manhattan, where friends and colleagues can relate. The freak, rejected partly for her willingness to be confrontational, used her place on the margins to become a shrewd people observer."

Setting aside the ways these supposed "real" people are described—Robbins could be writing about the extras taking up space behind Zack and Screech on *Saved by the Bell*—I have two issues with quirk theory.

(1) In my experience, very few kids are completely "mainstream" or "on the margins" at school. Yes, there are a small handful of preternaturally good-looking and wealthy students. And there are an equally small handful of outcasts who have been conditioned to live as trench-coat-donning misanthropes. Extremes command an inordinate amount of attention in discussions about teen culture, just as extremes dominate societal discourse everywhere else. But the vast majority of teenagers are somewhere in the middle.

They are neither popular nor unpopular. They have at some point been picked on by another student, and they have at some point been the person who picked on somebody else. They might not be known by everybody in the school, but they have at least a couple of friends. (Imagine the "just-right" offspring of cool jock Emilio Estevez and nerdy psychopath Ally Sheedy in *The Breakfast Club*.) Status tends to be fluid when you're growing up: there might be a semester or two when you feel weirdly popular, then it goes away the next semester and you're suddenly friendless. But in the end it usually evens out.

(2) The net result is that almost everyone remembers being less popular than they really were in school. Because most of us associate this time in our lives with feeling alienated, awkward, and insecure, and there's a misconception that some kids *don't* feel that way, even though I've never met a single person for whom that was true. We therefore wrongly assume that these feelings make us special, when in reality they are an inherent part of growing up.

If you're the sort of person inclined to talk self-deprecatingly about your geeky childhood, I have an experiment for you: dig out your high school yearbook and look up the most attractive people from your class. When I did this, I was shocked to discover that they were gawky, goofy, or flat-out weird-looking. They weren't the untouchably cool creatures I cast in my pathetic geek stories. They were in fact not much better off in the awkward department than I was.

My adult perspective allowed me to see the truth: the popular kids back then were having their asses kicked by the horrors of puberty, just as I was. I was just too narcissistic at the time to see it. But that's how school is: you base your self-worth on comparisons made against an extremely small sample size.

One time in high school I was hanging out with my friend Mike and bored out of my mind. I was seventeen, and being bored out of my mind was my job. I decided it would be a good idea to call a local pizza place, order the most expensive pie, and have it delivered to a kid who had bullied me in grade school. Then I decided it would be a great idea to call five or six other pizza places and do the same thing. You can guess what happened next: said pizzas were delivered, the calls were traced to Mike's house, he got in a lot of trouble the following day, and I got off scot-free. I felt triumphant.

Now, I realize this story makes my childhood sound like an episode of *Happy Days*. I was lucky to have a pretty wholesome upbringing, all things considered. (I would joke that Mike and I went to the local burger stand to celebrate, but I'm pretty sure we actually did that.) Anyway, looking back on this incident, I feel some shame. At the time, I believed I was striking back against my oppressor. Now it just seems like I acted like a total jerk for no reason against a kid who hadn't teased me in years. I probably should've just gotten over it.

I'm not saying that there aren't true outsiders in schools who are picked on a disproportionate amount. Nor am I minimizing the hell that it is being a teenager. I have no sentimentality for childhood. I hated being a kid—all I wanted to be was older, and when I *was* older, I found that I was right all along about adulthood being way better.

It's just that the older I get, the more I believe that being quirky is sort of common and boring. Everybody has quirks. An intense curiosity about museums, classical music, and books doesn't make you unique. People have been caring about that shit for literally hundreds of years. What is weird is being really, really popular.

One clique at my high school labeled themselves the Love Posse and wrote "LP" on their arms—purely from a sociological perspective, that's strange. Even if that sort of thing happens all the time at other schools, I still can't wrap my head around it. What motivates people to draw letters on their bodies in order to signify their allegiance to a clique with perceived status among minors between the ages of fourteen and eighteen? Did they do it to feel superior to other students? Or were they protecting themselves from those students' resentment?

It's one thing to self-identify as a geek—doing so inoculates you against judgment. But if you seem to have it all, people have license to hate you, and if your hormones are already making you hate yourself, being popular must really suck sometimes. In the long run, I'd rather be Prince than Michael Jackson.

Perhaps it shouldn't be surprising that the very albums that derailed Prince's career in the mid-'80s have in many ways proved to be his most influential. The most interesting artists from the past two decades who have attempted a hybrid of classic rock, soul, and hip-hop with psychedelic imagery are biting at least partly from Prince's "weird" era: *Speakerboxxx/The Love Below*–era Outkast, *The ArchAndroid*–era Janelle Monáe, *channel ORANGE*–era Frank Ocean, *Yeezus*-era Kanye West, plus the Roots and Common on any number of their albums.

The hits from *1999* and *Purple Rain* will forever ensure that Prince lives the high life at Paisley Park. But artists don't emulate *Purple Rain:* they avoid doing so for the same reason that writers don't emulate Shakespeare—achieving that level of cultural significance seems inhuman. It would be wrong to describe any incarnation of Prince as his "everyman period," but holing up and making music that sounds like John Lennon and Sly Stone commiserating over an 808 drum machine seems more attainable than changing the world with another "When Doves Cry."

Prince's most profound cultural contribution was creating a blueprint for artists who seek to present aesthetically idiosyncratic music as both art and pop. Prince was a superstar who acted like a cult artist, which afforded him the wealth and status of the former and the license to flout commerciality, as artists in the latter group do. Prince has a huge audience but isn't beholden to their judgments or expectations. People actually get mad at Prince for not being weird *enough*.

It was different for Michael Jackson. It's trite to say that fame killed him. (His habit of taking enough sleep medication to quell a humpback whale is what killed him.) But MJ's death was awfully convenient for a lot of his fans. It became much easier to say that you liked his music without having to contend with all the baggage of his life once he was no longer a living person. Death also indirectly helped Jackson make better records—his 2014 album, *Xscape*, is the most enjoyable top-to-bottom MJ release since *Dangerous* (though I'm a defender of the non-greatest-hits half of *HIStory*).

Of course, *Xscape* isn't really an MJ record—it's just demos and sketches that other people (most notably Timbaland) completed after his death. But it's the sort of Michael Jackson record many fans would've preferred he had made in his later years. *Xscape* is a relatively straightforward collection of pleasing love songs with zero traces of the toxic self-pity or turgid balladry inspired by *Free Willy 2*. It's also (because of those omissions) likely the kind of album that could only be made over Michael Jackson's dead body.

So why did Prince win out over Michael Jackson? Well, for one thing, Prince lived, which enabled him to stick around long enough for his weirdness to become acceptable. MJ just got weirder and weirder until he stopped living. Only after dying did he become acceptably normal. If Michael Jackson were still around, I suspect his quirks would have continued to be amplified by his former popularity, which would've made him increasingly unpopular. He would still be one of the world's most recognized men, and one of the strangest—but not the right kind of strange. It was one thing for Prince to sequester himself at Paisley Park after *Purple Rain* and record songs that mashed up Curtis Mayfield, *Sgt. Pepper*, and *Penthouse* magazine. Prince's weirdness comes with a volume dial—he can turn it up or down as needed. When Prince guest-starred on *New Girl* in 2014, it seemed perverse for him to show up randomly as Zooey Deschanel's latest pal, but it proved to be odd only for how banal it was to see Prince be Prince on a network sit-com. Prince seems to understand that "being Prince" is now the most crucial part of his art. Prince can play the role of eccentric artistic genius with the same flair he brings to the guitar or his songwriting—it's sort of the only thing keeping him culturally significant at this point.

For a while, Jackson existed in the same "charismatic strange guy" zone, but his extreme fame eventually stripped him of the power to control his persona. Over time, the weirdest thing about Jackson was the way every aspect of his life was analyzed, publicized, dissected, and dismissed. Even now, Jackson's popularity is freakish and sort of terrifying. He will never be banal in any context. Anyway, this is my version of quirk theory, and I'm sticking to it.

CHAPTER 4
Gorilla Meets Gorilla

(White Stripes vs. Black Keys)

WHY CAN'T JACK WHITE and Dan Auerbach be friends?

Jack White is the former front man for a two-person blues-rock band called the White Stripes. Dan Auerbach is the current front man for a two-person blues-rock band called the Black Keys. The obvious answer to "Why can't Jack White and Dan Auerbach be friends?" is that Jack White has explicitly stated that he hates Dan Auerbach and that this hatred stems from White's belief that Auerbach copied his musical style. Even before he said it outright, White strongly implied his disdain for years. In a 2010 *Rolling Stone* interview, in response to a question about the White Stripes getting lumped into the "garage rock" movement that White was principally responsible for mainstreaming in the early aughts, White said his style had "a lot more to do with Jay Z than the Black Keys," a mysterious statement that's all the more enigmatic by virtue of its not being the least bit true. Fairly or unfairly, White's oeuvre is inarguably connected more strongly to that of the Black Keys than to the storied career of the artist presently known as Beyoncé's husband. White insisting otherwise is like Jay Z claiming he has more in common with a plate of garlic bread than with Kanye West.

Also, in a 2012 *Rolling Stone* profile of the Black Keys, there's a passing reference to White blocking Auerbach from entering his Nashville studio, a thoroughly awesome scenario straight out of *Road House* (with insecure guitarists subbed in for burly bouncers) that, disappointingly, isn't examined in detail.

In 2013, White's disgust for Auerbach was finally spelled out in an angry public screed disseminated by the tabloids. Perhaps in an effort to make her ex-husband appear insane, White's ex-wife Karen Elson submitted a bunch of his e-mails as evidence in a child custody fight, and the correspondence was later reported by *TMZ*. The most quoted snippet from these e-mails was White's dismay over his children attending the same Nashville school to which Auerbach sends his kids.

"My concern with Auerbach is because I don't want the kids involved in any of that crap," White wrote to Elson. "You aren't thinking ahead. That's a possible twelve fucking years I'm going to have to be sitting in kids' chairs next to that asshole with other people trying to lump us in together. He gets yet another free reign [*sic*] to follow me around and copy me and push himself into my world."

Let's set this e-mail aside for now. Imagine for a moment that White and Auerbach aren't successful musicians but merely two guys whose kids go to the same school. Now let's ask the question again: Why can't Jack White and Dan Auerbach be friends? They obviously should be friends, right? Frankly, it's kind of idiotic that they're not friends. I can't think of two contemporary rock stars (hell, people) who have as much in common. White and Auerbach were both born in the latter half of the '70s. Both were raised in hardscrabble middle-American cities (Detroit and Akron respectively). As teenagers in the '90s they obsessed over Delta blues musicians such as Robert Johnson and Son House, in spite of the fact that most people their age were obsessing over the authenticity of Gavin Rossdale at the time. Both formed bands with unconventional lineups that played music considered to be at least forty years past its commercial prime. Both released several albums on obscure indie labels years before their bands became modern rock-radio staples. Both have collaborated with Danger Mouse. Both claim to be fans of RZA of the Wu-Tang Clan. Both are divorced fathers. Both reside in Nashville and have been featured in some form on the ABC prime-time drama *Nashville*—Auerbach appeared as himself in a cameo, and White is the basis of a semiregular character named Liam McGuinnis, a sexy, principled rock-and-roll record producer. It's not impossible to talk about one without mentioning the other, but White and Auerbach seem to be grouped together more often than not.

If White truly were forced to sit in a kid's chair next to Auerbach for the next twelve years, at least he would have his choice of potential conversation starters. "Do you think the antimainstream Gen-X orthodoxy of grunge subliminally drove you into a moribund genre such as the blues?" "Why do dead-end rustbelt American towns foster such thriving rock scenes?" "What do *you* have against bass players?" This sounds like a dream come true to me. For many men with young children, finding a Relatable Dude in the midst of little-kid situations involves a never-ending and often fruitless search. After my wife and I had our son, I went through a period when I made no new "dad" friends. Whenever I took my son to his play group, I fantasized about running into an interesting guy with whom I'd be able to connect as our respective toddlers ritualistically disassembled Spider-Man toys. But it never happened. Over time I convinced myself that I was simply bad at meeting people. I felt lonely and alienated. Doors songs would come on the radio, and instead of laughing or changing the station, I *related*.

When Thurston Moore and Kim Gordon broke up, melodramatic indie-rock fans declared that they no longer believed in true love. I have similar feelings about Jack White and Dan Auerbach. I get that "Why can't Jack White and Dan Auerbach be friends?" might seem like a frivolous question: speculating on the status of the relationship between two similar celebrities is a silly exercise. But what I'm really asking is this: Why can't *I* make more male friends?

A while back, many years ago now, a guy named Eric, whom I used to work with at my hometown newspaper, invited me to his wedding. We had both moved on to different gigs: I was an editor at an alt weekly one hundred miles away in Milwaukee at the time, and he was doing some job at the University of Wisconsin in Madison, which I know he told me about but which at the moment escapes me. A lot of mutual former coworkers were at the wedding as well, so I knew a solid one-third of the guest list. But Eric didn't seat me next to any of those people during dinner. Instead I was placed next to three of Eric's friends from Madison—two of his then coworkers and a woman one of those coworkers was dating.

Now, I never spoke to Eric about this, but I assume I was put in that particular metal chair because one of his then coworkers wanted to meet me. He had read a series of articles I had written about '90s rock, and apparently he had a burning desire to speak to me about them. I realized this pretty quickly—somewhere between my first dinner roll and the arrival of my rubbery chicken and lukewarm vegetable mix—because the guy was very aggressive about making it known. After briskly introducing himself and verifying my identity as a holder of publicly stated opinions about the alternative era, he pressed me on an essay I wrote about the contentious relationship between Kurt Cobain and Axl Rose, which culminated in a backstage confrontation at the 1992 MTV Video Music Awards, my number one favorite awards show of all time. (Seriously, I'm going to talk about the 1992 VMAs a lot in this book. I suggest making it a drinking game.)

This coworker of my former coworker was really worked up over my assertion that Guns N' Roses was a genuinely subversive, even frightening band in its day. I based this thesis on my impressions as an eleven-year-old seeing the "Welcome to the Jungle" video for the first time. As you may remember, at one point in the video, Axl is in an electric chair, twitching like an ant under a magnifying glass, and a piercing scream is exiting his throat. It reminded me of the bloodthirsty gangs pouring out of New York City subways in *The Warriors*. Most metal bands that tried to be scary in the '80s were obsessed with Satan, but Satan never bothered me. (Satan was not a tangible concept in northeastern Wisconsin.) What scared me was fucking crazy people, and GNR acted like psychotics with swastikas carved into their foreheads.

That's what I believed when I was a kid, anyway. But this guy was having none of it. To him, GNR was no better than Poison. Now, if I enjoyed arguing about ye olde rock bands with strangers, I would happily point out that this is a plainly moronic thing to say. *Of course* GNR is better than Poison and every other poofy-haired joke from the late-'80s Sunset Strip music scene. But at that point in my life I didn't enjoy arguing about rock bands, like, at all. I did when I was twenty and felt the need to constantly assert my opinions in every social situation. But honestly, at that precise moment, all I wanted to do was finish my damn poultry. If this stranger equated *Look What the Cat Dragged In* with motherfucking *Appetite for* motherfucking *Destruction*, what did I care? It had no impact on my personal enjoyment of "Rocket Queen."

Only this guy wouldn't respect my polite but firm attempt to set some glam-rock boundaries. Not only did he have a problem with my Guns N' Roses opinions, he also had a problem with all my opinions. And not just my opinions, but the opinions of all rock critics. He hated the very idea of anyone writing about music professionally. He (apparently) deemed the act of grading records an affront to human decency. He was the most militant anti–Lester Bangs-ite I'd ever encountered. I couldn't believe my bad fortune. When I sat down, I had expected merely to be confronted with a mediocre meal. But my entire way of life was being called into question.

What gives? We already had a friend in common. We were both passionate about rock music. We were both drinking heavily in the late afternoon. What else do you need for a cordial interaction? But from the moment I sat down, our interaction was anything but cordial. We didn't have a conversation, we had a competition. His offense was challenging my defense. Instinctively, I put my guard up and pushed back, because I didn't want to be bested. I wanted to defeat this dickhead with the full force of my quip arsenal. I felt that instantly.

You could minimize this anecdote by saying, "Oh, that guy

was just a jerk" or "Well, Steve, you're probably overly sensitive about defending Axl Rose's honor." Both statements are true. But I remember this story because a similar scenario has played out countless times when I've encountered a fellow adult heterosexual male out in the wild. To borrow Jack White's phrase, it always feels like he's trying to push himself into my world, and I don't want any part of that crap.

Before we get further into that, let's delve into the particulars of the White-Auerbach rivalry. For starters, White's belief that Auerbach copied him is plausible, if not self-evident. It's likely that the Black Keys were at the very least inspired by the success of the White Stripes; dismissing *any* sort of connection between the rise of the White Stripes and the formation of the Black Keys strains credulity. It would be like Mumford & Sons claiming to have never heard of Bob Dylan. At the same time, the whole idea of blues-rock "originality" in the twenty-first century is itself a little ludicrous. Even the supposed novelty of a two-person lineup was hardly novel by the time the White Stripes became reluctant MTV stars. Before the White Stripes, two-person groups were de rigueur in '80s synth-pop—Jack and Meg were like Yaz if Yaz had listened to Hound Dog Taylor. If you count instrumental duos, you had Local H doing the two-person thing in the '90s. And don't forget the Beatles and Stones of alt rock's "quirky" wing, Ween and They Might Be Giants.

Then there is Flat Duo Jets, from Chapel Hill, North Carolina, fronted by the formidably monikered Dex Romweber. Flat Duo Jets started doing the stylishly primitive twoperson bluesy rock thing way back in the mid-'80s, when Jack White only fantasized about marrying his pretend sister one day. White has repeatedly cited Flat Duo Jets as an inspiration, and his label, Third Man Records, even reissued FDJ's pretty good 1991 album, *Go Go Harlem Baby*. (The LP includes a rendition of the Andrews Sisters' "[I'll Be with You] in Apple Blossom Time" that White closely mimicked onstage with the White Stripes in the mid-aughts.) But if anybody should have a gripe about interlopers pushing themselves into his world, it's Romweber. White has been pushing himself into Romweber's world for years.

So once again, we can see that nothing is ever truly original and that everything has roots in something else. Jack White might be a genius songwriter and the most singularly charismatic rock star of his era, but he didn't invent anything. Even if he put the idea in Auerbach's head, White doesn't have a patent on danceable gutbucket blues. The blues, by its nature, is based on recycling riffs and lyrics (even band lineup configurations!) drawn from a single communal well. I think this is pretty clear to anyone who isn't Jack White.

But let's say none of this is true and that White really is the inventor of two-person blues bands. How has White been harmed by the Black Keys? The Black Keys have not impinged on the White Stripes' legacy one iota. Jack White towers over Dan Auerbach in terms of celebrity and prestige. They exist in entirely different strata. That's the oddest thing about White's all-generations boycott of Auerbach and his kin: he's picking on someone who's nowhere near his status.

The White Stripes and Black Keys aren't really even part of the same era. The White Stripes formed in 1998, broke through to the mainstream in 2001 with *White Blood Cells,* peaked in popularity and critical esteem in 2003 with *Elephant,* and were basically finished by 2007, when Meg White's anxiety issues cut short a tour in support of the band's final album, *Icky Thump*. (The White Stripes officially broke up in 2011.) The Black Keys formed in 2001, had a middling career until 2010, then became an arena act when *Brothers* and 2011's *El Camino* went platinum, which for a rock band in the '10s is the equivalent of being Bon Jovi in the "Wanted Dead or Alive" video.

The White Stripes and the Black Keys appear to be contemporaries, but they're really not—their career arcs are situated about three years apart, which might not seem like a long time, but it's greatly affected how they're perceived. The Black Keys could potentially end up being the more successful band, but the White Stripes will always seem more important. Auerbach's songs have infiltrated deeper into the mainstream than White's, but there's no question that Jack White is the more prominent star. Auerbach is more popular, but White is more famous. This dichotomy can be illustrated most vividly in two ways:

(1) The Black Keys famously went on a licensing bonanza in order to promote *Brothers*, which at the time was a no-lose proposition because the Black Keys (like 99 percent of indie bands) were broke and largely unknown. For a few years the Black Keys provided the sound track for seemingly every commercial that advertised shitty American cars, shitty American TV shows, and shitty American "neighborhood" chain restaurants. It was a very wise move—licensing so many songs made the Black Keys one of the world's top bands. *Brothers'* biggest single, "Tighten Up," became a crossover hit the way few rock songs are in the twenty-first century. It was as overly familiar as a Katy Perry song—even people who couldn't pick Dan Auerbach out of a police lineup recognized it as "that fucking

song I hear every time there's a commercial break during the football game."

Jack White, meanwhile, wrote "Seven Nation Army," whose riff was transformed organically into a rallying cry that has been chanted by millions of people at countless sporting events around the world, ensuring that it will outlast every other rock song of its era.

(2) When Dan Auerbach had a messy divorce from Stephanie Gonis, in 2013, it was reported that he bequeathed a lock of Bob Dylan's hair, which he had previously purchased, to his ex as part of the settlement. Auerbach later said "Bob Dylan's hair" was actually a nickname for a psychedelic poster the couple shared, not Dylan's actual hair, which sort of ruins the story. But nevertheless: Dan Auerbach once had a poster hanging in his house called "Bob Dylan's hair."

Jack White, meanwhile, once told *Rolling Stone* that Bob Dylan offered to fix the gate outside his house.

In conclusion: The Black Keys are successful, but the White Stripes are legendary.

All this is true but also irrelevant: no matter the reality of White's relation to Auerbach in the universe and the fact that he *should* have no reason to feel threatened by Auerbach, White *does* feel threatened. White is not attracted by what he shares with Auerbach, he's repelled by it. He sees it as an invasion of his carefully curated personal space. To a person who has been so dutiful (OCD, even) about cultivating an air of iconoclastic eccentricity, the knowledge that there's another person hawking a more palatable version of the same shtick (and making tons of money off of it) must be maddening. Commonality is anathema to Jack White, and commonality, for Jack White, is represented by Dan Auerbach.

In an interview that White conducted with the *New York Times Magazine* in 2012, there's an interesting digression about White's preference for working with women rather than men in bands. In addition to Meg White there's Alison Mosshart, the lead singer of White's side project the Dead Weather, as well as the numerous undead Goth girls whom White has shaped into semiprofessional musical combos for his Third Man releases.

"When you're in a room of five guys, it becomes a bunch of gorillas in a cage," White said. "Girls don't have those hang-ups."

The *Times* profile suggested that White might also like working with women because he needs to be in control of everything he does, and the women he's chosen to collaborate with have been successfully (if not always happily) subjugated. That hypothesis seems to be supported by the album that White was promoting at the time, his first-ever solo LP, *Blunderbuss*, which underwent thorough analysis by music critics interrogating White's so-called problem with women. It's true (if you're inclined to read lyrics as a literal first-person representation of the writer's own experiences) that Jack White comes off like a dick on *Blunderbuss*. It's also true (as White himself pointed out when I interviewed him shortly after the record's release) that in the traditional narrative of blues songs—the milieu that White continues to draw from—*all* men come off like dicks.

The most remarkable song on *Blunderbuss* is "Hypocritical Kiss," in which White appears to playact an argument between himself and a person to whom he's very close but is about to become estranged from. Set to the prettiest and most delicate piano lick in White's canon — a far cry from the elbow slamming he gave the keyboards on the penultimate White Stripes LP, *Get Behind Me Satan* — "Hypocritical Kiss" enters the conversation after White has already said something unforgivable. "I know that you're mad at me / But if you're thinking like that, I think you'll see that you're mad at you, too." He's apologizing, but in that backhanded, deflecting way common to all night arguments between people who love each other so intensely it feels like hate sometimes.

Then White seems to switch perspectives, taking on the role of the other person in the argument. Strangely, White decides to give this person the best and most penetrating lines. "You're the boy / That talks but says nothing," the person says. "A big game to the ones / That you think will believe you."

In just a few lines, this person has accused White's first-person protagonist of being a phony, a liar, a big shot in an empty suit, and a blowhard. The last verse seems to switch back to White's perspective, and it's clear that those accusations have gotten under his skin. "Who the hell's impressed by you?" he thunders over those incongruously beautiful keys. "You would sell your own mother out / And then betray your dead brother with another / Hypocritical kiss." That's right: this conflict turns biblical in just two minutes and fifty seconds.

Perhaps because I happen to be a meddlesome music critic, I hear *Blunderbuss* as White's divorce record — though not about his divorce from Elson but rather from Meg White and the White Stripes.

In the *Times* story, White pushes back against the argument that White was essentially Meg's boss, calling her "the most stubborn person I've ever met," a person who "completely controlled the White Stripes" by deciding when the band would and wouldn't perform and therefore necessitating the dissolution of the band, which White still seems to actively regret and even resent. It sounds a lot like the scenario depicted in "Hypocritical Kiss."

Does "Hypocritical Kiss" really re-create the dynamic between Jack and Meg White? The only honest answer is, "I have no idea." White, for one, soundly rejected the idea when I asked him about it. "I think it's very funny that people nowadays still think if you use the word 'I' or 'she' you are talking about yourself or your girlfriend at the time," White said in an e-mail. "I mean, what year is it? Didn't they get rid of that prison in the '60s? If I say, 'I want to kill that man that came to my door' in a song today, by that logic a detective should be calling my house."

That is both a credible deflection and, in my view, kind of horseshit. White might not be a confessional songwriter, but the thematic consistency of *Blunderbuss* (elusive, treacherous women loom large in the lyrics) and the place the album occupies in the arc of White's life (it came out the year between the breakups of his band and second marriage) are a little too coincidental to be dismissed so easily. At the very least, "Hypocritical Kiss" can be appreciated as a critique by White of his own persona and a window into his perception of the way women complement and neutralize his worst character traits.

Jack White doesn't want to be friends with Dan Auerbach. I, on the other hand, would love to hang with half of the Black Keys. I would buy him drinks until he started venting about White. I'm desperate to know what he really thinks about the guy. Auerbach hasn't spoken about White publicly. If journalists have tried to get Auerbach to launch a shit-talking crusade against White, those attempts have apparently proved unsuccessful. But Auerbach has certainly been asked enough about White throughout his career.

From a 2003 interview with *Guitar World:* "When we started out, we had no idea who the White Stripes were. We never would have named ourselves the Black Keys if we had known about them."

From a 2009 interview with the music blog *Aquarium Drunkard:* "When Pat and I started, we were really sick of the White Stripes questions. *You sound just like the White Stripes,* or something ridiculous. We didn't know the White Stripes, we weren't part of that scene in Detroit, we didn't know anyone up there, it was annoying."

From a 2010 Artist of the Year profile in *Spin:* "We were in the shadow of the White Stripes when the garage-rock thing happened, and then we never felt like we fit in anywhere."

In 2012, David Lindquist of the *Indianapolis Star* asked Auerbach directly if he was "friendly" with White. "I don't know Jack," Auerbach replied, though he added that they had many mutual friends, including Patrick Keeler, the drummer for another Jack White side project, the Raconteurs.

"Not all musicians hang out," Auerbach concluded. "Not all writers hang out just because they're writers."

From virtually the beginning of his career, Dan Auerbach has been cast in the media as Jack White's twerpy little brother. Auerbach has been pretty gracious about it, all things considered, though over time the constant comparisons have obviously rankled him. Only once the Black Keys became massively popular was Auerbach allowed out of White's shadow. But if you've ever been somebody's little brother, you know that you never totally stop feeling the presence of that shadow.

Once the Black Keys rose to the level of superstars, a new undercurrent of resentment toward privileged indie rockers started appearing in the band's interviews. For instance, in that 2012 *Rolling Stone* profile of the Black Keys, Auerbach and his bandmate, Patrick Carney, complained bitterly about silently suffering slights from more fashionable bands during the Black Keys' formative years. Auerbach and Carney painted themselves as working-class plebs who had to find a way to make it in order to survive, in contrast with the so-called trust-fund babies they came to see as the enemy.

Auerbach picked up this narrative thread in a *Billboard* profile from the same period. "There's this weird thing that happened with being a successful band, and it has to do with rich, private-college kids who rule the indie rock world," he said. "We're both college dropouts. Driving around the country, paying for everything ourselves—this is the backup plan. The *only* plan, really."

Raised in Detroit as the youngest of ten children in a Catholic family, Jack White hardly comes from a privileged background. But as a self-appointed paragon of virtue who has relished casting public judgment on Auerbach's credibility, White all too easily fits the role of an indie-snob straw man, the sort of reductionist caricature that Auerbach and Carney tore apart out of frustration in the press. For Auerbach, White will forever be the most hulking gorilla in the vicinity of his cage.

Our culture isn't quite sure what to make of male friendship. Two dudes meeting each other and bonding over dude stuff is described with patently belittling nomenclature such as "bromance" and demeaned as a dullard bastion of frat parties and beer commercials. I wonder if men on some level have internalized this—I say this as a guy who reflexively recoils at any situation that seems a little too guy-centric. It's true that I like to hang out in bars and watch sports, but there's usually a voice in my head mocking me throughout. If you're a man with even a minimum level of self-awareness, it's difficult to be with other men in traditionally male situations and not feel at least a teensy bit bro-ish.

There's another problem with male friendship, which is that most guys are really bad at it. There's even a sociological theory, supported by decades of research, elucidating this phenomenon. It's called the male deficit model, and it postulates that men slot their friendships into categories such as "convenience friends" (guys who exchange favors but don't hang out) and "activity friends" (guys who play sports or go drinking together but otherwise don't experience true intimacy). In most cases, these friendships end once the respective needs of the men involved are satisfied.

"Of all people in America, adult, white, heterosexual men have the fewest friends," sociologist Lisa Wade observed in 2013. Wade writes that "when men get together, they're more likely to do stuff than have a conversation." This is classified as a "shoulder-to-shoulder" friendship, which is generally more superficial than the "face-to-face" friendships that women typically enjoy. This is to say that men generally don't like conversing, even with men they ostensibly like.

Now, I don't see anything wrong with shoulder-to-shoulder friendships. If you're married, sometimes the best part of hanging with the buddies is *not* having to talk. Often when I come home from hanging out with pals my wife will ask for updates on the personal lives of my friends—the state of their jobs, the health of their kids, and so on—and I'll have no idea. I've just spent three hours ranking NFL tight ends from the '80s and '90s, not hashing out my feelings. If I need to unburden myself about anything, that's what my wife is for.

According to Wade, that is such a *dude* thing to say: three-fourths of straight male Caucasians list their wives as their only confidant. Wade's data suggests that men desire those face-to-face relationships with other men, but for whatever reason they can't sustain them. Wade's theory (again supported by research data) is that men are essentially conditioned to be alienated from each other, because socially mandated "masculine" traits such as competitiveness and self-sufficiency undermine the ability to be vulnerable and empathetic (qualities associated with feminine behavior). This can cause (to cite two random examples) guitarists in competing rock bands to automatically see each other as enemies rather than compatriots, and strangers sitting next to each other at a wedding reception to argue rather than bond over '80s hair metal.

The core human need for companionship is constantly undercut by the core masculine need to be perceived as masculine by other men. You know those terrible *Hangover* movies in which a group of bachelor-party knuckleheads refer to themselves as a wolf pack? A wolf pack is actually a pretty decent metaphor for male friendship—it's a life-or-death battle disguised as a nurturing relationship, one in which one wolf "must" assert control over another.

Why should I expect Jack White and Dan Auerbach to sit next to each other for twelve years when I can't stand the company of another guy for one meal? I am bad at meeting people, and the people I most often try to make friends with are equally bad at meeting people. But I hold out hope for change. The next time I take my son to the park and I see another dad playing with his kid, I will tell myself that my need for intimacy must overpower the wiring in my brain that compels me to assert my superiority. I will try to look at this man as a brother. Because he's a nice gorilla, and I'm a nice gorilla, and deep down we both want out of solitary confinement.

CHAPTER 5

We Crash into Each Other Just So We Can Feel Something

(Taylor Swift vs. Kanye West)

THE MOST OVERANALYZED ninety seconds of the early twenty-first century begin with one Taylor (the one we call Lautner) announcing that another Taylor (the one we call Swift) has won a Moonman for Best Female Video at the 2009 MTV Video Music Awards.

The one we call Swift registers her surprise via circular, ruby-red lips. "What?!" she exclaims. Her perfect enunciation makes lipreading as easy to understand as audiotape.

She approaches the stage. Unlike the usual displays of Taylor Swift awards-show incredulity, this one seems genuine. Swift looks legitimately stunned. "I always dreamed about what it would be like to win one of these someday, but I never actually thought it would happen," she says. "I sing country music." She's like Carrie before the pig's blood hits.

Then it happens, though the tape doesn't show exactly when it happens. When it comes to documenting controversial coups d'état, MTV is no Zapruder. Instead of showing us how Kanye

West approached the stage—was he tentative or did he just barrel forward guilelessly, as he did with Kim on the motorcycle in the "Bound 2" video?—there's a brief cutaway to the audience. Then Kanye is just there, next to Taylor, microphone already in hand, like we're watching a Friars Club roast of Taylor Swift all of a sudden.

Kanye begins by halfheartedly congratulating a by then even more genuinely overwhelmed Taylor Swift. "I'm really happy for you," he says, which is even less credible than that sitcom pilot he did for HBO. (Look it up. I'm not joking.) Then comes the meme: "Imma let you finish."

Could Kanye have foreseen how often people would rehash *that?* (Answer: probably. This is Kanye West we're talking about. He pops wheelies on the zeitgeist.) He then proceeds to demolish the credibility of the MTV Video Music Awards, which isn't hard, as the credibility of the VMAs is constructed out of sand and Scotch tape. But it's still a ballsy move, given how uncomfortable the moment already is.

"Beyoncé had one of the best videos of all time!" Kanye declares. In subsequent discussions about what Kanye did, this part tends to be overlooked: Kanye was being chivalrous! Or, rather, he was *attempting* to be chivalrous. (In reality, Kanye overshadowed Beyoncé, a very unchivalrous move, which is why we're talking about him and not her.) Theoretically, he was standing up for the wife of Jay Z, his friend/benefactor/rival. This is what Kanye always does at awards shows. He did it again at the 2015 Grammys, when Beyoncé lost in the Album of the Year category to Beck's *Morning Phase.* Now, it's clear why *Morning Phase* won—it's Beck's Christopher Cross album, and the Grammys love it when formerly hip artists enter their "two turntables and a badass pink flamingo album cover" period.

Reasonable people who get what the Grammys are (i.e., stodgy and lame) understand this.

But it's never Kanye's job to be reasonable. It's his job to be the opposite of reasonable, though he wasn't *totally* in the wrong there. Beyoncé was nominated for "Single Ladies (Put a Ring on It)," which went on to win Video of the Year but lost to Swift's "You Belong with Me" (which wasn't nominated for Video of the Year) in the category of Best Female Video. So when you take the awards-show calculus into account, Beyoncé probably should have beaten Swift in the lesser category. Nevertheless, the audience at New York's Radio City Music Hall rained boos on Kanye after he handed the mike back to Swift and swiftly exited. Having a decent argument doesn't always make you right.

That was the beginning, middle, and end of the Taylor Swift–Kanye West incident. Taylor and Kanye have long since made up, though the rivalry continues to live on in the public imagination. It's just too irresistible. Here you have the two most impactful pop stars so far this century, and they're squaring off at the most culturally significant awards show, and no matter how silly the whole thing seems on the surface, you don't have to dig deep to see the symbolism.

For those inclined to view awards shows as fundamentally prejudiced against artists of color (an impression supported by the historical record) Kanye interrupting Taylor in order to complain on Beyoncé's behalf seems like a righteous "fuck you" move in response to a multitude of past sins. For those inclined to view awards shows as fundamentally prejudiced against female artists (another impression supported by the historical record), Kanye interrupting Taylor seems like another instance of a man saying "fuck you" to a woman finally getting her due recognition. For those inclined to view awards shows as props for a celebrity-obsessed media, Taylor Swift vs. Kanye West strongly reiterated that impression as well. Those ninety seconds are still being replayed, rehashed, and recontextualized over and over again, even as Taylor and Kanye move through new sounds and guises. No way that happens if we're talking about two other people.

For the sake of this discussion, I'm going to focus on just two aspects of Taylor vs. Kanye—one pertains specifically to how it affected both parties, and the other explores one way this rivalry resonated broadly. First things first: Taylor vs. Kanye sort of made Taylor and Kanye. Not that they weren't already made, but the 2009 VMAs crystallized the way we've come to perceive their respective career arcs.

Let's start with Taylor: as Swift herself acknowledged during her truncated acceptance speech, winning a Moonman was a huge step toward becoming a dominant mainstream pop star. "I sing country music," she said, leaving the second part of that sentence—"and country singers don't win VMAs"—unspoken. It's easy to forget that Swift was once considered a niche artist. Five years after the VMAs, when Swift released *1989*, she insisted on calling it her pop record, even though her previous LP, *Red*, had spawned several pop hits and moved more than four million units. By 2014, Swift had already assumed her place at the center of pop music; nobody was more popular or more representative of the pop establishment. Positioning *1989* at that point as a crossover move seemed redundant. Sure, Swift had stopped taking cues from Tim McGraw and was by then aping Jan Hammer's soundscapes from the *Miami Vice* sound track, but she had been running the Hot 100 for years. Swift didn't need to "cross" into the mainstream. She *was* the mainstream.

Back in 2009, however, Taylor Swift beating Beyoncé at the VMAs represented a major paradigm shift. There had been major crossovers before: Swift will likely never approach the sales statistics racked up by Garth Brooks and Shania Twain—the Mark McGwire and Sammy Sosa of the record industry's steroids era, in the '90s. But Swift attained a level of prestige in pop circles that Garth and Shania never had. Garth and Shania were always interlopers; Swift was an insurgent. She took over.

From the VMAs onward, Swift began separating herself in earnest from the "country singer" label. And she kept on winning awards—at the Grammys, just four months after Kanye bogarted her moment of MTV glory, Swift became the youngest person ever to win Album of the Year, which she was awarded for her second record, *Fearless*. Swift started winning so many awards that her so-called surprised face became the basis of every Taylor Swift impersonation, from *Saturday Night Live*'s Kristen Wiig on down.

What the awards did was give Swift credibility with an audience that might've otherwise ignored her. The recognition also made it easier for Swift to slowly back away from the country audience that had originally sustained her. This put Swift in a unique position. No matter how many millions of albums Twain sold—1995's *The Woman in Me* and 1997's *Come On Over* have been certified platinum a combined thirty-two times—she never had the license to become a full-on pop star. Shania had to play a different version of herself, depending on the format; any given song might have steel guitars and fiddles on country radio and dance beats and synth splashes on pop radio. For 2002's *Up!*, Twain made separate pop, country, and international versions of the album—the international version, weirdly, was done in Twain's music-gone-Bollywood style—so that the subsections of her audience could remain comfortably segregated.

Awards shows are the entertainment industry's way of anointing its most valuable stars and turning them into institutions. For Swift, her voluminous trophy case empowered her to dictate the terms under which her music would be received. Swift could do whatever she wanted, and it would automatically register as pop music just by virtue of its being hers. If Taylor Swift had decided that she wanted *1989* to be a Bollywood record, the pop charts would've suddenly been overloaded with songs and videos featuring sitars and manic dancers traipsing joyously through the streets of New Delhi.

As Swift was busy being crowned amid the post-VMA fallout, Kanye was fighting for his damn life as a viable artist. The degree to which people demonized him for being disrespectful to Taylor Swift is comical now, but at the time it seemed like his career might really be over. Ice T once said that he knew Body Count's incendiary anthem "Cop Killer" had crossed the line from run-of-the-mill controversy to national disgrace when President George H. W. Bush spoke his name in anger during a press conference. Kanye, incredibly, found himself in a similar predicament after the VMAs when Barack Obama reportedly called him a jackass during an off-the-record conversation with a reporter.

Obama was just echoing the prevailing (or at least most loudly articulated) sentiment about West at the time. Hating Kanye became a brief form of monoculture: people who normally disagree about everything came together to denounce him. Even publicly avowed birther Donald Trump joined the president in deriding West's actions, though Trump inevitably took it a step further and demanded a Kanye boycott. (As if any transgression could usurp "Gold Digger" from wedding reception playlists.) Perhaps the worst indignity that West had to endure was his public apology on Jay Leno's disastrous post–*Tonight Show* prime-time chat program.

"I feel like Ben Stiller in *Meet the Parents* when he messed everything up and Robert De Niro asked him to leave," West told Leno, using an analogy that, like Kanye's music, demands to be appreciated on multiple levels of irony and earnestness. "That was Taylor's moment, and I had no right in any way to take it from her. I am truly sorry."

At the time, a lot of people doubted whether Kanye was truly sorry. And apparently they were right to doubt him, as West later claimed in an interview with the *New York Times'* Jon Caramanica that he was pressured into apologizing. He insisted, "I don't have one regret" about barging in on Swift. Part of his penance for the Swift episode, West said, was making *My Beautiful Dark Twisted Fantasy,* a sprawling statement of purpose self-consciously crafted as a "mind-blower" that was instantly dubbed a classic upon its release, fourteen months after that fateful night at the VMAs. West characterized *Fantasy* as "a long, backhanded apology."

"I was like: 'Let me show you guys what I can do,'" he told Caramanica. "'And please accept me back. You want to have me on your shelves.'"

Now, it's possible that West was full of it there. The record he was promoting at the time of the Caramanica interview, *Yeezus,* was the opposite of a crowd-pleaser, and he clearly intended to position *Yeezus* as a more daring statement than *Fantasy,* in the way that artists often disparage their previous album when promoting their new album. But it's also plausible to take West's words, if not entirely at face value, as a valuable insight into his head space as he embarked on *Fantasy*. West had to audition for the public's affection again. You can hear this eagerness to please echoed most obviously in the self-deprecating chorus of "Runaway" ("Let's have a toast for the douchebags!"), but it also comes through on undeniable killers such as "Power" and "All of the Lights," which stand as some of the most purely likable music of West's career.

If Swift was already ascending as a pop commodity before West accosted her at the VMAs, Kanye was in something of a holding pattern. His fourth record, *808s & Heartbreak*, polarized fans in a way that none of his previous records had. It's still the weirdest LP in West's discography. *808s* is an epic, self-pitying wallow, a breakup LP as well as a "mourning the recent death of my mom" record. The music is sparse, chilly, and vocoder-heavy. The intent is to express profound alienation from the rest of mankind. Not exactly a party record, but it grows on you. Plus, *808s* proved to be hugely influential for sensitive-guy MCs such as Drake and Childish Gambino, who used "sad Kanye" as a starting point for a soft-rock revolution in hip-hop.

Sometimes I think I actually prefer *808s* to *Fantasy*, which is overly padded with interstitial skits, the "drum solo!" of rap albums. My favorite Kanye LPs—*Graduation*, *808s*, and *Yeezus*—are his "no skit" albums, which I'm more apt to put on for fun than his "plus skits" records, *The College Dropout*, *Late Registration*, and *My Beautiful Dark Twisted Fantasy*. In some ways, the "plus skits" records are more cohesive as statements, but I'm not going to sit through that endless Chris Rock bit in "Blame Game" if I'm punching up songs in a bar. Give me the robo-voiced death ballads any day.

Ultimately, I regard Kanye West albums the way I regard Beatles albums and Stanley Kubrick films: it's more about how each piece fits together in the overall body of work than about my feelings for any particular piece. Kanye had to make *My Beautiful Dark Twisted Fantasy* to win people back and because it made sense to go big after *808s & Heartbreak*. Then he made *Yeezus* because going grimy and angry made sense after the double shot of coke-and-caviar excess served up on *Fantasy* and the Jay Z collaboration, *Watch the Throne.*

Kanye might be a pop star, but as an artist he's expected to be deep and idiosyncratic, rather than just churn out obvious hits. You digest his music as you would a prestige cable drama. You study it closely to see how each new record connects to what came before it, and you assume that whatever seems unexpected or random will pay off later on, upon future listens or even future records.

Taylor is the center of pop, and Kanye is the pop outlaw—that's the dynamic that was established for the first time at the 2009 VMAs. Taylor and Kanye get a little farther apart each year, but this symbiotic connection will probably never be broken as long as either one of them still matters.

The worst part of the post-VMA Kanye West pile-on was the rank hypocrisy on display. Wasn't Kanye acting like *every single person on the planet* when it comes to awards shows? Granted, he shouldn't have stormed the stage and embarrassed Swift (and Beyoncé, who got the rawest end of the deal there). But the substance of Kanye's protest—the wrong person won an award!—is the basis of nearly every conversation that's ever taken place in the history of our moronic televised arts contests.

You could even argue that provoking those conversations is the main reason awards shows exist. In his book *The Economy of Prestige,* author and professor James English suggests that awards serve a dual, seemingly contradictory role in society: first, they exist in order to bestow a marker of quality on items (such as films, music, and TV shows) that don't have any intrinsic value. But awards also create a forum where the value of what awards represent—the commodification of art—can be debated. If you're a person who believes that art should be "above" awards because it "reduces" the form to a sport, you are inadvertently reiterating the importance that awards have in our culture. It's all part of the same matrix. No matter what we do, we're all Oscar's bitch.

Kanye somehow got punished for both respecting the VMAs too much and respecting the VMAs too little. When he "Imma let you finish"-ed Taylor, Kanye looked like a jerk for upstaging Swift during a big moment. And when he complained that Beyoncé should've won instead, he seemed callow for caring about a dumb Moonman.

Give this to Kanye: at least he let it go. Kanye even showed he could laugh at himself when he smirkingly bum-rushed Beck at the Grammys six years later. (And then, in Kanye-esque fashion, the irony reverted back to earnestness when West told a reporter that Beck should've really handed his award to Beyoncé.) The same cannot be said for the rest of us when it comes to awards show controversies that never seem to go away.

Look at the never-ending preoccupation with *Crash* beating *Brokeback Mountain* for Best Picture of 2005. Complaining that *Brokeback Mountain* was "robbed" by *Crash* has become an annual tradition—it comes up any time some website wants to preview the Oscars by ranking the worst Best Picture winners ever. *Crash* inevitably ends up near the top of the list, if not at number 1. Hating *Crash* has become what I like to call a Default Smart Opinion. A Default Smart Opinion is an opinion that's generally considered to be inarguable because it's repeated ad nauseam by seemingly intelligent individuals. Other examples include "Nickelback sucks!," "*The Big Bang Theory* sucks!," and "Kim Kardashian is dumb and also sucks!"

Now, I'm not necessarily disputing the truth of those takes. But I'm not a fan of Default Smart Opinions as a concept. A Default Smart Opinion is like a pair of pants—you just put it on. No additional thought is required. The usual formula for a regular smart opinion—research plus careful consideration plus nuanced analysis—doesn't apply. You needn't actually listen to a Nickelback album or watch *The Big Bang Theory* or study Kim Kardashian's collected philosophical scrolls. You merely have to recite recycled bits of conventional wisdom.

The subtext of a Default Smart Opinion is that the person holding it is seeking to assert his or her superiority over those who might feel differently. It's more about setting yourself apart from an anonymous mass of people that you've decided to stigmatize than it is about assessing the actual work in question.

For instance, consider the following passage taken from a conversation between two writers discussing *Crash* that was posted on the website *The Awl* eight years after the movie was released:

> Liking *Crash* is a symptom of the worst kind of moral and cultural laziness. I feel free to make the wildest assumptions about *Crash* enthusiasts: they probably also enjoy Dave

Matthews' "Crash" and making Guy Fieri jokes. They pronounce it "cue-pon," not "coo-pon." They eat at the kind of restaurant where the provenance of each ingredient is carefully listed but the servers and bussers don't get health insurance. They buy scented candles and the wrong kind of disposable napkins. *Crash* fans also wade into the comments of news articles to take issue with referring to George Zimmerman as a murderer because "we don't have all the facts yet" and pride themselves on their objectivity.

Earlier in the conversation, the same writer asserts that "one can plot a straight line from *Crash*'s Best Picture win to Californians passing a proposition banning gay marriage *and* a proposition making chickens being raised for slaughter more comfortable in the same year *and congratulating themselves for doing so.*" So not only is liking *Crash* a symptom of being a simpleton, *Crash* is also the very virus that causes people to hold terrible opinions subsequent to viewing and enjoying it.

Now, you could point out that ascribing a whole set of values to a sizable group of strangers based on those individuals' feelings about a particular movie also represents "the worst kind of moral and cultural laziness." But let's set that aside for now. We clearly have a dangerous situation on our hands. *Crash* is contagious. *Crash* is here to destroy us all. *Crash* is the worst "good" movie ever made.

This characterization of *Crash* really made me want to rewatch *Crash*.

If you haven't seen it: *Crash* is one of those movies in which there are a dozen or so characters who seem to be unrelated at the start of the movie, then as the plot unfolds you learn that (aha!) they are connected after all. (Other examples of this genre include Robert Altman's *Short Cuts* and Paul Thomas Anderson's *Magnolia*.) Another important point about *Crash* is that everybody in the film is racist. Matt Dillon plays a racist cop; Sandra Bullock plays the racist wife of a semiracist politician portrayed by Brendan Fraser; Don Cheadle is a cop who is prejudiced against Puerto Ricans; Ludacris is prejudiced against anyone who isn't black; Ryan Phillippe seems like a nonracist but then he winds up being the most destructive racist of all.

You get the picture. Every character in *Crash* is defined by his or her views on race. That's not an oversight by the filmmakers. The characters aren't accidentally single-minded archetypes. Rather, *Crash*'s one-note hectoring was wholly intentional.

In a 2014 interview, the film's director and cowriter, Paul Haggis, said he made *Crash* in order to "bust liberals," referring specifically to "those people who think, 'We have it all figured out,' [and] who think, 'We're good people, we're good liberals' —those are the people you can't trust, because there's a level of denial." This worldview (that "good people" are really just bigots in denial) pervades *Crash*. A person who appears to be noble in the early scenes will be revealed to be flawed later on, whereas a person who seems to be bad will later be redeemed. If this idea seems a little obvious or trite to you, then the execution of *Crash* won't make it seem any less heavy-handed. This movie addresses race the same way Liam Neeson greets Albanian human trafficking syndicates.

I originally saw *Crash* when it was released in theaters, and I thought it was okay. It wasn't the best movie I'd ever seen, and it wasn't the worst. It was just...a movie. It didn't seem exceptional in any way. If it hadn't won Best Picture, I doubt I'd be thinking about it more than a decade later.

Back then, I remember several scenes that actively annoyed me, particularly the part in which a locksmith (played by Michael Peña) is confronted at gunpoint by an Iraqi business owner (Shaun Toub) who believes that the locksmith conspired to have him robbed. When the man pulls the trigger, he appears to accidentally shoot the locksmith's daughter at point-blank range, only...she's not shot after all. It turns out that the shop owner's gun is loaded with blanks, but when you watch the scene for the first time, it's implied that she's saved by divine intervention. (And yes, if you haven't seen *Crash*, I just spoiled the most dramatic part of the movie. You're welcome!)

This struck me as the epitome of cheap audience manipulation. But overall I thought *Crash* was well acted—especially by Dillon, who spends the majority of the film jutting out his chin in a convincingly "redneck cop" sort of way. At any rate, I'm pretty sure I didn't stop supporting marriage rights or start supporting the mistreatment of chickens after watching *Crash* and not despising it.

In 2005, I was primed to like *Crash* by the reviews, which were mostly positive. Roger Ebert gave *Crash* four stars out of a possible four and later declared it the year's best film. A less favorable and more prescient take was offered by David Edelstein, who marveled at the "spectacle of all those terrific actors (of all those races) working together and giving such potentially laughable material their best shot." That sounds about right to me.

When I revisited *Crash* a decade later, I was primed for the opposite reaction: I was sure I would fucking loathe it. *Crash* is one of the rare films whose reputation actually suffers because it won Best Picture. The award forever compelled people who might otherwise be indifferent about *Crash* to formulate a passionate yay-or-nay opinion, and *Crash*'s naysayers have always been way more strident. But hating *Crash* has had another weird side effect on the film's legacy: those inclined to argue vehemently against *Crash* being an important film are most responsible for keeping *Crash* meaningful years later. Hating other undeserving Best Picture winners from the '90s and '00s— *Titanic, Shakespeare in Love, Slumdog Millionaire*—isn't all that interesting. But hating *Crash* will still matter thirty years from now.

Going into my second viewing, I was keenly aware of the potential for overrating *Crash* in reaction to the hyperbolic criticism it has received. I'm inclined to defend anything that "smart" people go out of their way to hate. But even I would never argue that *Crash* deserves to be considered the best of anything. Rewatching *Crash* did provide a few surprises—for instance, I forgot how much *Crash* resembles the talky ensemble dramas (such as *2 Days in the Valley* and *Things to Do in Denver When You're Dead*) that followed *Pulp Fiction*. An early scene between Ludacris and Larenz Tate in which they talk about how much to tip a coffee shop waitress before pulling a carjacking seems like a deliberate Tarantino homage.

Also, the scene where the little girl almost gets shot made me choke up, because I have a kid now, which has made me soft and sentimental and easy to manipulate. But overall, my original impression was unchanged. *Crash* is still just...a movie.

Film historian Mark Harris has a theory about movies that don't win Best Picture (which he calls X films) and their relationship to movies that do (these are Y films). Y films are often derisively viewed, he writes, as "bromidic, blandly messagey, or hopelessly anodyne (there's potential in all of us; you never know what might happen; everyone has something to overcome). And when they're not telling you that everything will be OK, they're addressing important subjects with noncontroversial philosophical shrugs (racism is bad; if you repress emotions, they'll come back to hurt you; *we're all connected*)." Harris is referring to films such as *Dances with Wolves, Forrest Gump,* and, obviously, *Crash.*

X films, meanwhile, include *Goodfellas, Pulp Fiction,* and *Brokeback Mountain.* These films "tend to be dark, cynical, existential or nihilist, physically or emotionally violent, R-rated, and somewhat savage in outlook," Harris says. "They are often by, about, and for the alienated, the skeptical, and the enraged." Harris admits (as I do) that "'X' movies are more to my personal taste than 'Y' movies—but the least of them still reassure and flatter their target audience by congratulating it for its worldview in *exactly* the same way that 'Y' movies do."

What Harris doesn't (or perhaps can't) explain is why the Y movie always seems to beat out the X movie in the short term and then suffer in reputation over the long haul as the X movie grows in stature. I suppose you could just say that X movies are inherently better and therefore have a better shelf life, but that view seems to flatter the people who do the remembering. Those inclined to feel affinity for "the alienated, the skeptical, and the enraged" also tend to be the ones writing the history books.

What if the defining characteristic of an X film isn't that it's dark or innovative or "better" but *only* that it didn't win the big award? If *Crash* winning Best Picture ultimately hurt the film's overall legacy, it's possible that *Brokeback Mountain* seems more significant because it didn't win. Not winning exaggerates *Brokeback*'s outsider appeal. *Crash* beating *Brokeback Mountain* is the best thing that ever happened to *Brokeback*'s street cred.

Awards shows wouldn't exist if you didn't have one group putting forward a highly flawed theory of what constitutes quality in a given field and another group complaining that this standard hopelessly misses the mark. You can't have an X without a Y, and vice versa. The Y side has the numbers, but the X side is more stalwart, in part as a reaction against Y's hegemony. Eventually, enthusiasm from the masses for Y moves on, allowing X to take over.

How does this apply to Taylor Swift and Kanye West? Taylor feels like a Y artist. Nobody currently has a better understanding of what the public wants and needs from pop music. She makes songs that even people who believe they are above enjoying Taylor Swift songs can't help falling for. A skeptic might very well call her music anodyne or bland, but millions of people from disparate backgrounds see their own lives in her songs. She has the profound gift of being able to speak broadly and have it resonate in uniquely personal ways.

Kanye, meanwhile, feels like an X. He can only speak for himself—sometimes he seems interested in communicating exclusively *with* himself. While he's one of the world's most recognized pop stars, he is only fitfully interested in playing the pop game. He's released at least two albums (*808s & Heartbreak* and *Yeezus*) so anticommercial they would've killed a lesser career. But it's generally accepted that West's most difficult music will only grow in esteem.

This analogy is not perfect. The main weakness is that Kanye has won a lot of awards, though he only brings this up when he's not winning the *right* awards. In 2013, when his dark, cynical, existential, nihilist LP *Yeezus* did not garner an Album of the Year nomination, he said this during a concert in Phoenix:

I'm thirty-six years old, and I have twenty-one Grammys. That's the most Grammys of any thirty-six-year-old. Out of all of those twenty-one Grammys, I've never won a Grammy against a white artist. So when the Grammy nominations come out, and *Yeezus* is the top one or two album on every single list but only gets two nominations from the Grammys, what are they trying to say? Do they think that I wouldn't notice? Do they think that, some way, that I don't have the power to completely diminish all of their credibility at this moment?

But no, no; only positive energy [and] only positive vibes. But when you see me talking about what people are doing when I say "marginalized," when I say "boxed in," when I say "hold back," when I say "people are afraid of the truth," that's one example right there in front of you.

As is the case when a person of notoriety says something interesting, this was widely reported as a "rant." It's true that Kanye was probably a little angry when he said it, and not everything he says is true: West has beaten Eminem and the Beastie Boys in the rap categories and numerous other white people in the songwriting categories. But in other, more important ways, Kanye is absolutely correct. On artistic merit, *Yeezus* deserved an Album of the Year nomination. Not nominating Kanye does marginalize him. But this does not matter, because Kanye's power to diminish the credibility of awards shows is real. It just takes a decade or so to kick in.

CHAPTER 6
We Finally Talk About Beatles vs. Stones

WHY DID IT take so long for me to get to the Beatles vs. the Rolling Stones? That we're just now getting to this rivalry at this point in the book I suspect will anger at least two groups of readers: people over the age of fifty and people who mistakenly believe that I'm ranking these rivalries in descending order of cultural importance.

(I'm not ranking anything. Each chapter in this book was assigned a number, and those numbers were printed on Ping-Pong balls that were subsequently chosen at random from one of those hot-air lotto tanks. This is how all great literature is organized.)

To be honest, I seriously considered not even writing about Beatles vs. Stones. Well, maybe I wasn't *that* serious: I knew I could never justify doing a book on pop-music rivalries that left out Beatles vs. Stones. It would be like writing about American history and not delving into the Civil War. Yes, the Civil War has been amply covered elsewhere, but leaving it out for dubious reasons (i.e., "Yawn; boring; go rent the Ken Burns thing instead") is untenable.

Let me be clear: I love both bands truly, madly, deeply. I'm a regular Alan Rickman when it comes to the Beatles and the Stones. I do not subscribe to the obnoxious notion that music that existed before I was born is somehow an affront to me. This idea is oddly common among music fans, even people who would never think that way about other forms of culture. You never hear cinephiles complain that people still care about dead white men such as Orson Welles and Alfred Hitchcock. Nobody is idiotic enough to classify Martin Scorsese movies as emblems of boomer culture. And yet this happens routinely with classic rock acts. Hating (or at least resenting) your parents' music is expected if not encouraged. You might even get your Gen-X or Millennial card revoked if you don't automatically classify Tom Petty as "dad rock." Pop still seems to bring out the provincialist in us all, I guess.

I never cared about whether a band was "new" or "belonged" to my demographic. My only concerns were "new to me" and "where can I find the best possible shit?" And when I started caring about bands, in my early teens, I soon learned that the Beatles and Stones were the best possible shit. It didn't matter that the Beatles broke up seven years before I was born or that the Stones were well into their "neon Arsenio suit jacket" phase by the time I was aware of them. I grew up with both bands because in their prime they made better songs than anybody else.

I got into the Beatles and Stones the way so many classic-rock heads from later generations do—through my dad's tape collection. I feel like I'm describing a scene out of a Cameron Crowe movie, but I swear that's how it happened. My entry points were *Sgt. Pepper's Lonely Hearts Club Band* for the Beatles and *Big Hits (High Tide and Green Grass)* for the Stones; from the beginning, it was madly ambitious art-pop on one side and filthy-ass garage punk on the other.

Like that, the dichotomy that was established for countless rock fans back in the '60s was set firmly in my mind. I loved the Beatles and Stones for completely different reasons, yet I knew they would always be connected. I needed them both.

Instinctively, I could sense that Beatles vs. Stones encompassed every essential attribute that I would subsequently seek out in every band I'd encounter afterward. Without realizing it most of the time, I've judged bands according to whether they're a "Beatles band" or a "Stones band." Nirvana, Wilco, Guided by Voices (on their albums), Animal Collective, and Real Estate are Beatles bands. Guns N' Roses, Guided by Voices (in concert), Queens of the Stone Age, and the White Stripes are Stones bands.

Sometimes these designations are based less on how the bands sound than on esoteric criteria that make sense only in my mind. The Hold Steady, for instance, is clearly a Stones band, because they make me want to live a stupidly decadent lifestyle, as if I were spending the night laying down tracks with Keith Richards in the basement of a sprawling mansion in the south of France. The National, however, is a Beatles band, because their songs seem like spiritual descendants of John Lennon's bitterest, quietest, most soulful tracks (e.g., "I'm So Tired" and "Sexy Sadie") on the White Album.

Here's my problem: we've heard all this before many, many times. What can I possibly say about Beatles vs. Stones that would seem original or even necessary? Beatles vs. Stones has to be the most discussed rivalry ever. People still talk about it all the time, even though the Beatles haven't been a working band since the mid-twentieth century and the Stones have been holograms since leg 2 of the *Voodoo Lounge* tour.

Everybody already knows that the Beatles represented witty mop-top purity and the Stones represented greasy big-dicked danger and that these opposing signifiers had great cultural significance that inspired a generation to protest the Korean War and investigate the Monica Lewinsky scandal and mow down mountains of blow with John Travolta and Mark Wahlberg at the Peach Pit. (Sorry, old people, but anything that happened before 2005 is part of the same historical soup as far as the young are concerned.)

Rather than regurgitate yet another iteration of the same old conventional wisdom on Beatles vs. Stones, allow me to quote the following passage from a 2013 book entitled (conveniently enough) *Beatles vs. Stones*, by Atlanta professor John McMillian:

> The Beatles and the Stones also represent two sides of one of the twentieth century's greatest aesthetic debates. To this day, when people want to get to know each other better, they often ask: "Beatles or Stones?" A preference for one group over the other is thought to reveal something substantial about one's personality, judgment, or temperament. The clichés about the two groups are sometimes overdrawn, but they still retain a measure of plausibility. With some qualifications, the Beatles may be described as Apollonian, the Stones as Dionysian; the Beatles pop, the Stones rock; the Beatles erudite, the Stones visceral; the Beatles utopian, the Stones realistic.

What McMillian describes is so ingrained in our conversations about pop that we don't really think about it. I'm pretty sure I've described *Exile on Main St* as Dionysian even though I know fuck-all about Greek mythology. I'm aware that "Dionysian" is defined loosely as "pertaining to a band that is featured in an unreleased Robert Frank documentary called *Cocksucker Blues*," which must mean that Apollonian is "related to musical combos who star in cartoons about colorful submarines." You don't have to be smart to understand Beatles vs. Stones. You just have to know the difference between light and shade.

I'm sure there are clever individuals chomping at the bit right now who will insist that Beatles vs. Stones isn't a "real" rivalry. This is a common "You can't handle the truth!" argument as it pertains to Beatles vs. Stones. If you'll recall, the 1992 Aaron Sorkin–scripted legal drama *A Few Good Men* famously climaxes with a courtroom scene in which Tom Cruise needles Jack Nicholson as only an exceedingly toothy Scientologist can. Finally Nicholson explodes and admits to all the wrongdoing. Did Jack order the code red? You're goddamned right he did!

In the context of the film, this moment is intended to be dramatic and surprising. But it's not. The moment you cast Nicholson to play the heavy in your movie, you are telegraphing the dramatic outburst that will inevitably come later in the film. If Jack is in the picture, he's going to be screaming at somebody before the credits roll.

Similarly, the people who argue that the Beatles and Stones weren't really rivals believe they are making a surprising and profound pronouncement. They will lay their case out methodically, starting with the fact that the Beatles and Stones always conspired to stagger the release dates of their singles and albums so as to not come in direct conflict with each other in the marketplace. If these people have read McMillian's book, they will explain that the Stones started out by imitating the Beatles' formal dress but soon realized that it was better counterprogramming to set themselves apart by dressing like the world's sexiest hobos.

If these people have watched documentaries such as *The Beatles Anthology* and *Crossfire Hurricane,* they will point out that Mick Jagger hung out during the recording of "All You Need Is Love" and that Paul McCartney and Ringo Starr attended Jagger's wedding to Bianca Jagger. The Beatles and Stones were friends! If you believe otherwise, you can't handle the truth!

People make this case about the Beatles and Stones all the time. When I told people I was writing a book about pop-music rivalries, and I inevitably mentioned the most iconic pop-music rivalry as my first example, roughly two times out of five the person I was speaking with would say, "Ah, but the Beatles and Stones weren't *really* rivals. It was all marketing." Okay, fine, it was all marketing. *Marketing works.* A billion people on the planet drink Coca-Cola every day. Do those people not count as Coke consumers because they were persuaded against their best interests to ingest unhealthy sugar water by a nefarious, omnipresent advertising campaign? Marketing may be fake, but diabetes is real.

So yes, Beatles vs. Stones is a rivalry because music fans have perceived it to be a rivalry for more than a half century, no matter what the real-life relationship between the bands was. The belief is what matters; whether Mick Jagger authentically hated Lennon's guts is beside the point. This is show business. None of it has any intrinsic meaning. The meaning is extrinsic: it comes from the audience. And the audience decided that Beatles vs. Stones is a meaningful dichotomy a long, long time ago. It matters because we say it matters.

Now, if you really want to undermine the veracity of Beatles vs. Stones, you could argue that the better rivalries existed within the bands rather than between them. Keith hated Mick, John hated Paul, and Mick and Paul seemed bemused by Keith and John respectively.

John Lennon famously slagged Paul McCartney shortly after the Beatles disbanded, in 1970, unloading on his former partner in an interview with *Rolling Stone*'s Jann Wenner. Lennon called McCartney's first solo record rubbish; he complained bitterly about Macca's control-freak tendencies in the band's creative and business matters, and he suggested that "Paul thought he was the fuckin' Beatles." Later, on 1971's *Imagine,* Lennon took a break from professing his undying love for Yoko and dreaming about a judgment-free society in order to denounce McCartney as an embarrassing phony on the bracingly cruel diss track "How Do You Sleep?" At the time, Lennon's "brotherhood of man" definitely did not extend to his former bass player.

Lennon and McCartney never publicly buried the hatchet: the closest the world came to witnessing reconciliation was a medium-terrible 2000 VH1 original movie called *Two of Us,* a sort of thought experiment that made up a scenario in which McCartney (Aidan Quinn, a.k.a. Madonna's love interest in *Desperately Seeking Susan*) visits Lennon (Jared Harris, a.k.a. Lane Pryce on *Mad Men*) at the Dakota in 1976. (Lennon and McCartney did hang out that April, but the film is mostly fictionalized.) You can guess what happens next: they bicker, they get stoned, they dance to a reggae band in Central Park, they awkwardly shoehorn references to Beatles songs for no reason into their regular conversation, they shed some tears, and they embrace poignantly, evoking a sense of oncoming doom over Lennon's tragic fate. It is not a good film, and I've watched it only three times on YouTube.

Keith Richards's dislike of Mick Jagger was aired most memorably in his 2010 memoir, *Life*, and he was even meaner than John was when going after Paul. The part everyone remembers is Keith referring to Mick's penis as a "tiny todger" that "doesn't quite fill the gap" between an "enormous pair of balls." Saying Mick had a small cock was bad enough, but the inherently comic juxtaposition of a small cock paired with oversize testicles is exhibit 243 in the case for Keith Richards being truly the greatest of all the world's unapologetic bastards.

Richards's depiction of Jagger as a vindictive prima donna in *Life* is arguably even more devastating than the Ballghazi talk—Richards claimed that by the '80s Mick had become so insufferable that he couldn't even stand to visit Jagger's dressing room. (This feeling, apparently, wasn't mutual; Richards writes that Jagger was possessive of Keith and outspokenly jealous of Keith's other male mates.) The funniest cheap shot at Jagger's expense in *Life* is when Richards likens Jagger's 1985 solo album, *She's the Boss*, to *Mein Kampf*, in that "everyone had it but no one [listened to] it." (Exhibit 244!)

What's striking about the intraband rivalries within the Beatles and Stones is that they had essentially the same dynamic. You had one guy who at some point assumed control of the band (Paul McCartney/Mick Jagger), and you had a guy who resented being subjugated (John Lennon/Keith Richards). In both instances, the subjugated party is the band's most romanticized figure—"cool" people generally prefer Lennon to McCartney and Richards to Jagger (because they are the souls of their respective bands), while pragmatists favor McCartney to Lennon and Jagger to Richards (because they held their respective bands together).

The hilariously trenchant East Nashville singer-songwriter Todd Snider explored this dynamic in his song "Brenda," named after Richards's disparaging nickname for Jagger. Snider likens the Jagger-Richards relationship to a long-running marriage—the relationship might be dysfunctional, but the faulty components complement each other and work better together than they do apart. "Mick Jagger was born on a Monday morning / Keith Richards was born on a Saturday night," he sings.

If Snider had been a Beatles guy, he could've very easily written the same song about Lennon and McCartney, particularly given the contentiousness of the Beatles' later years, when Paul rose to power as Lennon drifted away with Yoko. Albert Goldman's notorious biography *The Lives of John Lennon*—this is the book that caused Bono to threaten Goldman's life in the U2 song "God Part II"—is unsparing in detailing (some might say exaggerating) Lennon's personal peccadilloes, which included heroin addiction. "Is it any wonder that Paul got a little bossy," Goldman writes, "[with] a sullen, apathetic drug addict like John?"

Paul McCartney was born on a Thursday and John Lennon on a Wednesday, but spiritually they're a Monday morning–Saturday night combo.

A common thread in pop-music rivalries—the rivalries that mean the most to me, anyway—is that one party is always dominant over the other. There is a proactive side and a reactive side. In a sense, the rivalry is *only* about the reactive side. The proactive side might not care or even be aware that there's a conflict. It's the reactive side that has determined that the proactive side has to be countered in some way.

Oasis vs. Blur was really about Oasis trying to prove it was better than Blur. Nirvana vs. Pearl Jam might've been instigated by Kurt Cobain early on, but it is ultimately defined by Pearl Jam's deference to Nirvana's legacy. Prince vs. Michael Jackson was about Prince proving he didn't need MJ's support network. The White Stripes vs. the Black Keys was really about Jack White trying to set himself apart from Dan Auerbach. Kanye West vs. Taylor Swift was about Kanye being an impulsive gadfly who can't sit still.

The Stones are one of the most popular and important rock bands in human history. In every other context, the Stones reign supreme. But in Beatles vs. Stones, the Stones (and Stones people) represent the reactive side. Therefore Beatles vs. Stones is really about the hegemony of the Beatles.

No band or artist has ever dominated culture the way the Beatles have for the past fifty-plus years, which is why hating the Beatles remains a meaningful gesture. Hating the Beatles became relevant the moment it dawned on Andrew Oldham to tell the Stones to throw their neckties in the trash. For the first time, a significant stand was taken against the Beatles' place in youth culture. If you wanted to flip the Beatles the bird, you could do it by standing with the Stones.

Several decades later, hating the Beatles still matters because the band's most popular songs are still being repackaged into insanely popular compilations. A Beatles greatest hits LP released in 2000, *1*, sold more than thirty-one million copies worldwide and ranks among the bestselling albums of the SoundScan era (which dates back to 1991). It outsold every other album released in the aughts, barely nudging out 'NSync's *No Strings Attached*. The Beatles are arguably *still* the biggest boy band in the world. What hating the Beatles says, then and now, is, "I don't like this thing because it engenders near-universal agreement." This position will probably always be common. It's part of human nature. Disliking what everybody seems to revere is something everybody does at some point in life, and few things are more revered than the Beatles.

Even for groups that aren't the Beatles, there's a long history in pop music of snubbing songs that achieve mass acceptance. When Outkast had a hit in the early aughts with "Hey Ya!" everybody loved it. The appeal of "Hey Ya!" transcended all racial, gender, and generational boundaries. You could quote the line in which Andre 3000 implores the ladies to "shake it like a Polaroid picture," and frickin' grandmothers would nod in recognition.

If a poll had been taken measuring the popularity of "Hey Ya!" right as it was peaking on the charts, I suspect it would've done "George W. Bush right after 9/11" numbers. Flash forward ten years: the website I used to work for, *Grantland*, conducted a March Madness–style tournament to determine the most popular song of the twenty-first century, and "Hey Ya!" was voted the winner by readers. Because this occurred on the Internet, "Hey Ya!" winning our silly little competition inevitably inspired scores of complaints. People whined about "Hey Ya!" being overplayed. Outkast fans maintained that "Bombs over Baghdad" was better. The victory of "Hey Ya!" could only be interpreted as the tyranny of the middlebrow.

What the dissenters were really saying was: "I don't like this thing because it engenders near-universal agreement."

Another interesting instance of (mostly good-natured) Beatles bashing occurred in 2014, when fans of the Atlanta rap group Migos perpetuated a "Migos are better than the Beatles" meme on Twitter. This was hilarious on multiple levels: first, Migos's music was perceived even among rap fans to be simplistic and repetitive. (The group's most famous song, "Versace," repeats the word *Versace* approximately a trillion times in just over three minutes.) Second, asserting Migos's supremacy over the Beatles was bound to confuse and confound old white people, always the most enjoyable demographic group to irritate.

Then there were people who believed that Migos had made significant artistic strides on its mixtape *Rich Nigga Timeline* and used the Beatles comparison to make a case for a new generation aspiring to leave a similarly lasting impact. In that way, saying "Migos is better than the Beatles" could be construed as a sign of respect, utilizing the Beatles as an impossibly high standard that only the best of the best can hope to match.

Around the same time, Kanye West released a single, "Only One," which he recorded in collaboration with Paul McCartney. This song inspired an even more popular meme: "Who is Paul McCartney?" Like the Migos meme, "Who is Paul McCartney?" was a joke. Certainly there are thirteen-year-old Kanye fans who aren't well versed in seventysomething English rock stars. But the majority of tweeters were diminishing Macca in comparison to Kanye only in an ironic sense. This did not prevent scandalized local news channels from picking up the story and reporting it at face value. The sanctity of the Beatles' importance had to be protected.

As a Beatles fan, I was embarrassed by this overreaction.

Had these people never seen *A Hard Day's Night?* Didn't they know the Beatles are neither mods nor rockers but *mockers?*

I don't mean to suggest that hating the Beatles is always justified. I tend to believe that anyone who says outright that the Beatles suck is being willfully perverse if not just plain old ignorant. I recognize that everybody's taste is different. Maybe it's not your taste to appreciate consistently brilliant songwriting, stylistically diverse and adventurous albums, or art that provokes culturally momentous movements that echo for years afterward. I guess there are weirdos who also hate cheeseburgers and chocolate cake, too. It's just that, in my experience, people who attempt to discredit the Beatles purely on the merit of their music have a personal agenda, and they always end up sounding buffoonish.

For instance, one time I was at a Dirty Projectors concert seated next to a nice-enough dude who attempted to argue that the Beatles are overrated. Again, you can dislike the Beatles if you want. But the Beatles aren't overrated. The evidence of their reach and influence is irrefutable. Your personal opinion does not change that. It's like arguing that the president of the United States is overrated. How? Is the president not worthy of being the most powerful person in the free world? Perhaps, but it does not change the reality of that power. So shut up already. Hate the Beatles as much as you want, but accept that you've chosen a lonely road.

The rest of the concert was a little awkward after this diatribe. Still, totally worth it.

I love the Beatles. I love the Stones. But you can ultimately only be a Beatles or a Stones person. That is the law. You can disagree with the law. You can argue that there is no good reason to have to choose one over the other. But it's still the law. And you still must choose.

I am a Stones person.

I'm just more attracted to the Stones. The Beatles are the person you want to marry, and the Stones are the person you want to fuck. If I could marry a band, I would be a Beatles person. But our society has not yet recognized person–rock band marriage rights. I guess you can't have sex with a band, either, but *Sticky Fingers* is the closest that rock music gets to sex, so I'm a Stones guy.

Let's break it down mathematically. Paul McCartney is the most talented musician in either band. Mick Jagger is the smartest. John Lennon is the funniest. Ringo Starr is the dumbest (in a sweet way). Charlie Watts is the best at looking bored. George Harrison is the most resentful. Bill Wyman is also the dumbest (in a not-sweet way). Keith Richards is the first guy I'd save if both bands were trapped in a burning house. Add up their individual scores, and the Stones come out ahead in my book. (And I'm not even counting Brian Jones and Mick Taylor.)

The Beatles, overall, have the more consistent discography—they never made a bad record. (Even the *Yellow Submarine* sound track has "Hey Bulldog," which is tremendous.) But when the Stones were great, they were better than the Beatles. The run from 1968 to 1972—which covers *Beggars Banquet, Let It Bleed,* the live album *'Get Yer Ya-Ya's Out!,' Sticky Fingers,* and *Exile on Main St*—is the best for any rock band ever. Any time a new band comes out that promises "to bring back rock," that band will look, sound, and act like the Stones from '68 to '72. That shit is elemental. So the Stones win again.

Also: consistency isn't all it's cracked up to be. The Beatles are so perfect they can be a little boring. Nobody makes bad albums better than the Stones. The badness of *Black and Blue*, *Undercover*, and *Steel Wheels* is rich and fascinating. You hear something new each time you play those records. I listen to them more than I put on *Rubber Soul*. "Fool to Cry" is no "In My Life," but you don't need to hear "In My Life" ever again. If you play "Fool to Cry" twenty times in a row, you might still think it blows. But the twenty-first time, you could be just the right amount of drunk to suddenly realize that it's the most beautiful song you've ever heard. (This has not yet happened for me.)

And yeah, I guess my love of the Stones could be construed as a statement about the Beatles. I find all the Stones' "fuck you" moves against the Beatles to be highly entertaining. Ripping off *Sgt. Pepper* with *Their Satanic Majesties Request*? Fantastic. Introducing themselves as "the world's greatest rock-and-roll band" when the Beatles were still together? Awesome. Not breaking up and raking in all that nostalgia cash in the '90s and aughts that the Beatles could've had if Lennon and Harrison hadn't died? Cold-blooded, but admirable from a business perspective.

Something I forgot to mention: I have a personal rule about the Beatles, which is that I don't rank them—like, ever. Ranking the Beatles makes any list anticlimactic, because you can never pick against the Beatles. They have all the best songs and all the best albums. So if I rank my favorite songs or albums, I never include any Beatles music, because it would be *all* Beatles music and therefore boring.

If I'm honest, I'll admit to being a Stones guy because being a Stones guy just seems more interesting. The most common signifiers associated with the Stones—sex, drugs, danger, outlaw posturing—are synonymous with cool, and, like every-body, I want to be cool. Loving the Beatles is so ordinary by comparison; it says nothing about you other than your unques-tioning acceptance of inevitable truths. Siding with the Beatles is like siding with gravity. So I'm a Stones person, and I also ex-empt the Beatles from any comparison to another band. What can I say? When it comes to Beatles vs. Stones, I have Jagger-size balls.

CHAPTER 7

Right to the Ways and the Rules of the World

(Eric Clapton vs. Jimi Hendrix)

ERIC CLAPTON MAKES me contemplate the inevitable decline of my own life, and this makes me uncomfortable.

For one thing, I don't like to realize that, as I have grown older, my affection for blues-rock has increased. When I was in my teens and twenties, the idea of listening to a group of white guys playing overamplified approximations of classic Muddy Waters and Howlin' Wolf songs seemed like the lamest thing in the world. (The exceptions to this rule were always the Stones, Led Zeppelin, the Black Crowes, and the White Stripes. Also the Allman Brothers Band if I was high.) It wasn't so much the music itself that was lame but rather the people I associated with enjoying that kind of music — balding fortyish dudes named Gary or Glen outfitted in mint-condition leather jackets and perfectly pressed khakis. Now that I'm nearing forty and my resistance to blues-rock is weakening, I find that my vanity is flaring up. As a working music critic, I'm quick to share my love of the latest hip-hop or EDM record. That shit buys you street cred. But when it comes to the Gary Clark Jr. live LP that's been secretly dominating my listening habits, I'm selectively mum. It's stupid, I know, but I'm self-conscious about hewing too closely to my demographic stereotype. I guess you could say that my old-ass psyche is in crisis and wearing a bad toupee and driving a too-expensive sports car to compensate.

At least I've been slow to accept Slowhand. So long as I can avoid getting into Clapton, I can stave off the process of transforming into a full-fledged Gary or Glen.

This goes deeper than the reflexive shame that comes with a grudging appreciation of extended guitar solos and tinny-sounding horn sections. Eric Clapton solo albums are reminders that death, for most people, is not some darkly romantic denouement that gives our lives added resonance, as it was for Clapton's eternally youthful rival, Jimi Hendrix. Rather, death is a drawn-out process that takes place over the course of decades, weakening us every step of the way. Death is what starts to happen after you leave Cream.

What is life? It is a series of arrangements that each of us makes in order to slow down the deterioration process as much as possible. Everybody faces the same decisions as they advance in age — behavior that was fun when you were younger (excessive drug and alcohol intake, indiscriminate sexual encounters with the powerfully magnetic and questionably sane, residing in shitholes with hygiene-averse scumbags) can't continue when you get older or else the death march gets accelerated. Mature people learn over time how to structure their lives in such a way that the likelihood of dying is minimized. Eventually the menu of fun items that won't instantly kill you is reduced to a small selection of spicy entrees, then a zesty appetizer or two, then a glass of water and a spoon (because forks and knives could cut your terrifyingly translucent skin, you decrepit old coot).

I realize this might strike some as a rather morbid overreaction to *Old Sock*. But Clapton, more than any of his classic-rock peers, represents the compromises inherent in survival. Besides, I would never put on *Old Sock*, even though it is my go-to signifier for "comically forgettable Eric Clapton LP."

Instead I'm playing *Journeyman*.

Journeyman came out in 1989, which was around the time when I first became aware of Eric Clapton's existence. Cueing up the album on Spotify instantly reminded me of watching VH1 in the sixth grade, back when VH1 was a music-centric network that played Bruce Hornsby's "Mandolin Rain" all day long. (I guess I was always a closet Gary or Glen, even in grade school.) *Journeyman* is strictly okay. Clapton gets a sweet, piercing sound out of his ax, but it's a little antiseptic. Even the best songs ("Pretending," "Bad Love," "No Alibis") sound like bumper music for erectile-dysfunction ads.

Still, *Journeyman* is a crucial turning point in Clapton's career because it was his first LP after he got sober, in 1987. Clapton wavered between using and recovery throughout the '80s, but with *Journeyman* he embarked on the healthiest and most commercially successful period of his professional life. It culminated with 1992's *Unplugged*, when Clapton, his Jason Priestley haircut, and that lounge-lizard reimagining of "Layla" were inescapable in popular culture.

"I thought that if I stopped drinking and I stopped using drugs...I would not be able to play anymore. In other words, those were things that were necessary for inspiration," Clapton admitted in an interview years later. Drugs clearly weren't helping Clapton in the '80s. *Journeyman* was preceded by two nearly unlistenable albums, 1985's *Behind the Sun* and 1986's *August*. Now, to be fair, those albums do include a couple of songs I enjoy purely for nostalgic reasons: "Forever Man," which is featured in the oft-overlooked kiddie sci-fi epic *SpaceCamp*, in which a young Joaquin Phoenix manages to be innocuously cute for the last time in his life, and "It's in the Way That You Use It," a pivotal song on the sound track for the justly not-overlooked "I watched this as a kid in order to see Mary Elizabeth Mastrantonio naked" billiards movie, *The Color of Money*.

Behind the Sun and *August* are derided because they were produced by Phil Collins, who set out to make Clapton sound like a Patrick Bateman wet dream. But the blame should really rest with Clapton, who was gakked out of his gourd at the time. According to his memoir, *Clapton: The Autobiography*, it was typical for Clapton in the mid-'80s to stay up every night until six in the morning doing blow, then go to the studio and attempt to play while suffering from a screaming hangover. Plasticky synths and booming drums sound good only to people in that sort of condition.

"I now realize that there was no reason for me to be making records at all," he writes in *Clapton*. It's a pretty stunning and wholly appropriate conclusion, if only for the soulless cover of "Knock on Wood" from *Behind the Sun,* in which Clapton supplants Robert Johnson as his muse with *The Return of Bruno*–era Bruce Willis.

Cocaine, to quote Rick James, is one hell of a drug.

Clapton comes off as surprisingly levelheaded in his book. (*Levelheaded* is an adjective I'd apply to precisely zero of the other rock memoirs I've read.) Generally, he seems genial and self-aware. As a musician, Clapton has always been deferential—probably too deferential. He's a superstar who has frequently relegated himself to the role of sideman going back to the late '60s, when he guested with Delaney & Bonnie and stood behind Steve Winwood in Blind Faith. Clapton always seemed content to regard himself as a mere "journeyman," even as his fans declared him a god.

Perhaps that's a commendable attitude—this is the man who wrote the riff for "Sunshine of Your Love" while in the midst of an acid trip, so his stature as a classic-rock badass is more or less secure. But Clapton's modesty also has resulted in a catalog that is overwhelmingly innocuous. Clapton never seems to be pushing himself that hard. If Clapton was a talented though underachieving point guard, sportswriters would accuse him of not being an alpha dog. The will to be great just isn't there for Clapton most of the time. He's the Vince Carter of guitar legends.

I would never argue that Eric Clapton needed drugs in order to be a brilliant musician. I would, however, point out that the most fucked-up period of his life happened to coincide with his sole masterpiece, 1970's *Layla and Other Assorted Love Songs*. The story behind *Layla* has been told and retold many times— in short, Clapton was in love with the wife of his best friend, George Harrison, and he wrote an entire album about it, which eventually aided Clapton in stealing her away from his pal. Clapton was a man on fire with unrequited love on *Layla*, and he channeled that self-destructive passion into his music. In his memoir, Clapton recalls endlessly jamming with his band (which became known later as Derek and the Dominos) and subsisting solely on a diet of cocaine and Mandrax tempered with vodka and brandy. When the musicians traveled to Miami to record, they added heroin and PCP.

My point is not that Clapton needed drugs in order to be

great. My point is that Clapton did drugs because he *believed* they gave him the fuel to be great. Whether drugs truly helped him is beside the point — it's the level of commitment that matters. Clapton on *Layla* was willing to do anything to make a great record, even getting junked out. It's that state of mind more than the actual stimulus of the drugs that give *Layla* an urgency that none of Clapton's other albums have. *Layla* feels like a true life-or-death proposition, and Clapton seems fine choosing death.

Journeyman is not a life-or-death record. *Journeyman* is a record with a respectful fear of death. It doesn't tiptoe to the edge of the black void; it calmly punches coordinates into the GPS and gingerly backs the fuck away. *Journeyman* is a sound track for settling into a quiet, comfortable life. It's the sort of album you make if you feel reasonably confident that you'll live to record another twenty LPs. Maybe the next one will be great, and maybe it won't. Either way, so long as the sun rises tomorrow, ol' EC will be a-okay.

When I put on *Journeyman*, what I hear are the gears that keep my own life grinding monotonously forward. Eric Clapton is not my hero, but he is my avatar.

Some rivals aren't really rivals, they're just friendly combatants. That's how Quentin Tarantino refers to his homie Paul Thomas Anderson. When PTA made *There Will Be Blood*, QT was inspired to swing for the fences with *Inglourious Basterds*. That is the dynamic of their relationship: QT and PTA are friends who compete in order to inspire each other to be great. The same can be said of Eric Clapton and Jimi Hendrix. In life, they formed a mutual appreciation society — Hendrix made his manager promise to introduce him to Clapton, the only British player he admired, when Hendrix visited England for the first time. Clapton, in turn, was dazzled by Hendrix's revolutionary technique and devastated by his tragic death. Clapton was supposed to meet up with Hendrix at a Sly and the Family Stone concert the night that Hendrix died. Clapton even brought a gift—a left-handed Stratocaster, a rare find. But the friends never connected that night.

On YouTube there's an unreleased documentary filmed in 1978 called *Eric Clapton and His Rolling Hotel*. In one scene Clapton launches into an emotional, semidrunken monologue when the interviewer asks him about Hendrix. Clapton still seems crushed by the loss. "After Jimi died, I was very angry. It wasn't selfish on his part, but it was a lonely feeling to be left alone," he says forlornly.

Even after Hendrix died, he was linked with Clapton in the public's imagination, and this conflation typically diminishes Clapton. If Hendrix is the most obvious example of "burning out"—he arrived, he was the best in the world at what he did for a brief time, then he ceased to exist—Clapton is an equally archetypal signifier of "fading away." By virtue of having a career that has lasted into his senior-citizen years, Clapton will never be as cool or sexy as Hendrix, who is forever fixed as the guitar-burning wild man who air-humped rock audiences into states of ecstasy. For all his innovations as a guitarist, Clapton's most vital music drifts further into the past with each passing year. Meanwhile, any Hendrix career survey has to account for only a small body of work that has virtually zero percent fat.

This dichotomy influences how people talk about Clapton, even when they're trying to be complimentary. When *Rolling Stone* ranked the best guitarists ever and predictably put Hendrix in the top spot, above Clapton, Clapton was praised (by

Eddie Van Halen) for the "basic simplicity to his playing, his style, his vibe and his sound," whereas Hendrix was credited (by Tom Morello of Rage Against the Machine) with "explod[ing] our idea of what rock music could be." For Morello, Hendrix's guitar represented nothing less than the "divining rod of the turbulent sixties."

Clapton is basic and simple, and Hendrix is explosive and turbulent—this squares with the conventional wisdom and encapsulates the way these guys are perceived, now and probably forever. Hendrix will always rank higher than Clapton on these "best guitarist" lists because Hendrix will always be viewed as the ill-fated genius, while Clapton is the steadier, less adventurous foil. I'm not disputing these classifications or arguing that Clapton is a better guitarist than Hendrix. Even with his limited discography, Hendrix's original three studio LPs are better than the best of Clapton's output. I would happily listen to *Axis: Bold as Love* over *461 Ocean Boulevard* any day. What I'm suggesting is that Clapton's continued survival has, in a strange and accidental way, enhanced Hendrix's legacy. Clapton's steadiness makes Hendrix's life appear all the more incredible, while Hendrix's volcanic recklessness makes Clapton seem all the more safe.

Survivors can't help but pale in comparison to dead people. A rare exception is Dave Chappelle. After Chappelle famously walked away from *Chappelle's Show,* he got to be Hendrix and Clapton at the same time. These days, whenever Chappelle chooses to reenter the public consciousness for a stand-up comedy tour or talk-show appearance, he still gets to be the person he was more than a decade ago. Reporters will ask about why he walked away from his $50 million contract with Comedy Central, and he'll explain that his personal sanity was more important than money. He will then proceed to be funny or not funny, and it won't matter. Dave Chappelle is already defined by the moment when he walked away from his career in the mid-aughts, and he can leverage that infamy to encourage people to spend money on his subsequent projects. He has the benefits of living and dying simultaneously.

What if Clapton had died of a heroin overdose after he put out *Layla*? Because that easily could've happened. Clapton and Hendrix were both living on the edge in the early '70s—it's just that one of them fell off the ledge and the other appeared in Ken Russell's bonkers adaptation of *Tommy*. At that point in his career Clapton's output was pretty sterling—stints with the Yardbirds and John Mayall and the Bluesbreakers, a starring role in Cream, one good record with Blind Faith, a solid self-titled solo record, and of course his defining masterpiece with Derek and the Dominos. Not a bad résumé to leave behind should you end up making an early exit.

Here's another question: What if Hendrix had lived? What if he were the one who attempted to form an unholy alliance of blues licks and *No Jacket Required* before checking into rehab and launching a comeback tour sponsored by Michelob? Would we remember him differently? Would Clapton be regarded as Hendrix is now? Would Hendrix be thought of as Clapton is now? Does a lightly balding Hendrix softly stroking a bossanova rendition of "Purple Haze" represent a fate worse than death?

When I feel anxiety about getting older, I put on *The Pod*, the second album by the two-man death-comedy jam band Ween, because I know it will make me feel anxious about being young. *The Pod* was an obsession for me during the summer of

2004, which was right before I turned twenty-seven, the magical death year for Jimi, Janis, Jim, Kurt, Robert Johnson, Brian Jones, D. Boon, Amy Winehouse, the singer for Canned Heat, the original keyboardist for the Grateful Dead, and a lot of other famous and semifamous musicians. The big two-seven didn't kill me, but *The Pod* sort of made me wished it would.

If you're a Ween fan, you know *The Pod* as the band's "difficult" record, a grimy, seventy-six-minute endurance test recorded on a Tascam four-track cassette recorder that doesn't seem to be working properly, possibly as a result of a toxic infusion of bong water, Mountain Dew, Doritos dust, and farts. The vocals are distorted to the point of near incomprehensibility, and the guitars sound like trapped rodents squealing in a distant attic. Even the drum machines act like they're stoned. Gene and Dean Ween claimed to have made *The Pod* while continuously huffing Scotchgard fumes—they were joking, but it suits the mood of the music, which is blurry and grotesque.

I was jamming on *The Pod* that summer because the woman I had asked to marry me—who had in fact *agreed* to marry me — was in the process of extricating me from her life. Not that I would ever wish that sort of heartache on anyone, but should it happen to you, I heartily recommend burying your head in *The Pod*. It's an ideal sound track for the worst period of your life. When the world is making you feel like unlovable lo-fi scuzz, unlovable lo-fi scuzz speaks to you like nothing else.

I also loved *The Pod* because I was a committed pothead. From the ages of twenty-two to thirty-two, I was high probably 70 percent of the time, excluding the parts of my day reserved for work and sleep. As soon as I was finished performing those essential duties, I would immediately spark up and watch episodes of *World Poker Tour*. (Is there anything more early-twenty-first century than the brief fad of people caring about televised poker competitions?) Honestly, if I hadn't suffered the occasional loss of a good weed hookup, that 70 percent figure would probably be closer to 100 percent. I don't think I was addicted; I was just really into what the "stoner lifestyle" signified in my mind. Becoming a pothead is the easiest way for lazy, apolitical people to feel like they're outlaws from mainstream culture. And I was a regular Billy Joe Shaver.

Also, being high all the time is really fucking fun until it stops being fun, at which point it becomes depressing and inhibiting. That was the arc of my experience with habitual pot intake, at any rate. Surely Seth Rogen would disagree. YMMV.

Ween was my favorite "drug" band—I loved doing drugs while listening to Ween, and I loved that Ween made me feel as though I were already on drugs when I wanted to do drugs but was temporarily out of them. The second time I saw Ween in concert is probably the druggiest live-music experience I've ever had. Within twenty seconds of finding my seat, I was offered mushrooms by the guy sitting in front of me. I declined—'shrooms had a way of making me behave like a lunatic. The first time I did 'shrooms, I chewed the bark off a tree and openly wept while listening to Bob Dylan's Royal Albert Hall bootleg. I was like a cross between a squirrel and Greil Marcus.

I also turned down the mushrooms because I was already very drunk. Before the show, I spent a few hours at the bar next door to the theater slamming whiskey cocktails, as the thought of listening to Ween sober inspired a mania in me that had to be curbed with enough chemical stimulation to quell an alcoholic lion. Adding hallucinogens to my body chemistry wasn't appealing, though I was hoping somebody would offer me weed. Nobody did, but the contact high from those people who were selfishly bogarting their joints around me proved a sufficient consolation prize.

When Ween came out, they sounded fantastic and looked terrible. Gene, in particular, seemed worse for the wear. I guessed that he was fifty pounds heavier than when I had seen Ween the previous year. If I hadn't been so fucked-up myself, I would've been more concerned for Gene's well-being. But I had to keep my buzz going in order to prevent the concert from bumming me out.

I finally had the chance to interview Gene Ween — who now goes by his proper name, Aaron Freeman — five years later. By then we had both come out of our drug phases. I swore off weed at my wife's request when we decided to have a baby; Freeman had checked himself into rehab after a widely reported onstage meltdown in Vancouver. He was still living at the rehab facility when he phoned me from somewhere in the middle of Arizona.

I felt nervous before the interview, as I always am before talking to an artist I admire. Freeman had a reputation for being surly and taciturn with reporters. But with me he was warm and friendly. I attributed this to his ongoing recovery — Freeman above all sounded like a man who was grateful and maybe slightly amazed that he wasn't dead.

Freeman was promoting his first solo record, *Marvelous Clouds*, a relatively straightforward tribute to the songwriter and poet Rod McKuen, whose songs had previously been covered by Frank Sinatra, Johnny Cash, and Dusty Springfield. The album was fine if a little, well, *adult*. Freeman didn't monkey up his vocals, as he did with Ween — he sang in a normal-guy croon that had the mind-altering power of decaf coffee.

Clearly Freeman was determined to leave his identity as Gene Ween behind; while he didn't state it outright, he implied that Ween was probably finished. (A few weeks later Freeman officially confirmed the band's dissolution, though Ween later announced a round of reunion gigs for 2016.) The decision appeared to be motivated by personal reasons rather than artistic impulses, a perfectly understandable position for a forty-two-year-old man to take.

"It gets to a point where you realize that you've been in this rock-and-roll world for so many years, and it's time to just take responsibility," he told me. Freeman wanted his music to grow up as well, in ways I assumed he couldn't possibly be serious about but insisted that he was. "I've always said from a young age that as I get older, I want to get lamer, in a good way. I want to morph into, like, Phil Collins– and Elton John–type shit, so that's kind of what I'm doing with this. This is like a little stepping-stone. It's going to get much worse, in a great way, but that's how I want to evolve, or devolve, as it were.

"It's the process of life," he argued. "You're just not as hip as you were, and it's always bothered me when I see aging rock stars who don't embrace that fully and [who] try to be young and hip. You see some wrinkled-up old rocker with tattoos all over him; he's not fooling anybody, you know — he's like an old fart. When I'm an old fart, I want to really embrace it."

I've thought a lot about what Freeman said and how it applies not just to rock stars but also to anybody approaching middle age. Freeman's attitude seems so healthy if also a little defeatist. It accepts the paradigm of "drugs equal dangerously awesome, sobriety equals comfortably stodgy" as a given. It puts me back where *Journeyman* left me, wondering if waiting out the clock is truly preferable to going out in a blaze of glory.

While I'm glad Freeman made it to his "Phil Collins– and Elton John–type shit" phase, I suspect that it won't ever move me as much as *The Pod.*

The lowest point of my *Pod*-scored dark period was a road trip I took to Kalamazoo to visit my ex-girlfriend. I wish I could say that the decision to drive six hours to see the woman I had dated before I got involved with my (by then) ex-fiancée was motivated by noble intentions. But the truth is that I wanted to distract myself with a meaningless hookup, and one of the few people on earth with a track record of hooking up with me happened to live in Kalamazoo. So that's where I went.

Before I left, I decided to take somewhere between eight and a dozen caffeine pills. Now, this was obviously a dumb decision for which there is no excuse. There is, however, an explanation, which is this: I had previously taken caffeine pills with my friend Nate, and they had given me an invigorated, confident feeling for a few hours. I assumed that doubling, then tripling, my dose would only intensify this feeling in the best possible way. I assumed wrong.

Instead I was filled with unresolvable dread as I approached the Wisconsin-Illinois border. As I was already filled with unresolvable dread, I initially surmised that the pills had merely failed to give me a decent high. By the time I reached rush-hour traffic in Chicago, however, I realized that this wasn't exactly true. The muscles in my face were throbbing maniacally, and my heart pounded as though Mola Ram from *Indiana Jones and the Temple of Doom* was about to rip it out of my chest and set it ablaze. I felt my right hand clench and close up into a meaty hook. I don't think I had a stroke, but my body was nevertheless seriously fucking pissed that I had dumped the equivalent of three pots of coffee into my system at once.

It got so bad that I had to pull over and check into a hotel near O'Hare airport. When I got to my room, I stripped down to my boxers and paced, my body dripping with sweat. I turned on the TV and tried to cool out to a *Seinfeld* rerun. It was the Kenny Rogers Roasters episode. I took a shower. I lay down and persuaded my heart not to perform a running leap out of my chest. Three hours later, I checked out of the hotel and resumed my trip to Kalamazoo, my bank account one hundred and eighty dollars lighter. Long story short, the combination of my lateness and the lingering effects of the caffeine killed any chance I had for a weekend of blissful carnality in Michigan.

I wish I could say that this incident was an aberration easily chalked up to lovesick depression or temporary insanity. But for most of my twenties there was nothing I loved more than getting high while driving around in my Toyota Corolla. When I was single and working as a reporter at my hometown newspaper, my weekend routine was to get hammered in my apartment until nine or ten, then go out to bars with friends and get *extremely* hammered. I drank like I was a character in a Cassavetes film: hard, fast, and with great instinct. I drank like I was living inside the Silver Jews song "Trains Across the Sea"—in my twenty-seven years I had had *at least* fifty thousand beers.

After the bars closed, I wouldn't go straight home. I'd go to Walmart—the only place still open at 2:00 a.m.—and shop for bargain-priced CDs and DVDs. And *then* I'd go home and watch my newly purchased copy of *Pretty in Pink* until I passed out on the couch.

In Wisconsin, there's a saying: "It's not 'Don't drink and

drive,' it's 'Don't drink and drive *far*.'" I never drove *far* to any of these places. The benefit of living in a small town is that everything is less than ten minutes away. The downside is that there is so little to do that drunkenly shopping at Walmart can become a staple of your weekly routine. Again, that's not an excuse. I was a stupid, stupid person who was very, very lucky he didn't hurt himself or anybody else. But it is an explanation.

Drunken fools typically need a higher calling in order to change their behavior. For Eric Clapton, it was the birth of his son, Conor. "I suddenly became aware that it was time to try and stop fucking around," he writes in the memoir. I came to the same realization in a similar way: I never realized how badly I needed structure in my life until I married my wife. Then I had to figure out how to not fuck myself up whenever she was gone.

It was shocking to realize how inept I was initially at not fucking myself up in her absence. The moment she left on a weekend trip—whether it was for work or to visit her sister—I immediately reverted to my long-lost bachelor self.

The routine was always the same:

• I would purchase the most rancid fast food I could find.
• I would pour myself the stiffest possible whiskey drinks and consume them as though I were a resident of Deadwood.
• I would play my Strokes records way too loud.
• I would feel crushing loneliness around bedtime, causing me to repeat the food, whiskey, and Strokes steps.

In the excellent *Mad Men* episode "Souvenir," Pete Campbell is left alone in his Manhattan high-rise apartment by his vacationing wife, Trudy. At first he drinks heavily and watches television. Then Pete decides to seduce his neighbor's nanny, though his "seduction" looks an awful lot like sexual assault. When Trudy returns, Pete feels guilty and helpless. He wanted to feel powerful, but he was only reminded of his powerlessness to control himself. "I don't want you to go away anymore without me," he tells Trudy at the end of the episode, a non-confession confession of his infidelity and a form of surrender. Pete needs Trudy to save him from himself.

I suppose that somebody will care about whether Jimi Hendrix is a better guitar player than Eric Clapton for as long as guitar-based music still exists. (I give it another ten years.) But I don't care who's better, and I'm sure Clapton doesn't, either. On his records, Clapton sounds like a guy who doesn't care about anything beyond living his life, and I'm just now learning to hear the beauty in it. When I was younger, I lived like Jimi Hendrix. I aspired to be a divining rod. But eventually you find out that divining rods aren't meant to go the distance. You have to surrender if you want to live. We're all just journeymen hoping for another gig.

CHAPTER 8

The Pope > Robin Thicke

(Sinead O'Connor vs. Miley Cyrus)

BEFORE WE CONTINUE, I want to take a moment to thank you for reading this book. I'm blown away that you've decided to spend some of your precious time on me. I wish I could express my gratitude to each and every one of you in person. Alas, we'll probably never meet. Or if we meet, I'll pretend that I'm not the author of this book, because strangers frighten me.

Let me instead share with you my best anecdote. I've retold this story in countless conversations, and subsequently it's become an oft-requested favorite among my friends. I'm not saying I've recited it as many times as U2 has played "Where the Streets Have No Name," but I bet I could give "Mysterious Ways" a run for its money.

It's about the time when I subscribed to *Playboy* under an assumed name. (I told you this was a quality anecdote.)

The story begins in 1990 at a Waldenbooks inside the Fox River Mall in Appleton, Wisconsin. I was twelve and perusing the magazine rack, searching for the latest issue of *Mad* or

Premiere, because even though I was still in junior high school I had already evolved into exactly the person I am today. Suddenly I noticed a subscription card lying on the beige-carpeted floor. It was emblazoned with an iconic logo familiar to fathers, suave bachelors, college bros, and young boys everywhere.

In a flash, I had a vision: What if I took this card, put my address on it, and used another person's name? That way, I could enjoy the convenience of *Playboy* magazine being delivered directly to my home and not suffer the consequences should my mother retrieve one of the issues from the mailbox before I did. (And my mother never got the mail before I did, because I walked the five blocks from school to eat lunch at home nearly every day.)

I already had the perfect front man for this brilliant scheme: Dean Kapinski, a man I did not know but whose name was already infamous among my family members. (His name isn't really Dean Kapinski—I've changed it to protect the unfairly exploited.) Dean was a guy who used to rent the duplex where my family and I lived. We still received the occasional mailer addressed to him from some Atlantic City casino he must've visited once. One of these mailers featured a scantily clad woman on the envelope.

"What a lowlife," my mom said.

Mr. Dean Kapinski was the perfect cover for my own lowlife activities.

I don't know how I came up with this frankly inspired idea, but it was the smartest brainstorm I've ever had, before or since. I will forever be haunted by the fact that I will never be as clever again as I was at that very moment. Now, to be honest, I didn't think it would actually work. But sure enough, six weeks later, my first *Playboy* arrived. La Toya Jackson was on the cover.

She resembled Michael Jackson with the wrong surgically enhanced body parts. The sexual underworld of adulthood was even more frightening than I had imagined. But I was riveted.

It continued like this for a few months. My life was like the first half of *Goodfellas*—I was a young guy enjoying the exciting, flashy parts of a life of crime. Life was like one long, nostalgic Bobby Vinton song. Then came the "everything turns to shit" Billy Batts moment: I started getting bills, which didn't seem like a big deal at first because I assumed I could just cancel after the first few issues and not have to pay. (This might be the dumbest idea I ever had, before or since.) Eventually a collection agency started hounding me. If I had been mature enough to subscribe to *Playboy* legitimately, I might've shrugged off those bills, too. But the words *collection agency* sounded ominous to my seventh-grade ears. I envisioned coldhearted men in sharp suits visiting my house and informing my mother that her son was a pervert.

I started to freak out a little.

My older brother, Paul, found out what I was doing—he snooped in my room like a KGB spy and found my stash of mags and invoices—and decided to mentally torture me. "You know, Steve," he said one day, casually, like a snake, as we both watched MTV in the living room, "I just learned in my social studies class about this crime called mail fraud, which is when you use the United States Postal Service to pose as another person. Apparently it's pretty serious."

Then I was full-blown freaking out.

(There's a subplot to this anecdote involving my accidentally breaking one of the legs of my mom's prized living room chair, which I concealed for three months with an ungodly amount of Super Glue as my *Playboy* scheme went sideways. I got busted the night of my mom's New Year's Eve party. My brother and I went out that night to see *Home Alone,* and came home just in time to see my scheme finally fall apart. My comeuppance occurred when the huskiest person at the soiree sat in the chair. She sat down and swiftly rolled forward like the boulder in *Raiders of the Lost Ark.* There's more to this part of the story, but I'll save it for the director's cut of the book.)

Anyway, I had to shed my false Dean Kapinski identity immediately. This required writing a letter to Hugh Hefner's representatives posthaste. I had no sense of how a grown-up was supposed to cordially end a *Playboy* subscription, so I had to improvise. Clearly I had to write the letter in pen; only kids used pencils. I also assumed that adults wrote exclusively in cursive—otherwise, why spend so much goddamn time on that flowery nonsense in elementary school? I suspected that writing the letter on notebook paper would hurt my credibility, but I was out of loose-leaf paper. Dean would have to be a notebook man.

Finally I labored over the closing signature. I must've rewritten the letter a dozen times before I got it right. Should I sign it as "Dean Kapinski" or the classier and more enigmatic "D. Kapinski"? I went with the latter. It felt right for the character. I folded up the letter around a crumpled twenty-dollar bill, a small fortune for me at the time, and mailed it off.

Seeing as how the *Playboy*s stopped coming and I'm not writing this while serving a life sentence in mail-fraud prison, I assume the letter must've worked.

The other reason I wanted to share this story is so that future generations understand that teenagers once had to work really, *really* hard to procure pictures of naked people. Anyone who entered and exited puberty before the advent of the Internet has at least one story about sneaking adult mags from a parent's stockpile or staring at scrambled cable channels late at night, hoping for the occasional boob, wang, or ass cheek. Today you have to consciously decide *not* to look at porn—unimaginable filth is only a quick Google search away, rendering terms like "unimaginable filth" meaningless. The early '90s was practically the age of innocence by comparison.

When I was a kid, and I thought about having my own kid someday, I wondered what it would take to shock me when I was a parent. Culture seemed to have reached the apex of graphic sex, violence, and language in the late '80s and early '90s. By the time I was twelve, I had been exposed to 2 Live Crew, Guns N' Roses, and Andrew Dice Clay. I had seen *Lethal Weapon 2* in a movie theater and watched Mel Gibson blasting holes through South African diplomats after screwing Patsy Kensit and her bouncing, perfectly tanned breasts. I was allowed to rent *Taxi Driver* from the local video store, no questions asked, which gave me a sense of '70s-era Times Square seediness. A few years later, *NYPD Blue* aired on network television, and, like the rest of America, I contemplated the vastness of Dennis Franz's backside. I assumed I had seen the worst the world had to offer at that point. How could my theoretical child sink any lower?

Now that I am an adult and a parent of a small child, it's obvious that the world my son is growing up in is much skankier than the one where I spent my childhood. I've accepted that I can't shield him fully from the reality of this, though I'm committed to guiding him through the digital slime as safely as possible.

I just have no idea how the reality of omnipresent Internet

porn is going to affect my son. There are basically two schools of thought here, both of which I buy into to a degree. Part of me thinks that Internet porn will inevitably warp all the impressionable, horned-out minds that seek it, creating a world that resembles a Harmony Korine movie. (I'm talking about the early, truly disturbing films, like *Gummo,* not the relatively commercial stuff, like *Spring Breakers.*) But for the most part, I tend to believe that easily accessible porn could have a positive long-term impact because it will make sex seem so much less mysterious than it was for me. I thought my generation would be the first to not be shocked by the sexual misadventures of their kids' heroes in pop culture. But it's probably going to be my son's generation. Having porn everywhere feels like the end of sex being something that people get upset about or even notice. If you're young, sex is wallpaper, banal and largely invisible. And maybe that's a good thing, because we can finally get past it and talk about something else for a change.

You can already see this happening. I first noticed it in the aftermath of Miley Cyrus's performance at the 2013 MTV Video Music Awards. If you'll recall, Miley strutted out of an oversize teddy bear—her tongue hanging out, her hair done up into two spiky devil horns, her nightie stitched with a cartoon mouse sticking its own tongue out. Cyrus sang her best song, "We Can't Stop," which is both an uplifting anthem of generational inclusiveness ("It's our party, we can love who we want / We can kiss who we want / We can screw who we want") and a depressing character study of an impulsive nihilist who "can't stop" getting fucked-up all the time. "We Can't Stop" is like "We Are the World" meets *Less Than Zero.*

Then Robin Thicke came out, dressed in a ridiculous white-and-black suit that made him look like a *Batman* villain, and performed his most famous track, "Blurred Lines," as Cyrus ground on Thicke's diabolical crotch. Of all the unforeseen consequences of allowing Alan Thicke and Billy Ray Cyrus to become celebrities a quarter century prior, their offspring faux-fornicating on an awards show was certainly among the worst-case scenarios.

Predictably, the immediate reaction to Cyrus's VMA appearance was moral outrage. Cyrus rose to fame as the star of the enormously popular Disney Channel TV show *Hannah Montana,* which was about a normal girl who lives a double life as a wholesome pop star. Now she was gyrating like some kind of Whore-ah Montana, all while wearing a debauched parody version of Mickey Mouse on her underwear. Cyrus seemed to be deliberately fucking with the parents who once entrusted her with their children, and those people naturally responded by gnashing their teeth and lamenting the lost sanctity of their precious babes, who were presumably cowering in fear over the VMAs in family rooms across the nation.

This is precisely the kind of response you'd expect from such a provocative performance: what's surprising is how quickly it passed. Eventually the conversation about Cyrus's showstopping outrageousness at the VMAs pivoted from the oversexualized text of the performance to the subtext of what it all "really" meant. Sex, for once, was secondary to other topics. The outrage derived from those who believed that Cyrus's inclusion of black backing dancers—and her playfully grabbing the butt of one of those dancers—was reminiscent of minstrel-show imagery. This allegation was rapidly countered by those who approached Cyrus's iconography from a more knowing metaperspective—they argued that a would-be provocateur such as Cyrus is supposed to be outrageous on the VMAs,

therefore her performance should be appreciated as a reitera-
tion of that cyclical show-business ritual known as "scare the
squares." If the performance seemed forced or even maniacally ill-conceived in places, this was just evidence that Cyrus
was being authentically herself, like "a 14-year-old in the mall
with tissues in her bra, rouge on her cheeks, and lipstick on her
teeth," as the website *Gawker* observed.

Whether people loved or hated Cyrus, the accepted "smart"
position was to move beyond the sexy superficialities and take a
broad view of the implications of her performance. But Cyrus
herself didn't care about any of that. In a *Rolling Stone* cover
story that ran shortly after the VMAs, the writer asked Cyrus
about the dialogue her performance provoked. After rejecting
the "minstrel show" argument out of hand, Cyrus proceeded to
dismiss the "provocateur" position as well:

> I'm from one of the wealthiest counties in America.... I
> know what I am. But I also know what I like to listen to.
> Look at any 20-year-old white girl right now — that's what
> they're listening to at the club. It's 2013. The gays are get-
> ting married, we're all collaborating. I would never think
> about the color of my dancers, like, "Ooh, that might
> be controversial."... Times are changing. I think there's a
> generation or two left, and then it's gonna be a whole new
> world.

Cyrus appeared amused by all the old people working so
hard to make sense of something that to her seemed natural
and sort of thoughtless in the best possible sense. What's particularly stinging about Cyrus's comments is that she implicates
the "cool" grown-ups who would otherwise be inclined to

defend her against the knee-jerk judgments of the Moral Majority crowd. She's laughing at anyone—her critics *and* her defenders—who thinks about what she is doing too deeply. Cyrus simply doesn't see what the big deal is.

Cyrus wasn't merely putting forward a postracial view of the world—it's a postcultural view that erases stratification of all kinds, especially that pertaining to race, class, sex, sexual orientation, and taste. It's a perspective born of experiencing media via the leveled-off landscape of the Internet, where an infinite number of realities exist in neighboring silos that stretch on forever and ever. Cyrus grew up in a time when the old division between high and low culture (and good and bad taste) was rendered nonexistent. Everything is up for grabs now, because none of it really matters. Cyrus understood that she was creating disposable content on the way to being replaced by more disposable content.

If you're in your teens or twenties, this point of view is so ingrained that it might seem intuitive. If you're older, it might make you a little uncomfortable. Or perhaps the fact that it might make you uncomfortable might make you uncomfortable.

Comedian Patton Oswalt once did a bit, before he had children, about his "duty" to be a stereotypically square parent should he ever have any offspring. "When I have kids, the most recent CD I will own is Phil Collins's *No Jacket Required*," he declared. The crux of the joke is a familiar idea about the way generations relate to one another. Oswalt was arguing that children need rigid, out-of-touch authority figures to react against, and he based this on his own experience. When he was growing up, his parents were repressive, which inspired him to care about underground music and obscure movies and eventually move to a big city. Meanwhile, his friends with permissive hippie parents stayed in the suburbs back home, because there was nothing driving them away.

If there's a flaw in Oswalt's parenting theory, it's this: no matter what authority figures do, kids will generally be compelled to rebel against them. "Cool" authority figures are still authority figures, which negates their coolness. Affected coolness in a parent may in fact accentuate his or her otherness from young people—there's really nothing worse than an old person who thinks he "gets" what kids are into when in reality simply being an adult with a modicum of real-world responsibility automatically excommunicates you from their world. After a certain age, you can try to understand youth culture, but you'll never be *of* it. You are inherently, inevitably lame.

There are unofficial signs of not being a kid anymore—your first child, your first mortgage, your first colonoscopy. But entering adulthood isn't like a graduation ceremony. It's an ongoing process that your brain never quite accepts as final. If you're in your late thirties or early forties and feel a measure of vanity about your cultural literacy, you might still be in the denial stage.

As a professional member of the media industry, I felt my own growing pains kick in as I watched my colleagues comment en masse on Miley Cyrus's VMA debacle. I read a lot of trenchant, insightful commentary on Cyrus's 270 seconds of notoriety, but underpinning many of the think pieces was a familiar anxiety about how exactly to make something, *anything,* of what seemed like a seminal cultural event. I wonder if those writers suspected, as I did deep down, that Cyrus was punking all these Gen-X writers rushing to either lionize her as the epitome of a twenty-first-century pop star or demonize her as the personification of white privilege. By commenting on Miley, we could stand with Miley, share in Miley's moment, and believe that Miley's moment was reflecting something in our own lives, no matter how far removed we are from our early twenties. But was it really all just ridiculous, "Ooh, that might be controversial"–level drivel?

Miley froze me up. When it came to offering my own hot take, I punted. I told myself that this was because I didn't want to join the click-bait scrum. I tried to believe I was noble for keeping quiet. But looking back, I think I was afraid that it wasn't my place to have an opinion. I feared that whatever I wrote would sound reactionary by virtue of its being written by a straight white male in his late thirties. I didn't want to be "that guy," and being "that guy" was unavoidable because I was that guy. My demographic profile would speak louder than anything I could possibly write.

In case it isn't already obvious, I am not as courageous as Sinead O'Connor. This is true for a variety of reasons, but in the context of Miley Cyrus, O'Connor is far ballsier than I when it comes to looking like a reactionary. Sinead leaned into her indignant impulses, then doubled, then tripled, then *quadrupled,* then QUINTUPLED (!) down on them.

Miley Cyrus vs. Sinead O'Connor isn't a typical rivalry. They aren't contemporaries vying for a similar audience. They do not compete with each other for album sales or cultural significance. They don't even seem to exist in the same universe. If you know about one of them, you are likely completely clueless about the other. They only briefly collided in the aftermath of the 2013 VMAs and created the unlikeliest '90s-'10s mash-up ever.

If you want to get technical about it, Miley vs. Sinead should perhaps be classified as a feud rather than a rivalry. Their interactions were limited to tweets and media interviews that took place over the course of a month in the fall of 2013. Compared with some of the other rivalries discussed in this book, Miley vs. Sinead might seem a little marginal. But Miley vs. Sinead represents the oldest rivalry there is: old vs. young. And in their case, young—as it always does—trounced old.

Sinead first entered Miley's life in the least desirable way imaginable, via an open letter. I'm not famous enough to have ever had an open letter addressed to me, but if it happened, I know I would hate it. I have written a few open letters to celebrities in my time as a journalist, and I deeply regret it. It is the single most condescending form of correspondence there is. The idea is that you are offering advice or comfort to a person you've never met and who likely doesn't care about your opinion. But what you're really doing is holding this person up to ridicule by passive-aggressively pointing out to millions of people what they've done wrong.

Sinead was compelled to address Miley after Miley mentioned in *Rolling Stone* that Sinead's iconic video for "Nothing Compares 2 U" was an inspiration for her own "Wrecking Ball" video, a comparison that was already obvious to observers familiar with both videos. In the video for "Nothing Compares 2 U," O'Connor is viewed in a close-up, and her emotional performance culminates with tears running down her cheeks. In the video for "Wrecking Ball," Cyrus also breaks down with the camera right up in her grill. And she licks a sledgehammer, which didn't occur to O'Connor in 1990.

Anyway, O'Connor used this as an entry point to call Cyrus a whore.

Actually O'Connor's letter was a little more nuanced than that. After prefacing her comments with a promise that she is writing in the "spirit of motherliness and with love," O'Connor argues that it is not "in any way 'cool' to be naked and licking sledgehammers in your videos. It is in fact the case that you will obscure your talent by allowing yourself to be pimped, whether it's the music business or yourself doing the pimping." O'Connor also warns that "the music business doesn't give a shit about you, or any of us," and "none of the men ogling you give a shit about you either." Ultimately, O'Connor wants Cyrus to know that she is "worth more than your body or your sexual appeal."

While the language is a little hyperbolic and the format patronizing, I can't find much fault with the content of O'Connor's letter. What she's saying practically qualifies as conventional wisdom. The music business *is* seedy, young women *are* constantly being exploited sexually and then discarded, and even female artists who dictate the terms of that exploitation *do* often suffer in the long run as they age. The gist of what O'Connor is saying is, "Look out, because you might get hurt." If you take O'Connor's words at face value, they truly do seem like something your mom would say before allowing you to sign a record contract.

It's also pretty clear that O'Connor was only ever going to come off like a scold in this situation. "Put your clothes on, dear," will never be a forward-thinking position, no matter the context. And only a deluded person could seriously believe that Cyrus would react positively to such a gesture. Instead, Cyrus responded as you'd expect: she took to Twitter and suggested that O'Connor had lost her damn mind. This, in turn, inspired four more open letters in which O'Connor angrily insisted that she wasn't crazy (always the worst way to prove you're sane) and denounced Cyrus for slandering her. But the battle had already been lost. The media sided with Cyrus, no matter the consternation over the VMAs, because nobody wants to be aligned with a killjoy who no longer sells records and is locked in a no-win battle with the hottest pop star of the moment.

The obvious irony here is that Sinead O'Connor was once a young woman who caused a spectacular media uproar after provoking moralists on national television. But whereas Miley Cyrus made her career on the VMAs, Sinead O'Connor destroyed her livelihood in October of 1992 (one month before Miley Cyrus was born), when she appeared on *Saturday Night Live* and tore up a picture of the pope.

I was fifteen when it happened, so I'm not sure I can trust my memory of the aftermath. But I lived through the Miley furor just a few years ago, so I can confidently recount the way it seemed to consume the Internet with a white-hot intensity for weeks—although it petered out after only a few days in all my IRL encounters. (In the modern online think-piece economy, Miley was like an influx of subprime mortgages.) As for Sinead, I remember the reaction seeming wider and shallower. The following Monday, it seemed like everybody in my school was aware that Sinead O'Connor had performed an a cappella version of the Bob Marley song "War" on *SNL* that culminated with O'Connor admonishing the audience to "fight the real enemy" and tossing torn-up bits of a John Paul II photograph at the camera.

What followed was, in a way, more alarming: the audience didn't make a sound. It didn't applaud, and it didn't boo. Everybody just sat there. According to *Live from New York: An Uncensored History of Saturday Night Live,* the show's director, Dave

Wilson, deliberately didn't hit the applause button, ensuring a weirdly quiet studio.

Stunned silence was also the consensus where I lived. People seemed to think that defacing pope pics was sort of a nutty thing to do between Matt Foley and Canteen Boy sketches. But I don't recall much outrage in my immediate community. Granted, I was surrounded mainly by Lutherans in northeastern Wisconsin—if O'Connor had torn up a picture of Martin Luther, perhaps there would've been more of an uproar in my town.

However, the people who were pissed off at Sinead O'Connor in the waning days of 1992 turned out to be *extremely* fucking pissed. In retrospect, the repercussions she suffered for ripping up a photograph were so over-the-top that it almost seems funny. (Comedy isn't just tragedy plus time. It is also furious people plus physical distance.) But the aftershocks were undeniably swift and devastating for O'Connor.

On the following week's *SNL*, Joe Pesci half jokingly expressed a desire to hit O'Connor in the face, and this time nobody stopped the audience from applauding. When O'Connor appeared at a Bob Dylan tribute concert a week later, she was roundly jeered by thousands of people expressly assembled to salute a man associated with left-wing protest. Even those who should've been aligned with O'Connor turned out against her. O'Connor's CDs, tapes, and LPs were smashed and burned by disgruntled mobs. Overnight, she was ostracized, and her career never recovered.

Over time, pundits came to view O'Connor's actions in a more sympathetic light. O'Connor was protesting the Catholic Church's complicity in widespread instances of physical and sexual abuse of children in Ireland. The issue was personal for O'Connor: she had also been abused as a child.

This was lost in the hysteria over O'Connor's provocation, but in retrospect she was obviously prescient. In subsequent interviews, O'Connor explicitly stated her criticisms of the church's role in child-abuse cases, yet those accusations remained curiously ignored. Most of her stateside supporters interpreted O'Connor's actions as a protest against the church's stance on abortion or as a stand against religion-based violence in Northern Ireland. Her detractors simply saw her as a crazy person and marginalized her as such, just as Cyrus did two decades later when O'Connor again spoke out on behalf of a young person being victimized (in her view) by a corrupt bureaucracy.

Rewatching the *SNL* appearance on YouTube, I see that O'Connor is overwhelming in her intensity and earnestness. While it's understandable that American TV viewers didn't immediately understand the full meaning of O'Connor's statement, she can't be accused of caginess. On the contrary, O'Connor could hardly be more direct. There is nothing playful or ironic about what she's doing. You can laugh at it, but only as a by-product of discomfort.

The clip lasts for only two and a half minutes, but watching a person throb with self-righteous fury for that long feels like an eternity. Most people cross streets, change phone numbers, and invest in extra padlocks in order to keep out that kind of unbridled rage. But that could just be my age talking. Somebody who wasn't alive at the time might even find it dull. O'Connor's statement is strong, but it's all text. There's not much to parse with a ripped-up photo. It means what it means, and what it means is that you're either with me or against me.

If something like Sinead O'Connor ripping up a photo of the pope happened today—I guess the modern equivalent would be Lorde urinating on a Bible and posting a photo of the soiled book on Instagram—I suspect it wouldn't have nearly the traction that it did in 1992. Simple, overtly serious statements devoid of subtext don't work as well on the Internet. Ridiculous spectacles that can be deconstructed for their hidden meanings have a longer shelf life. Miley Cyrus was tasteless, silly, and inept on the VMAs, but those were the attributes that made her performance ideal for viewers accustomed to consuming everything through multiple screens and several levels of appreciation. If she were a joke, Miley would be "the Aristocrats," whereas Sinead would be:

"Knock, knock."

"Who's there?"

"Pain."

"Pain who?"

"I told you the first time. Pain. Just pain."

If I go with my gut-level, unthinking reaction, Sinead seems more righteous to me. She put herself on the line in 1992 and challenged the culture on an important topic in a substantive way. No matter how she was treated, Sinead O'Connor was always right. I think she was probably right about Miley, too. Miley should be careful, lest she be chewed up, spat out, and reduced to writing open letters to pop stars in twenty years.

But again, this is only my unthinking reaction. It's the reaction of a person my age with my generational biases. Old people always think that young people don't care as much as they once cared. And old people are correct. Young people don't care. Young people don't care about old people. And this will never not stop offending old people. The kids, meanwhile, will continue to be all right.

CHAPTER 9

Competing with Yourself and Losing

(Roger Waters vs. the Rest of Pink Floyd)

WHEN ASKED WHAT my favorite TV show is, I always say *Saturday Night Live,* even though I know this answer is likely to start an argument with the sort of person who cares what your favorite TV show is. Since 1980, when Lorne Michaels and the original cast left and the show was taken over by infamously ill-equipped replacements, including executive producer Jean Doumanian and "stars" Charles Rocket and Denny Dillon, it has been fashionable for intelligent, television-savvy individuals to dismiss *SNL* as terrible. (This is another example of a Default Smart Opinion.) To be fair, there have been many times in the past thirty-five or so years when those intelligent, television-savvy individuals were absolutely right. Nevertheless, the conversation about whether *SNL* happens to suck *at this very moment* is boring. I'm not interested in attempting to prove that Kate McKinnon is as valid as Gilda Radner, because it has nothing to do with why I've remained loyal.

What I love about *Saturday Night Live*—more than any cast

member or recurring character—is the format, which never changes and is helpfully stated right in the title. *Saturday Night Live* airs on Saturday night, and it is live. That is all the information you need to know going in. There are other aspects of the *SNL* formula that go beyond the brand name: the cold open that ends with "Live from New York, it's Saturday night!"; the monologue; the first musical performance, which takes place before "Weekend Update"; the second musical performance, which takes place before the weird "10-to-1" sketch. Ultimately, I appreciate both the consistency with which *SNL* is delivered—always on the same day of the week, and never via prerecorded video (commercial parodies and Digital Shorts aside)—and the consistency with which it is crafted: the product is always the same, no matter who happens to be making it. I like this because it re-creates a familiar experience that has resonated with me in the past, and I want to continue experiencing it.

I love *SNL* for the same reason I love the NFL. It doesn't matter if my team, the Green Bay Packers, has a great season or a bad season. I won't stop watching because I happen to think the current crop of Packers isn't as talented as the Packers from ten, twenty, or forty years ago. I would never argue that the NFL should pack it in for the good of its legacy because the most recent Super Bowl was unsatisfying.

When I watch professional football I am first and foremost enjoying the ritual of watching football. This is an uncomfortable truth that sportswriters who write columns criticizing the public for not caring more about concussions in football (or steroids in baseball) will never understand. They're focused too much on the sanctity of the game (or the good of society) and not on what actually draws people to sports. Sports fans want stuff to do. We want to watch football games on TV in the fall because it's an excuse to eat junk food and engage in excessive daytime drinking in our living rooms. We want to have tail-gate parties outside baseball stadiums in the summer because it's an excuse to eat junk food and engage in excessive daytime drinking in an environment that's not our living rooms. These activities always take precedence over whatever happens to be horribly wrong about sports at the moment. I'm not saying this is right or even defensible, only that it's true. Taking a moral stand against the latest scandal du jour instantly becomes un-tenable for most sports fans if it means giving up our snacks.

The most egregious example of this is probably the 1987 NFL players' strike, which resulted in one week of canceled games and three subsequent weeks in which "replacement" players filled out the rosters of professional teams. Instead of Joe Montana and Lawrence Taylor, fans were treated to Doug Hoppock and Jim Crocicchia. It was the worst.

But it was also acceptable. The '87 strike is largely forgotten now; its most lasting legacy is that it inspired the lesser of two movies in which Keanu Reeves, improbably, plays a quarter-back. (I refer to *The Replacements*, a supremely crappy film I have seen ten times, which is inferior to *Point Break*, a supremely ex-cellent film I have seen one hundred times.) Unless you were alive at the time (I turned ten right before the strike began), you probably aren't aware that the striking players were trying to secure free-agent rights and a better portion of the league's rev-enue, both worthy causes.

What's notable to me in retrospect is that the majority of NFL fans watched the replacement games knowing full well that they were getting a fraudulent product (as well as undermin-ing those aforementioned worthy causes). Ratings after the first week dropped about 20 percent compared with regular NFL games, and the numbers for *Monday Night Football* at the time were the game's second lowest since 1970. But the TV networks had expected ratings to be far worse; *MNF* still attracted more than twelve million viewers, and the Sunday afternoon games on CBS had between nine and ten million viewers. That's far less than the average NFL game draws now, but still, given the NFL's relative popularity in the late '80s, the replacement games were much closer to "business as usual" than they had any right to be. A *New York Times* story published after the first weekend of replacement games confirmed that the networks would carry the subsequent contests "because they have no alternative programming that would draw a bigger audience."

The same month that the '87 NFL strike commenced, Pink Floyd released its thirteenth studio album, *A Momentary Lapse of Reason*. Like the NFL, Pink Floyd was an insanely successful and prodigiously well-off institution experiencing serious dissension in its labor force. Two years earlier, bassist and principal songwriter Roger Waters quit via a letter sent to Pink Floyd's US and UK record labels. Because Waters was the chief creative force behind the group's most popular albums—*The Dark Side of the Moon, Wish You Were Here,* and, most crucially, the twenty-two-times-platinum double LP, *The Wall*—he assumed that his departure meant the end of Pink Floyd. However, because Waters had voluntarily relinquished rights to the Pink Floyd name during a power struggle over the firing of the band's manager, Steve O'Rourke, his former bandmates David Gilmour and Nick Mason believed that it was their right to continue without him. Waters sued, unsuccessfully, arguing that Pink Floyd was "spent" creatively. "If one of us is going to be called Pink Floyd," he declared, "it's me."

Waters made his case with characteristic eloquence in a *Rolling Stone* cover story parsing the details of his feud with the rest of Pink Floyd. "There is the legal issue, which is the only thing that can be resolved in court. And that is, who owns the piece of property that is the name Pink Floyd?" he said. "The other issue is completely separate, the whole issue of what is and isn't a rock group. What is the Beatles? Are Paul McCartney and Ringo Starr the Beatles? My view now is they're not, any more than the Firm should have been called Led Zeppelin, even if John Paul Jones had been there."

"What is and isn't a rock group?" is a fascinating and profound question that, like other fascinating and profound questions posed by Roger Waters in the context of Pink Floyd, Gilmour and Mason were no longer interested in pondering. By all accounts, Waters had been a domineering and arrogant bandleader who for years publicly undermined the contributions of the other band members. "Back in the early '70s, we used to pretend that we were a group," Waters told *Rolling Stone* in 1982, right as the film version of *The Wall* was released. "I could work with another drummer and keyboard player very easily, and it's likely at some point that I will."

Waters not only disrespected the other people in Pink Floyd, he also took the power of the Pink Floyd brand for granted. Surely he *could* work with different musicians, but would anybody care? Waters seemed to think so, though five years later that theory was being put to the test.

As for "what is and isn't Pink Floyd," the majority of people not named Roger Waters seemed to believe that Pink Floyd was whatever entity happened to be calling itself Pink Floyd, no matter who was involved. In spite of Waters's legal efforts— Gilmour claimed that he met with his attorneys nearly every day while making *A Momentary Lapse of Reason* because Waters's attorneys were constantly threatening to shut him and Mason down—the album was completed, it was released by the Floyd's longtime label, Columbia, and it went on to sell three million copies. Gilmour and Mason (with ousted keyboardist Rick Wright rejoining as a hired gun) then proceeded to make tens of millions of dollars touring stadiums around the world for nearly three years.

Waters responded by expanding his media offensive. "I think the songs are very poor in general," Waters said of *Reason*. "The lyrics I can't believe." The dig on the lyrics (mostly written by Gilmour) is telling, as Waters had been the acknowledged intellectual in Pink Floyd. It was Waters who devised the big concepts that Floyd albums were known for in the '70s, while Gilmour was recognized for accenting Waters's ideas with grand musical flourishes. ("I didn't play the guitar solos; he didn't write the lyrics" was how Waters put it.)

Lack of tact aside, Waters has a point: *Reason*'s best-known song, "Learning to Fly," features the truly stupid lyric "Can't keep my eyes from the circling sky / Tongue-tied and twisted, just an earth-bound misfit, I." (Think Gilmour's cowriter on this was Yoda, you?) Waters's singular lyrical obsession in Pink Floyd was reconciling his admiration for the band's original front man, the infamous acid-case recluse Syd Barrett, with his fear that rock stardom would render him similarly crazy. (Waters did end up like Barrett in one respect—they both watched Pink Floyd flourish after they left the band.) This colors all of Pink Floyd's best and most resonant work, from *Dark Side*'s climactic cut, "Eclipse," to "Shine On You Crazy Diamond" to the entirety of *The Wall*. "Learning to Fly," meanwhile, is about David Gilmour's joy in flying his own fucking plane. It was, to put it mildly, inferior Pink Floyd product.

After he was out of Pink Floyd, Waters had bigger problems than Gilmour's inane lyrics. A few months before the release of *Reason*, Waters put out his second solo record, *Radio K.A.O.S.*, the most concept-intensive concept record of his career. What is the concept of *Radio K.A.O.S.*? I could tell you, but then I'd have to kill myself. Allow me instead to quote from the liner notes:

> Benny is a Welsh coal miner. He is a radio ham. He is 23 years old, married to Molly. They have a son, young Ben aged 4, and a new baby. They look after Benny's twin brother Billy, who is apparently a vegetable. The mine is closed by market forces. The Male Voice Choir stops singing. One night Benny takes Billy on a pub crawl. Drunk in a brightly-lit shopping mall, Benny vents his anger on a shop window full of the multiple TV images of Margaret Thatcher's mocking condescension.

I'm going to stop here—there are approximately thirty-eight more characters and 1.2 million additional words to get to—because I'm already tired and I'm guessing that you want to put this book down to listen to a song about a rich guy flying his own fucking plane.

Suffice it to say that *Radio K.A.O.S.* did not sell as well as *A Momentary Lapse of Reason*.

Gilmour's advantage (and Waters's insurmountable problem from a commercial perspective) was that Gilmour's vocals and guitar playing were Pink Floyd's first and second most recognizable musical attributes. *A Momentary Lapse of Reason*, unlike

Radio K.A.O.S., sounds almost exactly like a Pink Floyd record if you aren't listening to the songs all that closely. Fortunately for Gilmour and Mason, this was precisely the way Pink Floyd's audience chose to listen to Pink Floyd in 1987. Pink Floyd exclusively played the sort of venues where the people standing onstage appeared to be small and distant abstractions surrounded by dry ice and retina-shearing lights. Close listening was out of the question, which meant it didn't really matter what the songs were about or who was playing them. What mattered was the ritual of seeing Pink Floyd, which Waters had actively worked to dismantle for years.

When the supporting shows for *Reason* were announced, there had not been an extensive Pink Floyd tour in a decade. In late 1980 and early 1981, Waters devised the stage show for *The Wall*, which was too elaborate and expensive to tour outside of a handful of cities. A traditional round of concerts was discussed for 1983's *The Final Cut*, but Waters opted out of those as well. Pink Floyd became even more popular in the interim, and the band's scarcity heightened its mythic status.

Pink Floyd (rivaled only by Led Zeppelin and possibly Bob Marley) became the signature act of a certain kind of teenage suburban drug-culture lifestyle. If you were into smoking pot and traversing metaphysical realms of the mind while physically situated inside the confines of unsupervised basement rec rooms, Pink Floyd's '70s work was required listening, regardless of how removed each new generation was from those old records.

The unrequited demand for a Pink Floyd live experience is conveyed by an episode of *Freaks and Geeks* in which the freaks (played by Linda Cardellini, Seth Rogen, Jason Segel, James Franco, and Busy Philipps) talk about hitting up the local planetarium on Friday night to check out the Pink Floyd laser show, which Segel's character, Nick Andopolis, describes as a "transcendental experience." *Freaks and Geeks* takes place in 1981, roughly at the midpoint between major Pink Floyd tours, but it really could've been any year, then or now. (There are *still* Pink Floyd tribute shows performed by hundreds of bands around the world.)

What Gilmour and Mason were offering with *Reason* and the accompanying tour was the ultimate Pink Floyd laser show, an ideal venue for aging fans to relive their glory days and for kids who missed the "real" Floyd to take drugs in the midst of a credible approximation. What must've been extra galling for Waters was that he predicted this on *The Wall*. In *The Wall*'s initial, preposterously expensive stage production—which was presented in only four cities—a band of four musicians dressed up like Pink Floyd performed the album's bombastic opening number, "In the Flesh?" The point was to underline the dehumanizing impersonality of arena shows, but what it ultimately illustrated was how Pink Floyd's propensity for emphasizing iconography and visuals over the band members' names and faces would neutralize the damage of Waters's eventual departure.

No musician has ever argued in an interview, "I am as important as my songs—in fact, I'm *more* important." It is required to at least pretend that "the music comes first." No band is more associated with this idea than Pink Floyd. The band members have rarely appeared on their own album covers. (The exceptions are Floyd's first album, *The Piper at the Gates of Dawn,* and the tedious double LP *Ummagumma.*) Even as *The Dark Side of the Moon* became one of the most popular LPs ever, the men who wrote and recorded it barely qualified as rock stars. This was by design.

"Oh, I wanted anonymity," Waters said in 1987. "I treasured it. And somehow we made it big and stayed private and anonymous. It was the best of both worlds." Now Waters wanted to retroactively assert his identity in Pink Floyd as a crucial aspect of the band's aesthetic. But he was too late. (Perhaps not coincidentally, there are three photos of Gilmour and Mason in the liner notes of *A Momentary Lapse of Reason*—one duo shot and two solo pictures.)

"It is frustrating to find out how many people don't know who I am or what I actually did in Pink Floyd," Waters complained to *Rolling Stone*. "We get on a plane, and people ask what band we're in. I tell 'em I'm Roger Waters, and it doesn't mean a thing to them. Then I mention Pink Floyd, and they go, 'Yeah, "Money." I love *The Wall*.'"

But even fans who did know what Waters contributed to Pink Floyd didn't stop going to Pink Floyd concerts. Perhaps the music was worse without him, but the rituals associated with the music were essentially the same. More important, Waters's exit made the revival of those rituals possible. Pink Floyd would've been finished if Waters had his way. Siding with him as a fan would mean giving up the "transcendental experience" of hearing Pink Floyd music played by a majority of Pink Floyd's members with fifty thousand people consuming fifty thousand tabs of acid. Even if Waters was *right* about the validity of calling this enterprise Pink Floyd, he was not *correct* as far as judging the market is concerned. As Waters himself put it, "I'm competing with myself and losing."

What if *A Momentary Lapse of Reason* were structured around an obscure story involving radio waves and anti–Margaret Thatcher broadsides? What if *Radio K.A.O.S.* swapped out Jim

Ladd's interstitial DJ patter for some majestic David Gilmour guitar solos? What if Waters never left Pink Floyd? That would've been better for all involved, no?

Before we address all that, let's ponder a parallel topic: What if Conan O'Brien never left *The Tonight Show*?

The late-night wars ended when Jay Leno folded up his wacky small-town newspaper headlines and retired to his fifty-story garage in 2014. But I will never not be interested in talking about the behind-the-scenes wrangling that took place over *The Tonight Show* in the '90s, '00s, and early '10s. My interest in this topic far exceeds my interest in the actual *Tonight Show*. I honestly could not care less about *The Tonight Show*. I was sad when Leno retired, because I knew I could no longer hate him. Leno was an outstanding villain in a drama I couldn't get enough of—the quality of the talk show he hosted inside that drama mattered as much to me as *TGS* did in the context of *30 Rock*. To me, *The Tonight Show* is like one of those making-of-the-video music videos (e.g., Genesis's "Invisible Touch" and Paula Abdul's "Forever Your Girl")—you never see the actual video. Forget the corpse; I just wanted the dirt.

When people talk about the 2010 *Tonight Show* conflict between O'Brien and NBC/Jay Leno, they often overlook a vital detail: Leno did not "steal" *The Tonight Show* from O'Brien any more than Gilmour and Mason stole Pink Floyd from Waters. O'Brien decided to leave after rejecting a proposal forwarded by the network that would've placed Leno's denim-clad carcass in the 11:30 p.m. slot for a monologue-centered prologue to O'Brien's *Tonight Show* at 12:05 a.m. O'Brien subsequently released a statement maintaining that he would "not participate in the destruction of *The Tonight Show*" and demanded to be released from his contract.

I would normally characterize equating a half-hour time-slot bump with "the destruction of *The Tonight Show*" as hyperbole, but given my semantics-based argument for *SNL* earlier, I must let it slide for the sake of ideological consistency. O'Brien wanted *The Tonight Show* to air at night and not (technically) in the morning. I won't dispute any of that. Instead I'll just quote Jerry Seinfeld at the end of Bill Carter's definitive account of the Jay-Conan debacle, 2010's *The War for Late Night:* "It's all fake! There's no institution to offend! All of this 'I won't sit by and watch the institution damaged.' What institution? Ripping off the public? That's the only institution. We tell jokes and they give us millions!"

(How awesome is post-*Seinfeld* Jerry Seinfeld? Actually, it's more like post–*Bee Movie* / *The Marriage Ref* Jerry Seinfeld, but still: he's such an unrepentantly cranky bastard now. At some point Seinfeld decided to follow the Kobe Bryant model: he dropped the smiling, likable celebrity act and revealed the angry, misanthropic, and candid asshole underneath. Everything he says now is deeply cynical and coldly persuasive.)

O'Brien partisans will insist that even if Conan did voluntarily jump from NBC, the network escorted him to the ledge and then covered that ledge in rabies-infested rats. He was *practically* pushed from *The Tonight Show,* in other words. There is some validity to this argument: reinserting Leno into the late-night mix couldn't help but undermine O'Brien and his show. It was a humiliating vote of no confidence from NBC. But if you set aside O'Brien's bruised ego and look at this strictly in terms what was best for O'Brien's career, staying on NBC still seems better in retrospect then winding up on TBS (or Fox or ABC, if O'Brien had been luckier). Again, I'll quote Seinfeld, the Sage of Real Talk: "Hang around! Just stay there, just be there! The old cliché: 95 percent is just showing up. OK, I'm on at 12; I'm still showing up. You never leave!"

I have a theory about why O'Brien's *Tonight Show* pulled in mediocre ratings, and it goes back to viewing rituals. As a person born in the late '70s, I naturally believe that Conan O'Brien is funnier than Jay Leno. But I hardly ever watched his version of *The Tonight Show*, just as I never watched Leno's *Tonight Show*. Watching *The Tonight Show* was simply never part of my formative experience as a TV viewer. I appreciate Johnny Carson as a historical figure, but I was too young to see him in his prime, back when he could seduce sexy-as-hell Angie Dickinson, even while one of Jack Hanna's monkeys urinated on his shoulder.

I think I'm pretty typical in this regard—for people under the age of fifty, *The Tonight Show* is just another late-night talk show, not necessarily the greatest franchise in the history of TV. So if you supported the idea of O'Brien rather than Leno hosting *The Tonight Show*, there's a decent chance that this support didn't translate to actual viewership. Whereas the people who did watch *The Tonight Show* liked Leno, or else they wouldn't have sat through all those O.J. jokes for twenty years.

The conventional wisdom on O'Brien is that he was "too weird" to operate on *The Tonight Show*, which is true if by "too weird" you mean "utterly disconnected from Jay Leno's version of *The Tonight Show*." When Jimmy Fallon—who won the Jay-Conan war without firing a single shot—took over in 2014, he began by introducing himself to *The Tonight Show*'s core audience with an ingratiating display of boyish humility. He talked about his wife and child, his proud parents, and the honor of inheriting what Leno had shepherded since the early '90s. He courted the uncool Leno fans whom O'Brien seemed ambivalent about. If Fallon had been wearing a cap, he would have respectfully removed it and gripped it to his chest; if it were possible to mow 4.1 million lawns in a single night, Fallon would've chartered a jet and loaded it with his trusty mower immediately after stepping off the stage. Fallon's message was clear and reassuring. This was the gist: "I'm the new guy, but not really new. What you're about to see might seem different at first, but you'll discover that it's the same thing to which you've grown accustomed."

If O'Brien had stayed on *The Tonight Show*, his show probably wouldn't have been like that. It probably would've been more like *The Wall*—a late-night talk show about the ugly and dehumanizing environment in which late-night talk shows are created. I only became a regular viewer of O'Brien's *Tonight Show* during its final two weeks, when O'Brien steered his failing enterprise spectacularly off a cliff. As a person not emotionally invested in *The Tonight Show*, watching O'Brien self-destruct was way more entertaining than watching a conventional late-night talk show.

Could he have done that every week, with Leno as his lead-in? We'll never know, but Leno was clearly a valuable foil for O'Brien. The "Team Coco" protests that erupted in response to O'Brien's "firing" were rooted at least partly in generational resentment. Leno was a potent symbol of boomer cultural hegemony, and if you were conditioned as a Gen Xer or Millennial to hate Woodstock retrospectives and Eagles reunion tours, O'Brien was easy to root for. Putting Leno on directly before *The Tonight Show* under contentious circumstances would've given O'Brien license to be a dick to his network and Leno while remaining a sympathetic figure in the eyes of the media and viewers who might not otherwise care about *The Tonight*

Show. Perhaps NBC would've eventually replaced O'Brien with Leno on its own volition, but I doubt it, especially if the drama happened to gin up interest in O'Brien's otherwise indifferently received show.

This is all speculation, of course. What's known for certain is what happened to O'Brien after he left *The Tonight Show:* he was marginalized on a cable network best known for airing reruns of *The Big Bang Theory* 467 times per day (give or take a hundred airings), and he was defined by the row over *The Tonight Show* in a mostly negative way. Again, Conan O'Brien in my view as a non-Cocoite seems sad and sort of small on basic cable. It's similar to the way Waters receded in the public's estimation in the aftermath of blowing up his relationship with Pink Floyd. In the 2011 film *Conan O'Brien Can't Stop,* a concert documentary about O'Brien's post–*Tonight Show* Legally Prohibited from Being Funny on Television comedy tour, O'Brien is depicted as a man adrift. He is self-pitying, angry, and needy. He also seems to have temporarily lost his ability to discern irony: at one point O'Brien insists that he's "the least entitled person" he knows in spite of starring in a feature film based on the premise that he was persecuted by NBC because of a personnel decision that added tens of millions of dollars to his bank account.

That discomfiting impression is exacerbated by how unfunny the movie is, both when O'Brien is on the stage and when he's off it. No matter how hard his put-upon assistants laugh at his desperate mugging, O'Brien's bitterness is palpable. (If *Dont Look Back* had been filmed during Bob Dylan's *Self Portrait* period, it might've resembled *Conan O'Brien Can't Stop.*) It speaks to how deluded O'Brien and his camp were by the Team Coco bubble: they believed *Conan O'Brien Can't Stop* would make its titular star seem sympathetic. Instead the film unintentionally reveals O'Brien's "destruction of *The Tonight Show*" talk for what it is—self-serving and ultimately self-defeating.

This will strike some as counterintuitive and trollish but nevertheless I believe it's the truth: NBC was right. The public was comfortable with Leno doing a monologue at 11:30 p.m. and watching O'Brien after that. Leno was good at guitar solos, and O'Brien was good at lyrics. For his own good, O'Brien should've kept the band together.

So: What if Roger Waters never left Pink Floyd? This question was sort of answered in 2005, when Waters reunited with Gilmour, Mason, and Wright at Live 8 in London. Pink Floyd played four songs: "Breathe," "Money," "Wish You Were Here," and "Comfortably Numb," and nearly everyone who saw the performance agreed that it went as well as could possibly be expected. Pink Floyd sounded fantastic: considering the circumstances, it's probably the greatest reunion gig ever. Most striking was Waters, who bounded around the stage enthusiastically and stopped the show before "Wish You Were Here" to remark on how emotional he felt to be back with the Floyd again.

Big-money offers predictably poured in after the gig, rumored to top out at $200 million. Gilmour publicly rejected the idea of a tour; he likened playing with Waters to sleeping with an ex. "The Live 8 thing was great but it was closure," he said. "There's no future for Pink Floyd."

The apparent retirement of the Pink Floyd name prompted a stunning role reversal—now it was Waters's turn to satisfy the ritualistic needs of Pink Floyd's fan base. For three years after the Live 8 show, from 2006 through 2008, he toured the world playing *The Dark Side of the Moon* in its entirety. In 2010 he launched another three-year tour centered on *The Wall* that wrapped the month he turned seventy. While he didn't technically tour under the Pink Floyd banner, Waters was trading on Pink Floyd's music, and he benefited from Gilmour, Mason, and Wright essentially surrendering the brand name. Waters's ex-partners and longtime adversaries even offered public approval of his efforts: Gilmour and Mason joined him for a *Wall* show at London's O2 arena. Waters no longer had to compete with himself.

Perhaps Waters could be accused of hypocrisy, but "what is or isn't a rock group" is a question that time is in the midst of settling without the input of guitar-slinging mortals. I'm writing this two days after the death of Tommy Ramone, who had been the last original surviving member of the Ramones. It seems incredible that Joey, Johnny, Dee Dee, and now Tommy are gone forever, but it's really not incredible at all. What's incredible is that more top-line classic-rock bands haven't been wiped completely off the face of the earth. There are two surviving original Beatles, two surviving members of the Who, three surviving members of Led Zeppelin, and four original surviving Stones. All four guys in Black Sabbath are still alive in spite of eating LSD for breakfast throughout the '70s. U2 and R.E.M. are still intact, too. Axl hates most of the original Guns N' Roses, but a full reunion is still possible should cooler heads finally prevail. Every significant band you can think of— even a hard-luck outfit with a high body count, such as Lynyrd Skynyrd or the Allman Brothers Band—still has *somebody* who's around to answer the call if a concert promoter phones. When the final episode of *Breaking Bad* briefly reignited interest in the '70s power-pop group Badfinger by using the heartrending "Baby Blue" over the closing scene, that band was able to tour, even though the two main singers had committed suicide decades earlier. Against all odds, classic-rock bands have endured like termites.

Eventually, every single person in these bands and every other band you've ever loved or merely heard of will be dead. What then? Well, if there's still an audience of living music fans interested in seeing the music performed live, those bands will carry on in the form of holograms, jukebox musicals, and Cirque du Soleil extravaganzas. Consider that, in 2010, Elvis Presley had his best earnings year ever, thirty-three years after his death, raking in $60 million thanks to sales spurred by his seventy-fifth birthday and the launch of the *Viva Elvis* Cirque du Soleil show in Las Vegas. That same year, Cirque du Soleil announced that it would be mounting a Michael Jackson–themed show for a worldwide tour and a permanent installation in Vegas. Jackson, who died in 2009, became a bestselling artist again in the aftermath of his death, moving 8.2 million units in the United States and thirty-five million units worldwide. Sony paid a quarter of a billion dollars for access to his archive of unreleased music, the biggest contract for a single artist in history.

Over the next ten to twenty years, these stories will become increasingly common. Some people are too popular to ever leave show business, even after they stop breathing. But don't worry—there's no institution to offend. Ripping off the public is the only institution.

CHAPTER 10

Why Does the Thunder Pass Me By?

(A Short History of Unfought Celebrity Boxing Matches, Starring Axl Rose and Vince Neil with Cameos by Scott Stapp, Fred Durst, Kid Rock, Tommy Lee, Kurt Cobain, DMX, and George Zimmerman)

IF THIS BOOK were submitted to the Motion Picture Association of America, and the MPAA read only what you've read so far (assuming you're reading these essays in order), and the MPAA for some reason had been tasked with issuing potentially prohibitive consonants to books about musical rivalries, I'm guessing this book would be rated R. There has been a fair amount of bad language and a few scenes involving sexual situations. There has been virtually no violence, but this would actually make the book seem tawdrier in the MPAA's eyes, as the MPAA would rather see a person getting his head blown off than that same person getting head.

What this book needs is some real, bruising, dangerously physical altercations. We are talking about human conflict, after all, but thus far the fights have all been purely metaphorical. (You could maybe set aside that Ping-Pong game between Prince and Michael Jackson as an exception.) At some point, all this tension has to be released in the form of visceral action.

Humans yearn to tussle, and because we're only human, we must succumb to this impulse.

"It's to me one simple rule," cigar-chewing boxing historian Bert Sugar once said of the sweet science. "Who imposes his will on the other man?"

Damn right.

As an American, I'm naturally obsessed with violence. But being an American also means taking a reflexive (if also somewhat phony) stance against violence. So for the record: Violence is bad. Violence hurts. Violence will ruin your day and stain your clothes. Therefore we must talk about a version of violence without consequence, a violence that is basically imaginary. It is violence that feels real but is not; violence that is in fact another metaphor, only this time dressed in leather and scarves.

Let's talk about Axl Rose.

Now, I'll admit that I don't need much of an excuse to talk about Axl Rose. I've already inserted him into other chapters in this book. Axl is to this book what Drake is to R & B hits and major sports teams' locker rooms. Maybe Axl doesn't always belong, but I find that he, like Drake, is always a welcome presence.

When it comes to metaphors about fake violence, Axl Rose is the car-cutting scene from *Reservoir Dogs* in human form. What you imagine Axl is doing is always worse than what he's actually done, though either way it's still pretty gross. Actually, if we're talking about Erin Everly or Stephanie Seymour, it may well have been just as gross as you imagine.

Both Everly (his first wife) and Seymour (his girlfriend during the *Use Your Illusion* years) have publicly accused Rose of battery. But Rose was living an "It's So Easy" lifestyle several years before *Appetite for Destruction* dropped. In a great John Jeremiah Sullivan essay focused largely on Rose's childhood in Lafayette, Indiana, there's a funny-sad anecdote about Rose striking a classmate's mother over the head with his arm—which happened to be in a splint at the time. Rose's outburst stemmed from a disagreement concerning the kid riding his bike in front of Axl's friend's house and leaving skid marks on the sidewalk. That sort of shit is probably *still* a capital offense in Indiana.

So, it appears that Rose has acted monstrously toward women from the moment he could swing an injured appendage. For the purposes of this discussion, however, I am going to focus on why Rose seems uninterested in executing his threats to hit those with XY chromosomes.

Axl Rose is commonly perceived to be a tough guy. But Axl Rose is not a tough guy. Axl Rose was once beat up by Tommy Hilfiger.

"It was the most surreal thing, I think, that's ever happened to me in my life," Rose later told KROQ, to the agreement of every single person who's aware that Tommy Hilfiger once beat up Axl Rose. Hilfiger reportedly "smacked" Rose (to use Rose's word) in 2006 at a New York nightclub because Axl moved a drink belonging to Hilfiger's girlfriend, and you do *not* move a drink belonging to Mr. Tommy Hilfiger's girlfriend in the presence of Mr. Tommy Hilfiger. Hilfiger later said that he hit Rose because he feared that Rose would hit him first. (Hilfiger and Rose later reconciled.)

Hilfiger acted on a perception of potential violence from Rose that wasn't real, because people always believe Axl Rose to be more violent than he is. For a while that perception worked for him—it was the source of Axl's power, giving him the upper hand in every encounter. He was like a gangster or a lion that escapes from some crazy guy's backyard animal menagerie. Axl Rose intimidated people. He made you want to keep your distance. But the downside of being an anticipatory ass kicker eventually caught up with Axl Rose in a big way, long before Tommy Hilfiger handed Axl his ass.

In order to understand why that is, it's important to revisit "Get in the Ring," from 1991's *Use Your Illusion II*. "Get in the Ring" is not a distinguished song in the Guns N' Roses canon. It was never released as a single. It has never been performed live by any incarnation of GNR. If you were to poll GNR fans on the band's worst songs ever, "Get in the Ring" would likely garner more votes than any track from the classic-era records, with the possible exception of "My World." And yet "Get in the Ring" is one of those GNR songs that even non-GNR fans know—maybe not on the level of "Sweet Child o' Mine" or "Welcome to the Jungle," but the sheer ridiculousness of "Get in the Ring" (and the fact that *Use Your Illusion II* moved seven million units) has pushed the song into the general consciousness as an utterly insane gesture by a transparently deluded and extremely famous man.

"Get in the Ring" is perhaps better known as "that song in which Axl Rose threatens to throttle several journalists for highly questionable and vaguely articulated reasons." The crimes described by Axl in "Get in the Ring" include "printin' lies," "rippin' off the fuckin' kids," and "startin' controversy," all of which, in a conventional court of law, might call for a fine or even jail time but never corporal punishment. But Axl went rogue on "Get in the Ring" in more ways than one.

That "Get in the Ring" exists at all can be blamed on sub-standard early-'90s technology. Had GNR released the *Use Your Illusion* albums just a few years later, "Get in the Ring" would've been turned into a blog post about Axl's desire to box a cabal of music writers in front of a paying audience. It never would've been a song immortalized on an album by the biggest band in the world. Putting it on a multiplatinum record gave "Get in the Ring" a permanence it doesn't deserve. But "Get in the Ring" is part of the historical record now, which makes it easy to misconstrue Rose's bluster as fact. If your knowledge of early '90s GNR derives solely from the band's records, you might believe that Rose actually beat those people up. *But he so did not beat those people up.* On the contrary, Axl actively avoided the (metaphorical) boxing ring after the song came out.

If Rose had been serious about boxing his enemies, he would've counted "Get in the Ring" among his greatest accomplishments. It was very effective at provoking the people Axl said he hated. One of the journalists Axl Rose called out, *Spin* publisher Bob Guccione Jr., publicly accepted Rose's challenge. For a man named Guccione, boxing Axl must have seemed like a publicity stunt made in sleazeball heaven. But Rose never followed through.

Another writer named in "Get in the Ring," Mick Wall, later wrote an unflattering unauthorized biography of the singer that opens with a detailed account of Axl's beef with the author from the author's point of view. Wall published his first unauthorized book about GNR around the time that the *Use Your Illusion* albums were released, and it was assumed that Wall ended up in "Get in the Ring" for that reason. But in the Rose bio, Wall theorizes that Axl was actually upset about a story Wall wrote for *Kerrang!* magazine in 1990, in which Rose ranted about wanting to assault Mötley Crüe singer Vince Neil in connection with a previous altercation involving Guns

N' Roses guitarist Izzy Stradlin at the 1989 MTV Video Music Awards.

Here's Axl's money quote from Wall's story:

> I tell ya, he's gonna get a good ass-whippin', and I'm the boy to give it to him. It's like, whenever you wanna do it, man, let's just do it. I wanna see that plastic face of his cave in when I hit him!...Personally, I don't think he has the balls. But that's the gauntlet, and I'm throwing it down. Hey, Vince, whichever way you wanna go, man: guns, knives, or fists, whatever you wanna do, I don't care.

Unlike GNR's bloated music videos at the time, which provided more face time for animated dolphins than for Duff McKagan, Axl's taunt is concise and linear, and the meaning is unambiguous. It is a premeditated call to brawl—guns, knives, fists, Axl doesn't care. As Wall tells it, Rose even cleared the quote before the piece ran. And yet once the story was published, Rose proceeded to throw Wall under the bus in light of the predictable firestorm the interview caused.

The most damaging fallout from the story (this, again, is Wall's theory) was that Vince Neil eagerly accepted the invitation to "go" with Rose. Neil even went on MTV and challenged Rose to a charity boxing match. In the Mötley Crüe memoir *The Dirt,* Neil claims that Rose sent "little messengers to me," instructing Neil to meet Rose "in the parking lot of Tower Records on Sunset or on the boardwalk of Venice Beach." Neil says that he always showed up and Rose "chickened out a good half-dozen times."

The Axl Rose–Vince Neil feud began when Neil punched Stradlin at the VMAs in retaliation for Stradlin allegedly groping Neil's wife at Riki Rachtman's legendary Sunset Strip skeez haven, the Cathouse. That Neil punched Stradlin is undisputed. What's less clear are Axl's intentions vis-à-vis avenging Izzy. In retrospect, Neil's account seems the most credible— if he was willing to punch Izzy Stradlin, it's logical to think that he would also punch Axl if given the chance. He was also "in the right," as much as anybody in this moron circus could possibly be in the right. He went after a guy who attacked his wife. Neil's motivation to fight is clearer than it is for Rose, who seems to have been driven primarily by machismo and ego.

At the time, it was widely assumed that Rose would destroy Neil in a fight. People were projecting the qualities of GNR's music onto Rose as a fighter—he was presumed to have the battle skills of a starved alley cat injected with a potent speedball of crank and Jack Daniel's, because that's what he sounds like on *Appetite*. The media subtly reinforced this presumption of Axl's superiority in the way they presented the combatants. Neil appeared on MTV News articulating his challenge to Rose directly into the camera, like a C-list wrestler. Rose, however, was allowed to blithely dismiss Neil in an interview with the channel's avatar of seriousness, Kurt Loder. Vince Neil was unquestionably one of the biggest rock stars of his era, but Axl Rose was treated like a dignitary perched on a higher stratum.

Perhaps I should take a moment to explain the importance of MTV News to those of us who grew up in the '80s and '90s. Younger generations might not understand that MTV was once a trusted *news source* that provided valuable *information* on famous *musicians*. Kurt Loder was the Gen-X Walter Cronkite—his coverage of Kurt Cobain's suicide is my generation's equivalent of Cronkite's emotional yet steady hand in the aftermath of the Kennedy assassination. These days MTV is known for...I actually don't know what MTV is known for now. I haven't watched MTV regularly in at least fifteen years. I assume MTV's programming consists of reality shows in which twenty-one-year-olds flash their junk in exchange for Skrillex tickets, but don't quote me on that. Back then, MTV was like the CNN of music—or Fox News, if Fox News preferred redheads named Tabitha to blondes. In the pre-Internet era, MTV was where you went to find out about new albums, concert tours, or, in this case, a potentially violent rock-star rivalry.

GNR, no matter the boorish behavior of its front man, was granted a veneer of seriousness by MTV that the network never afforded to Mötley Crüe. When Vince Neil punched out Izzy Stradlin, Izzy was exiting the stage from a duet he and Rose had performed with Tom Petty and the Heartbreakers on the song "Free Fallin'." In 1989, GNR was already being integrated into the history of classic rock while Vince Neil fumed in the wings.

Rose's battle with Neil inevitably was viewed through this lens. Rose didn't have to fight Neil. Merely by talking about throwing down the gauntlet, Rose had already won. He had imposed his will on the other man.

The last time I challenged a person to a fight, I did not really want to fight. It happened when I was in my midtwenties. I was in a bar with my girlfriend at the time, and a guy walked up to her and made a vulgar comment. I felt obligated to confront him, so that's what I did. I stood over him at the bar—he was sitting on a bar stool—and made sure my chest grazed his shoulder. I informed the guy that he'd have his own girlfriend if he didn't say stupid bullshit to women in bars.

The guy kept his eyes locked on his beer. Meanwhile, inside

my head, I was praying he wouldn't call my bluff. This was my favorite bar. I drank at this place all the time. I did not want to look like an idiot by fighting this guy or, worse, risk getting kicked out and banned for life.

Fortunately, the guy did not want to fight, either. Instead he apologized.

By the way, this altercation was over the girlfriend I mentioned in the Clapton vs. Hendrix chapter, the one who later backed out of being my fiancée. We broke up five months into our engagement, and a year after that, we ate chicken strips at a Chili's by the mall and she told me she was a lesbian and living with our former neighbor. In life, sometimes you're Vince Neil standing in the wings with a balled-up fist, and other times you're an unsuspecting Izzy Stradlin walking offstage. So it goes.

We have been conditioned to expect brute force as a punishment against those who do us wrong. Our legal system sanctions it, and when our legal system fails, we look to other institutions to bring the pain in the name of justice. In 2014, a man who specializes in celebrity boxing matches proposed such a bout between George Zimmerman—the Florida security guard who shot and killed an unarmed black teenager named Trayvon Martin—and the rapper DMX. The proposed fight seemed to have a built-in audience: after Zimmerman's acquittal, millions of Americans were outraged. The promoter claimed that fifteen thousand people volunteered to fight Zimmerman. One of them was rapper the Game, who said he wanted to fight for "the legacy of Trayvon Martin and his family," but apparently he was insufficiently famous. (Zimmerman allegedly wanted to fight Kanye West.)

DMX, however, appeared to be an ideal adversary. DMX's popularity peaked in the early aughts with hits like "Ruff Ryders' Anthem" and "Party Up (Up in Here)," which showcased his perturbed bark lashing out over minimal beats, like a pit bull rudely introducing itself to a poodle. "I am going to beat the living fuck out of him," DMX promised. "I am breaking every rule in boxing to make sure I fuck him right up." DMX vowed that once he annihilated Zimmerman, he was going to take his cock out and piss on him, "right in his muthafuckin' face," because "Zimmerman is a piece of shit and that's what he needs to drink."

Perhaps DMX lacked tact, but his "George Zimmerman should drink DMX's urine" argument was otherwise sound.

Alas, neither blood nor piss was spilled in the name of justice. Zimmerman didn't fight DMX or anybody else. No matter how much the public hated George Zimmerman for killing Trayvon Martin, most people recoiled at the idea of Zimmerman fighting the ruffest of the Ruff Ryders on pay-per-view. People registered their outrage with the usual token gestures— Facebook pages protesting the fight were initiated, and online petitions were signed by tens of thousands of protesters. The fight was eventually canceled.

While Americans might have liked the *idea* of Zimmerman's face being forcibly converted into ground chuck, they understood that a circuslike boxing match would empower Zimmerman by feeding into his transparent need for attention (and this would diminish Martin's memory). Not assaulting Zimmerman in the virtual town square, therefore, was the tougher, more apt punishment for his crimes. In lieu of prison, marginalization as an eternal pariah would have to do.

This is basically what happened to Axl Rose after he tried to fight Kurt Cobain backstage at the 1992 MTV Video Music Awards.

*   *   *

Before we get to that: I really wanted to write about two other nonstarter rock-star boxing matches in this chapter. But they're not important enough to warrant much in the way of commentary or analysis. This book is about trying to find meaning in musical rivalries, but these conflicts mean zilch. Nevertheless, I find this stuff to be pretty hilarious. I'm sure my fellow slap-fight enthusiasts will agree. So I'll just present the facts of these "fights" and let you rubberneck to your heart's content.

FRED DURST VS. SCOTT STAPP

Hardly anyone remembers this, but at the time it was pretty big news on MTV, and in my mind it represents the great lost moment of mutually assured destruction between the two most popular bands from two of the worst rock subgenres, nu-metal and post-grunge.

Here's what happened: Creed and Limp Bizkit were on the same bill for a radio station–sponsored concert in 2000. Limp Bizkit was scheduled to go on before Creed. After showing up onstage late, Fred Durst called out Scott Stapp: "I want to dedicate this next song to the lead singer of Creed. . . . That guy is an egomaniac. He's a fucking punk, and he's backstage right now acting like fucking Michael Jackson. Fuck that motherfucker, and fuck you, too."

It's not clear what exactly prompted this outburst. Was Scott Stapp backstage treating a group of twelve-year-olds to free rides on his Ferris wheel? Did he have a pet monkey who mistakenly soiled Durst's collection of red caps? Whatever it was, when Creed came out to perform, Stapp fired back: "It takes a lot more guts to say something to somebody than from behind their backs." Stapp then sent Durst an anger management manual *and* challenged him to a charity boxing match, a mixed message on a par with naming a record *Human Clay*. Sadly, they never fought.

I'm torn: I feel like I hate Scott Stapp and Fred Durst equally, but I also sort of love Scott Stapp for wanting to fight Fred Durst, and I sort of love Fred Durst for saying that Stapp was "acting like fucking Michael Jackson." This fight was too good for this world, I guess.

KID ROCK VS. TOMMY LEE

Technically, this fight really did happen. At the 2007 VMAs, Kid Rock took a swing at Tommy Lee after years of enduring Tommy's taunts related to Pamela Anderson, whom both men married and divorced. (Rock alleged that Lee sent him "extremely disrespectful" e-mails from Anderson's BlackBerry.) On his website, Lee referred to Kid Rock as "Kid Pebble" and described his punch as a "bitch slap." A promoter stepped forward to propose a celebrity boxing match. "You send me two hundred and fifty thousand dollars, and I will sit in a room and talk about it," Rock told MTV. Later, Rock claimed that Lee phoned him to apologize and they were friends again.

If this boxing match had taken place, I'm sure Tommy Lee would've won. I guess I just have a natural fear of wiry guys who never wear shirts. I used to live next to a dude like that. One day he showed up at my apartment door and asked if I could drive him to the liquor store. It was the first time we had ever spoken. Apparently he woke up, saw that it was 9:30, assumed it was 9:30 *at night* (he was wrong), and was alarmed that he was not yet drunk. I told him I was busy. In reality, I suspected this guy was a full-blown alcoholic, and I felt ethically conflicted about enabling him. I also didn't want him to puke in my car. After that I was his sworn enemy. He would blast George Thorogood CDs at all hours just to spite me. When I moved out, I returned to my apartment to pick up some boxes and discovered a pool of liquid outside my door. I don't know what the liquid was or who left it, but any scenario is tied for the grossest possible cause. Anyway, I'm sure my wiry shirtless neighbor would've boxed me for twenty-five cents if it also included a free ride to the liquor store.

My only problem with Kid Rock vs. Tommy Lee is that it's a little too meta. It's like the *Snakes on a Plane* of rock-star feuds.

As previously mentioned in this book, my favorite awards show of all time is the 1992 MTV Video Music Awards. There is no second place because I am not interested in ranking awards shows, just in professing my adoration of this particular awards show. The '92 VMAs are just the best. You had Nirvana vs. Guns N' Roses. You had Nirvana vs. Pearl Jam. You had Dana Carvey as Garth Algar playing drums with U2. You had Bobby Brown performing "Humpin' Around" and Elton John performing "The One" on the same show. Bryan Adams was invited for some reason. Honestly, I think about the '92 VMAs all the time.

I love the '92 VMAs so much that I'm self-conscious about the fact that I never shut up about them. I talk about the '92 VMAs the way sportswriters blather on about "elite" quarterbacks. I just find them endlessly fascinating. If you and I were in a conversation and you were telling me about your kids, I would find a way to redirect the conversation back to the '92 VMAs. "Oh, your son isn't fitting in yet at his new school? That reminds me of how Nirvana's legendary performance of 'Lithium' with the 'Rape Me' intro was preceded by Def Leppard playing 'Let's Get Rocked.' Just to be clear, your son is Joe Elliott in this analogy."

Should I ever meet a Hollywood producer, I have a pitch for a movie about the '92 VMAs centered on a semifictionalized depiction of Axl Rose and Kurt Cobain's relationship. (Eddie Vedder and En Vogue would also have significant supporting roles.) I would want David O. Russell to direct, as he's become Hollywood's go-to director for period pieces that require silly-looking wigs. The best thing about this pitch is that it could work as either a drama or a comedy, though I suspect the dramatic version would be unintentionally hilarious and the comedy version inadvertently depressing.

Hold on: you don't know the story about Axl Rose's run-in with Kurt Cobain at the VMAs? Oh, man, I *love* telling this story! Here's the short version: It started when Courtney Love shouted a snarky comment at Axl, asking him to be godfather to her unborn child, Frances Bean. Axl (allegedly) told Kurt, "You shut your bitch up or I'm taking you to the pavement." Kurt then turned to Courtney and sarcastically barked, "Okay, bitch, shut up." Then Stephanie Seymour, *Sports Illustrated* swimsuit issue star and Axl's girlfriend, turned to Courtney and said, "Are you a model?" To which Courtney replied, "No—are you a brain surgeon?"

This actually happened! It wasn't made up by a screenwriter attempting to condense the cultural tensions of the early '90s—specifically, ascendant Seattle grunge vs. rapidly sinking LA hard rock—into a hackneyed confrontation between cultural icons. This encounter really occurred. Rose was an aggressor who secretly didn't want to fight but felt obligated to put up a front in order to assert his band's shrinking authority. Cobain was the antagonist who explicitly didn't want to fight, and he proved to be a superior nonfighter.

My friend Steve Gorman used to play drums in the excellent blues-rock band the Black Crowes, and he was actually *at* the '92 VMAs. (The Crowes opened the show with a performance of their unkillable hip shaker, "Remedy.") Not only did Steve perform at the VMAs, but his trailer was also situated between the Nirvana and GNR trailers. Now, he didn't see the actual Axl vs. Kurt confrontation, but he was close enough to be annoyed by all the gossip buzzing backstage. The Crowes were known to be occasional brawlers themselves, and Steve says he and his bandmates were "taking odds" that they could kick Nirvana *and* GNR's asses.

Now, Steve is a great guy and I'd be his friend even if he hadn't played at the awards show that I'm most obsessed with. But the fact that he did play at the '92 VMAs has caused me to exploit our friendship time and again. Any conversation with Steve has the potential to turn into a press conference about an incident he didn't witness and barely remembers.

Since the Crowes satisfied their VMA commitment within the show's first ten minutes, Steve went home early. He says, "By the time Nirvana was onstage and [Krist Novoselic] threw the bass on his head, I was already on the way to LAX." But Steve was around before the show, which is when the nonfight fight took place.

"It was just in the air that there was this war going on," he told me. "I remember the vibe actually being really serious. Do people actually care that a junkie and a poseur are going to fight? I picture it now like the *Anchorman* fights."

Steve came away from the VMAs with the same impression as most people did—that Axl was a joke and Cobain emerged as the clear victor. Then the media tilted its coverage away from Rose and toward the other guy. It was the beginning of Axl's marginalization, the worst beating of all. Axl was relegated to the Vince Neil role relative to Cobain, who went on MTV News and gleefully shared the story about the backstage encounter. Three years earlier, people assumed that Axl would win in a fight with Neil, and since they never actually fought, Axl scored an imaginary KO. But now it was the grunge era, and the idea of rock stars fighting just seemed stupid, which meant that Cobain looked like a winner for just being a bystander to Rose's ridiculousness.

Rose vs. Cobain was the bookend for Rose vs. Neil. No punches were thrown in either situation, and no punches were required. In the end, Tommy Hilfiger could whup 'em all.

CHAPTER 11
Geek USA

(Smashing Pumpkins vs. Pavement)

A COMMON MISCONCEPTION about critics is that we love writing
negative reviews. In my experience, writing about a record I
like is far superior to writing about a record I don't like. Sure,
if you happen to be a mean-spirited ass, you will relish trashing
somebody's art in print. (Admittedly I am a mean-spirited ass
when it comes to the output of indie wimps like James Blake
and How to Dress Well, who make R & B feel as sexy as a sur-
gical glove dipped in mayonnaise. See? I truly enjoyed typing
that!) But it feels a lot better to find something I genuinely love
so I can attempt to explain why I love it to readers. Sharing my
enthusiasm for great music (which will hopefully inspire readers
to check out worthwhile art, theoretically enriching their lives
in some small but not insignificant way) is the only socially re-
deemable aspect of my profession.

In 2014, I interviewed a singer-songwriter from Philadelphia
named Timothy Showalter, who has recorded several albums
under the name Strand of Oaks. The record we were talking

about, *Heal,* was easily my favorite thing he had ever done. *Heal* was great because it was more musically dynamic than Showalter's previous work (he had evolved from hushed folk to synth-accented arena rock), yet it wasn't so different that the record was completely unrelated to what preceded it (he's essentially an autobiographical songwriter, and *Heal* described his marital problems in startling detail). It's the kind of record I always hope for as a professional appreciator of pop music in that it showed me how completely wrong I was about everything else in Showalter's discography. I'm always excited when I'm proved wrong, and luckily it happens to me pretty often. I'm still waiting for the day when I hear "Cotton Eye Joe" in precisely the right context and realize that Rednex are fucking geniuses.

The most notable part of my conversation with Showalter was only tangentially related to *Heal.* On the record's first track, there's a line about Showalter singing in the mirror to Smashing Pumpkins songs back when he was a fifteen-year-old burnout growing up in Indiana. I immediately gravitated to this lyric, as it was describing something I had also experienced when I was a slightly older teenager living in Wisconsin. (Showalter told me later that his mirror-singing song of choice was "Muzzle," whereas mine was probably "Hummer" or "Here Is No Why.") I then explained that I was writing a book on musical rivalries and that one of the chapters was about the Smashing Pumpkins vs. Pavement. I said I had a theory that Billy Corgan's overreaction to a lyric on Pavement's *Crooked Rain Crooked Rain* was rooted in an inferiority complex common among Middle Americans such as Showalter and I and that this incident was really a metaphor for Corgan's overall worldview and that it contributed to the rise and fall of the Smashing Pumpkins.

This run-on sentence made Showalter very excited. It turns out that he'd already had the exact same thought. I was merely the latest person to enter into a conversation with him about it.

"I think Smashing Pumpkins and Pavement is [the] beginning of what indie rock is now. There's this, like, sarcasm and irony and these, like, arty fucking smart kids that I just want to punch in the face sometimes," he said. "Like, 'We don't like to try' or 'Our guitars aren't tuned.' And then Billy Corgan went, 'I want to change the world with this chorus' and 'My guitars *will* be in tune.' He was like, 'I just wrote the most beautiful melody that's ever been recorded.'"

Just like that, Showalter and I bonded like a couple of Siamese dreamers.

I should probably outline the particulars of the Smashing Pumpkins–Pavement rivalry, just in case Showalter and I are the only people who have thought way too much about it. Actually there isn't all that much to sketch out. Pavement was a highly celebrated indie band back when "highly celebrated indie band" wasn't considered an oxymoron. In 1994, they released a song called "Range Life," in which the band's primary singer-songwriter, Stephen Malkmus, sings, "Out on tour with the Smashing Pumpkins / Nature kids, they don't have no function / I don't understand what they mean / And I could really give a fuck." Because the Smashing Pumpkins were one of the era's most popular rock bands, and because Pavement was already considered the decade's coolest band, those twenty-seven words inspired much clucking in the rock press. The name Pavement immediately appeared in every Smashing Pumpkins magazine profile, even though many of the people who liked the Smashing Pumpkins probably couldn't name a single Pavement song.

The "Range Life" diss was a gift for rock journalists—conflict is salacious, of course, but "Range Life" also conformed to a media narrative that had already been established for the Pumpkins (and Corgan specifically) since the beginning of their career. In spite of the group's dominance of alt-rock radio and MTV, the Pumpkins were defined by criticisms lodged by semifamous hipsters (including Malkmus, Steve Albini, and Kim Gordon) who hated them. Every article about the band addressed the Pumpkins' "credibility issues" and inherent lack of coolness. Corgan was constantly dressed down in print for being either a whiny drama queen or an arrogant egomaniac. It was as if music reporters went into their Smashing Pumpkins assignments assuming the band members were assholes and put it on Corgan to prove that they weren't. Even if the Pumpkins successfully managed their PR problems for one writer, the scale would automatically be set back to "asshole" for the next writer.

The Smashing Pumpkins weren't the only alt-rock juggernaut besmirched by "Range Life." Malkmus arguably reserved his funniest put-down for Stone Temple Pilots, whom he classified as "elegant bachelors." Now, STP obviously had their own credibility issues—the Pumpkins were hated, but at least they were taken seriously by most rock writers. STP was both reviled and regarded as a joke. This is a shame, because as any dirtbag metalhead with a soft spot for pop hooks could've told you, STP wrote some of the catchiest anthems of the grunge era. Nirvana and Pearl Jam set the template, but they didn't craft singles as transcendent as "Interstate Love Song" and "Big Bang Baby."

STP had the misfortune of rising to prominence during the snootiest era in rock history. In any other decade, STP's ability to craft submental, gonad-rattling rock songs would have been better appreciated. But in a grunge context, STP's arena-rockin' ways stuck out like a hot-pink duster at a flannel convention. This didn't prevent STP from selling millions of albums, but it did undermine their long-term sustainability.

Oddly, Malkmus suffered no significant repercussions for taking an unprovoked shot at two bands that were far more popular than Pavement. Normally, it's the shit talker in these situations who gets lambasted, not the shit taker. Pavement's only tangible (alleged) punishment was that Corgan supposedly kept Pavement off Lollapalooza that summer. (The Smashing Pumpkins were headlining.) But Pavement ended up on the bill the following year.

Malkmus ultimately benefited from a unique (and in this case fortuitous) dichotomy—he was a member of a band that was a major success critically and a minor success commercially. The media was both sympathetic to Malkmus's cause and inclined to protect him against a more powerful adversary. It's the same dynamic that protects trolls from getting called out by the celebrities they spend all day denouncing online. It's expected that a celebrity should just take it because a troll isn't worth the effort. Everyone believes that punching down makes the person in the "higher" position look stupid, even though the constructs of class and professional privilege aren't supposed to matter online. Similarly, Corgan and Malkmus existed in the same context with critics even though they were on different planets commercially, and this situation made Corgan vulnerable.

Whenever Malkmus was asked years later about the Smashing Pumpkins, he tried to distance himself from "Range Life," claiming that he never *really* insulted Corgan. "I only laughed about the band name, because it does sound kinda silly," he told *NY Rock* in 1999. "And well, their status, that they were the indie darlings, the heroes of the indie scene. I never really dissed their music. I like their songs—well, most of their songs anyway."

Three things about this quote stand out: (1) It's impossible to tell exactly how much of it is sincere and how much is ironic, which means it's practically a Pavement song; (2) Malkmus weirdly describes the Smashing Pumpkins ("the heroes of the indie scene") in the way most people would describe Pavement; and (3) Malkmus saying "I didn't diss the Smashing Pumpkins" is not as convincing as hearing him very clearly diss the Smashing Pumpkins in "Range Life."

Corgan, for one, wasn't convinced by Malkmus's demurrals. Instead he internalized "Range Life," along with every other slight he was forced to suffer from the indie-rock community. In 2010, sixteen years after "Range Life" was released, Pavement reunited for a nostalgia tour that included no plans for a new album. In response, Corgan wrote on Twitter that Pavement "represented the death of the alternative dream," adding, "Funny how those who pointed the big finger of 'sell out' are the biggest offenders now." Corgan seemed to be physically incapable of letting "Range Life" go; it was as if the song had been absorbed into his very physiological makeup.

"It's easy to pick on the geek," Corgan complained in a 2012 *Stereogum* interview. (Notice that he's speaking in the present tense.) "My clothes are too tight, I'm always 10 pounds overweight, I've got crooked teeth, one of my eyes is bigger than the other one, I've got no hair, I sing with a funny voice."

Corgan could've probably stopped there and made his point.

But why would a man who once performed an eight-hour improvised jam inspired by Hermann Hesse's 1922 masterwork, *Siddhartha*, choose this moment to show restraint? He continued:

"They didn't pick on Kurt [Cobain] because they all wanted to be Kurt. They all wanted to be Beck, they all want to be Thom Yorke. Thom Yorke's okay because he's 'the right look' funny. I'm not 'the right look' funny, I'm 6'4", I've got my mother's hips, people are like, 'Who is this guy?' I wouldn't be up there if I weren't talented, you know?"

Malkmus never called Corgan a sellout. He called the Smashing Pumpkins "nature kids" without any "function" whom he otherwise didn't "give a fuck" about. As a critique it's not all that personal or specific—it's the sort of tossed-off remark that a snarky dude would make to crack up his buddies while watching cheesy alt-rock music videos, knowing that he'll never have to support it with a cogent argument or actually face the guy he's clowning. That's basically the spirit in which "Range Life" was written. It speaks to what was so appealing about Pavement for the people who liked them. "Range Life" is just some funny shit that was made up more or less extemporaneously. It's precisely the kind of impulsive artistic endeavor that's anathema to an innately calculating artist such as Billy Corgan—a straight-up lazy "we don't like to try" move, as Showalter put it to me on the phone. Corgan would rather write "the most beautiful melody that's ever been recorded," a goal I'm guessing Malkmus (along with most rational people) would find to be comically grandiose.

The paradox of stacking Pavement's body of work against the Smashing Pumpkins' body of work is that for all Corgan's plotting and Malkmus's flippancy, Malkmus is actually more consistent than Corgan. Even though I like *Siamese Dream* and

Mellon Collie and the Infinite Sadness more than I like any Pavement album, the overall arc from *Slanted and Enchanted* to *Terror Twilight* accidentally achieves a perfection that Corgan could not will himself to reach on purpose. *Slanted and Enchanted* is a prototypical debut—it falls together with an unstudied amateurishness that somehow coalesces into incredible songs. *Terror Twilight* is a prototypical last record—it's very clearly the work of a band that has reached the end of what it has to say. (Even the title predicts Pavement's eventual breakup.) In between, you have the "let's be popular" record (*Crooked Rain Crooked Rain*), the "let's be less popular" record (*Wowee Zowee*), and the "let's find a happy medium between the previous two records" record (*Brighten the Corners*).

The Smashing Pumpkins' career path is less direct. The band's 1991 debut, *Gish,* has some of the same debut qualities as *Slanted,* but it's less singular as a statement, sounding in retrospect like a rough draft for the superior (as opposed to merely different) *Siamese Dream.* The last Smashing Pumpkins album with the original lineup, *MACHINA/The Machines of God* (and the accompanying free album, *MACHINA II/The Friends & Enemies of Modern Music*), was a stab at reviving the grandiosity of *Mellon Collie* in the wake of the commercial failure of 1998's somewhat underrated (but hardly great) *Adore. MACHINA* has some incredible songs and some incredibly crappy songs, and in retrospect seems more like a failed reboot than a proper closing statement.

At the risk of reducing both men to regional caricatures, it more or less rings true that Malkmus personifies a casual confidence associated with California while Corgan embodies a gnawing insecurity that's inherent to the Midwest. Malkmus's artistic persona is the lack of a persona; he could be himself and attract admirers. In Pavement, the less he seemed like a rock star, the more he seemed like a *fucking* rock star. Corgan, however, had to invent a version of himself that people could believe actually belonged in a band. All rock stars who grow up in the Midwest do this—Bob Dylan, Prince, Michael Jackson, and Axl Rose might come from the same part of the country, but they all wound up in their own made-up solar systems. Corgan didn't have the luxury of simply screwing around with a four-track until music writers showed up to fawn over him: the only way he was going to make it was by writing and recording songs that were undeniable. As the '90s wore on, Pavement was allowed to mature naturally and remain tangibly human. Meanwhile Corgan just got loonier until he transformed into a pale, bald-headed Nosferatu around the time of *Adore*. (All significant midwestern pop stars inevitably devolve into freaks.) All the while, he kept working harder than anybody, even as the haters derided him for trying too hard to prove that he belonged.

Can you blame Billy Corgan for never getting over the bitterness of that? Can you blame the public for slowly backing away from him once he ran out of top-shelf material?

If I were to rank all the unlikable public figures whom I am ashamed to find relatable, Billy Corgan would be number 2. At number 1 is Richard Nixon. I blame Oliver Stone (number 3 on this list) for number 1.

Self-identifying as a "smart" kid in the late '80s and early '90s usually meant having an Oliver Stone phase. This seems curiously difficult for people who are concerned with retroactively "improving" their adolescent tastes to admit. But from the mid-'80s (when Ollie made *Salvador* and *Platoon*) to the mid-aughts (when his critical rep cratered with 2004's *Alexan-*

der), Oliver Stone was, to quote film historian Robert Kolker, a "more controversial, written about, admired, and despised figure than any filmmaker in recent memory." For nearly two decades it was acceptably adult to view Oliver Stone as a seminal cultural figure. Even people who found Stone's films reductive, self-important, obvious, or even incompetent still participated in the dialogue those films inspired. This registers as an obvious victory for Stone, who was frequently criticized for ham-fistedly inserting his political point of view into the most transformative historical events of modern times—Vietnam, the Kennedy assassination, the bitterly contested 2000 presidential election, 9/11. And yet Oliver Stone has left his mark on the way those events were subsequently discussed.

You could argue that a teenager watching Oliver Stone movies back when Oliver Stone movies were important was merely eager to be perceived as a grown-up, making this activity akin to sipping tea in a cafeteria full of soda drinkers. But when I rewatched Oliver Stone movies as an actual grown-up, I realized I was exactly the right age for *JFK* when it came out— during Christmas break when I was in the eighth grade. The ideal audience for an Oliver Stone movie has to be both cynical about the legitimacy of authority figures (a.k.a. "the system") and naive about the way the world actually works (i.e., they need to believe that "the system" is a tangible entity and not an overused metaphor). *JFK* flatters viewers who blindly buy into their own fake expertise, and no demographic puts more value on unearned experience than teenagers.

This explains why I, as an eighteen-year-old high school senior, really wanted to see 1995's *Nixon*—a 189-minute sort-of sequel to *JFK*—the weekend it opened in theaters. None of my friends were interested in seeing this film. I had to persuade my dad to go with me. But I'm pretty sure I loved it. After all, I was uniquely suited to enjoying an overlong meditation on a self-pitying, perpetually persecuted figure. *Mellon Collie and the Infinite Sadness,* which had come out just two months earlier, had primed me for *Nixon.*

The most obvious similarity between *Nixon* and *Mellon Collie* is their extremely long running times. The original version of *Mellon Collie* clocks in at nearly 122 minutes. The vinyl version is just over 128 minutes. The expanded reissue edition balloons to an ungodly 351 minutes, which, by comparison, makes the 217-minute director's cut of *Nixon* look like the most historically suspect Vine video ever made. But the most crucial parallel concerns the protagonists: Billy Corgan and Richard Nixon have essentially the same worldview, and it was shaped by a similar mix of insecurity, megalomania, talent, and an inability to discern legitimate grievances from paranoid delusions.

In his landmark 2008 book, *Nixonland: The Rise of a President and the Fracturing of America,* journalist and historian Rick Perlstein formulates the perfect metaphor to describe Nixon's perspective and strategy for attaining political power. While a student at Whittier College, Nixon founded a social group called the Orthogonians for a "silent majority" of unexceptional students deemed unworthy of the school's elite fraternity, the Franklins. Orthogonians, like Nixon, saw themselves as hardworking "regular" people fighting against a powerful elite (personified by the Franklins) for status and wealth. Perlstein convincingly argues that Nixon carried this dynamic over into his political career, which subsequently shaped the public discourse in ways that are apparent to this very day. Nixon understood better than anyone that Americans, no matter how well-off they are, can always find somebody to resent for the crime of appearing to be better taken care of than they are. (The Tea Party would not exist without Nixon.)

Stone explored the Orthogonian concept thirteen years earlier in *Nixon*, though he did it with a lot less nuance. The least debatable critique of Stone's work (even for people, such as I, stubbornly inclined to defend it) is that his characters tend to plainly state Stone's themes in the form of dialogue in lieu of allowing audiences to draw their own conclusions. This happens a lot in *Nixon*. "Why are these assholes turning on me?" Anthony Hopkins's sweaty, swarthy, nearly hunchbacked Dick Nixon seethes when reporters grill him about Watergate at a press conference announcing the end of the Vietnam War. "Because they don't like the way I look! Because they don't like where I went to school!" (Once again, the press corps is biased in favor of the Thom Yorke look.) Later, Paul Sorvino, as Henry Kissinger, solemnly intones to no one in particular, "Can you imagine what this man would've been if he had ever been loved?" In an earlier montage, Stone simply has a mock news announcer declare that Nixon "didn't have opponents, he had enemies" over a mix of newsreel footage and historical reenactments. The old journalism maxim "Show, don't tell" is bullshit in Stone's book.

At *Nixon*'s midpoint, there's a preposterous scene in which Nixon leaves the White House in the middle of the night to visit the Lincoln Memorial, where he encounters a group of college students who challenge him about the war. The setup for the scene is based on a widely reported incident that caused some in Nixon's camp to question his sanity, or at least his sobriety. According to Nixon's own account as well as interviews with the students he spoke with, what was discussed that night wasn't terribly consequential. Nixon was described as tired and disjointed in his thoughts—he wanted to talk about Syracuse football (the students were Orangemen) at least as much as he wanted to talk about Vietnam. The students, meanwhile, were understandably bewildered by Nixon's presence and overall weirdness. Nixon's most memorable quote from that night came during a tangent on the environment: "You must remember that something that is completely clean can also be completely sterile, without spirit." Nixon was arguing that pollution was good for America's personality.

In *Nixon*, the Lincoln Memorial anecdote is turned into another treatise on the powerlessness of Orthogonians in the midst of shadowy, all-controlling Franklins. Stone delivers his critique in the guise of a beautiful brunette coed who looks uncannily like Alyssa Milano. "You can't stop it, can you?" she asks Hopkins-as-Nixon, referring to Vietnam. "Because it's the system, and the system won't let you stop it."

There are plenty of smart people who would argue that Nixon could have indeed stopped the war much earlier than he did. Presenting Nixon's persecution complex as evidence that he was a pawn of the Man not only indulges Nixon's self-pity but absolves him of responsibility. Those inclined to attack Nixon on these grounds would argue that Orthogonian marginalization is largely, if not entirely, imagined.

I feel like the truth is somewhere in the middle. The fact is that Nixon *has* been stigmatized by history for reasons that seem to run deeper than the substance of his political record. He will never be regarded with the same affection afforded his most hated rival, John F. Kennedy, even though it's commonly accepted that JFK's campaign cheated its way to victory in the 1960 presidential election. JFK was smoother and more glamorous than Nixon, but he also grew up with far greater wealth and privilege. Kennedy could've slept through the first few decades of his life and still had the wherewithal to become a success; Nixon watched two of his brothers die before he finished college and had to scrape along for years just to survive.

That's just the way life is. The class system exists. Some people get breaks, and some people don't. However, it doesn't explain everything in the world. A quirk of being human is the tendency to personalize whatever happens to us in our daily lives, as if these events are judgments on who we are as people. But they're not. Sometimes, it's just stuff that happens.

Oliver Stone started out as a Franklin (his father was a stockbroker, and he was accepted to Yale) but opted to become an Orthogonian (he dropped out of Yale to go to Vietnam and later became an antigovernment conspiracy theorist). Billy Corgan is unquestionably an Orthogonian, and Stephen Malkmus was his JFK. In case it's not already apparent, I am an Orthogonian, too. I am loaded with middle-American resentment. Deep down, I suspect "they" don't like me because of where I went to school. Or maybe it's because I have my mother's hips. Either way, when I see guys like Corgan and Nixon seethe, I seethe right along with them.

The key to understanding Billy Corgan is assuming that every public statement he makes is in some way rooted in his indignation over how he's perceived by the media and "cool" musicians.

This is something that many of us who think Corgan is both brilliant and moronic know instinctively. When Showalter and I went on our Smashing Pumpkins tangent, he referenced Corgan's appearance in the excellent documentary *Rush: Beyond the Lighted Stage.* Specifically, Showalter singled out this Corgan quote from the film:

> Every once in a while you have an artist that is very sophisticated, but somehow in their sophistication they don't alienate the common person. They're really a people's band. The great hole in their career is that they've never been truly accepted by the intelligentsia.... What was it? They just don't fit in a neat box.

Unbeknownst to Showalter, I had referenced this exact quote in a *Grantland* column on the Smashing Pumpkins' surprisingly solid 2012 comeback record, *Oceania.* It's not that Corgan's observations about the way Rush had been perceived historically by rock's media gatekeepers aren't trenchant as they pertain strictly to Rush: besides the members of Rush, Corgan says the smartest things about why Rush matters in *Beyond the Lighted Stage.* It's just that this statement is even truer as it relates to Corgan's own career. Corgan's greatest demon—the greatest demon for *all* Orthogonians—is craving the acceptance he is forced to loudly deny wanting because he secretly knows it will never arrive. You have to act like you quit in order to conceal that you were really fired. It always comes back to "Range Life" for Corgan.

This is why (I think) Billy Corgan blames Obama for his bad reviews.

Let's back up for a second. In 2012, during the promotional cycle for *Oceania,* Corgan appeared on *Infowars,* a talk show hosted by paleoconservative conspiracy theorist Alex Jones. In case you're not a right-wing nut: Jones is perhaps our nation's highest-profile "truther"—he believes the US government was behind both 9/11 and the Oklahoma City bombings. Normal people might know Jones as a rotund, crimson-faced rageoholic who is occasionally invited on mainstream talk shows to scream about gun control. But when Corgan appeared on *Infowars*, Jones was suddenly more effusive than Jimmy Fallon greeting the sixth lead on *Modern Family*, praising not just Corgan's music but his ability as a "thinker."

Now, if you've ever been in the company of rich, middle-aged white men who subsist on a steady diet of conservative talk radio and self-sustaining smugness, you can probably guess the sorts of "thoughts" that plopped out of Corgan's mouth on Jones's show. In short, Corgan talked a lot about the importance of "rigorous debate" in light of "corporate interests" who are "stifling dissent" because of "crony capitalism." Jones, meanwhile, grunted approvingly as his own buzzwords were parroted back to him. At one point, Corgan claimed that he doesn't watch television because too many shows depict a "castrated" version of the American male, an odd argument coming from an artist who originated in the antimacho alt-rock era. (When Corgan sang about how he "used to be a little boy" in "Disarm," he was practically Sylvester Stallone's antimatter.)

Corgan (of course) spoke at length about the way the media controls reality, referring (of course) to how his recent appearance on a South by Southwest seminar panel was spun into a "rant" by *Rolling Stone*'s website. "I'm very keen to watch how other people are demonized . . . when somebody rises up with a grand idea," Corgan told Jones—an instance of one holder of grand ideas confiding in a fellow holder of grand ideas.

What's most annoying about libertarians is their astonishing mix of bravado (Corgan constantly refers to himself as a "self-made person") and sense of perpetual victimhood (Corgan also whines about being "attacked" online for questioning climate change, because he's the only person ever to be criticized for expressing a stupid opinion on the Internet). Somehow, in the minds of megalomaniacal blowhards, these otherwise irreconcilable polarities achieve a weird, toxic harmony. For Corgan, the music industry might as well be the government, and being a climate-change denier is merely an extension of loving *Permanent Waves* in high school when all the preppy kids preferred Rick Springfield.

This is what Billy Corgan has become, and it's the primary reason he—in spite of those old Smashing Pumpkins hits *still* dominating the dramatically reduced rock-radio landscape—is not held in the high esteem that his talents and body of work would normally justify. It's not the system, it's him. His insecurity over cool people believing that he's awful has made him awful.

And what of Stephen Malkmus—the actual Stephen Malkmus, as opposed to whatever "Stephen Malkmus" might signify in Corgan's mind? Corgan might be surprised by how much they share in middle age. Like Corgan, Malkmus split from his band in 2000; in a Corganesque gesture, Malkmus held up a pair of handcuffs at Pavement's last show and declared, *This* is what it's like to be in a rock group.

In the years after Pavement's breakup, the group's albums continue to hold up for many of us who liked them in the '90s. But for the rest of the world, Pavement's influence has shrunk, not grown. Shambolic guitar rock is now regarded as passé in indie circles; it's sort of incredible how much Pavement sounds like a jam band in retrospect. (Grimes would probably never cover "Gold Soundz," but Phish did.) Malkmus continues to tour small clubs and put out likable, guitar solo–heavy records with his current band, the Jicks. In magazine articles, meanwhile, he seems to talk exclusively about fantasy sports and rock documentaries. In a 2014 interview with *Rolling Stone*'s Rob Sheffield, Malkmus even demonstrated a working knowledge of Rush's catalog.

"I just listened to *Fly by Night* the other day—you know Side One? It really holds up," he said. "It gives you this rush, no pun intended, where you air-drum to it and it just makes you feel invigorated. Then on Side Two there's a horrible slow one about going to California like Led Zeppelin, and it just falls dead, like the dead owl on the album cover."

I like to imagine that in some far-off dimension, Billy Corgan and Stephen Malkmus are just two middle-aged white guys with an opinion about *Fly by Night,* showing the rest of us Orthogonians that the Franklins aren't so different after all.

CHAPTER 12

A Tour of Three Ultimatum Prison Cells

(Dr. Dre vs. Eazy-E; Dave Mustaine vs. Metallica; David Lee Roth vs. the Van Halen Brothers)

LET'S SAY YOU had access to a time machine, and you could only do one thing with it. What would you do?

Surely you have already been asked this, probably when you were younger and 100 percent more stoned than you are now. "What would you do with a time machine?" is a pretty common question among unoriginal deep thinkers. It's equally common to respond by saying, "I would travel back in time to kill Hitler." You're sort of obligated to say "kill Hitler" in this scenario. If you don't say "kill Hitler," you will appear self-involved and possibly even anti-Semitic. An interrogation of your personal ethics will inevitably follow. "While I understand that learning how to play 'Your Body Is a Wonderland' by John Mayer, then time-traveling back to the period right before that song became a hit might seem alluring—as you could persuade beautiful college girls to sleep with you by claiming that you and not John Mayer wrote it. But wouldn't you agree that preventing the Holocaust is more valid, you Nazi-sympathizing bastard?"

Now, if you're moderately clever, you'll recognize the flaw in this scenario: if you can go back in time once, you can go back a hundred times, and it will be imperceptible to anyone who isn't also time-traveling. In the time it took you to read that previous sentence, I could've paid visits to Woodstock, Woodstock '94, and Woodstock '99. To you, it passed by in a nanosecond; meanwhile, I was ingesting substandard acid during Santana's performance, suffering stomach cramps from swallowing too much mud during Green Day's set, and decapitating Fred Durst before he went onstage with Limp Bizkit.

So if I had a time machine, and if I had already corrected at least a dozen major historical injustices, I would travel back to 1999 in order to crash VH1's interview with Dr. Dre in the episode of *Behind the Music* that was devoted to him and his work.

(I realize that worming my way into a Dr. Dre interview might in fact be more difficult than time travel. But if I get a goddamned time machine in this hypothetical scenario, it's not as if having access to a sympathetic publicist willing to sneak me into a TV show taping is a less realistic disruption of the space-time continuum.)

If you've seen that episode of *Behind the Music*, you'll remember that a crucial turning point in Dr. Dre's rise-fall-rise narrative arc is reached when his former founding partner in N.W.A., Eazy-E, dies suddenly of AIDS, in 1995. This is what I would want to ask Dre about, because I suspect that the way he presents his feelings in the episode aren't totally on the level.

For years, right up until roughly a week before Eazy passed, he and Dre had been beefing bitterly. It started when Dre left N.W.A. because he believed that the group's manager, Jerry Heller, was unfairly aligned with the financial interests of Eazy to the detriment of the other members. There's a well-known (and possibly exaggerated) story recounted in John Borgmeyer and Holly Lang's *Dr. Dre: A Biography* about Eazy refusing to release Dre from his contract, which prompted Dre to dispatch future Death Row Records head Suge Knight and a gang of lead pipe–wielding goons to negotiate with Eazy on his behalf. Knight's strategy was two-pronged. First he claimed that he had kidnapped Heller and was holding him in a van. Then he threatened Eazy's family. "I know where your mama stays," he supposedly told Eazy after handing him a piece of paper with her address on it. Eventually, Eazy caved.

The public learned about the inner workings of N.W.A.'s split primarily via two songs: Ice Cube's "No Vaseline" and Dr. Dre's "Dre Day." Cube's song was meaner. (He refers to Eazy as both a "maggot" and a "half-pint bitch.") But Dre's track did more damage because it ended up in regular rotation on MTV. In the video, Eazy-E is referred to as "Sleazy E" and depicted as a clownish, Jheri-curled puppet for his craven, overweight, and pointedly Jewish-looking manager, who refers to "Sleazy" as "boy" in the opening scene. (The incendiary political incorrectness of the "Dre Day" video would've been nuclear in the social-media era.)

Simply put, the "Dre Day" video destroyed Eazy's reputation among casual rap fans. People who knew Dre from *Straight Outta Compton* could put the Eazy insults in context. But the success of Dre's *The Chronic* overshadowed everything he and Eazy did with N.W.A. in the minds of millions of pop listeners. Released as a single in May of 1993, "Dre Day" went on to quickly secure summer-jam status. It was one of those songs that just seemed to magically appear whenever a minimum of two people between the ages of sixteen and twenty-five congregated in a public space. For legions of white middle-American high schoolers like me, "Dre Day" was the first and last word on the Dre-Eazy rivalry.

Real rap fans knew better. At the end of '93, Eazy put out a furious answer with his EP *It's On (Dr. Dre) 187um Killa,* which included a G-funk parody called "Real Muthaphukkin' G's" in which Eazy called out Dre for being a phony gangster. (Whereas Eazy sold drugs before investing the earnings in his label, Ruthless Records, Dre was already trying to get a rap career going by the mid-'80s.) *It's On* sold two million copies to an audience predominantly made up of rapheads and N.W.A. fanatics. *The Chronic,* meanwhile, sold three million copies and made Dre a pop star. Authenticity didn't matter. Dre had a bigger platform and a long shadow that engulfed Eazy.

"Is there a more reviled name in hip hop than that of Eazy E?" *Vibe* asked when it interviewed Eazy in 1993. *Vibe* was quick to answer its own question, and that answer basically amounted to: "No. No, there is not." The magazine dwelt on Eazy's "thinly veiled obsession with the life and career of Dr. Dre," which was manifested by the way he "alternately rails against Dre and waxes nostalgic over the early days of N.W.A." The impression you get from the article is that Eazy is a broken man and Dre is the clear victor in their war of words.

In a famous essay, Chuck Klosterman argued that successful people need one nemesis and one archenemy. "We measure ourselves against our nemeses, and we long to destroy our archenemies," he wrote. Going by Klosterman's definitions of those terms, Ice Cube was Dre's nemesis (Dre insulted Cube when he left N.W.A. over a money dispute, but Dre soon followed him out the door for essentially the same reason), and Eazy-E was his archenemy. But then Eazy died—not a violent death, but certainly it was a shocking and surprising demise. Suddenly Dre couldn't use Eazy as his archenemy anymore. On the contrary, circumstances required Dre to speak of Eazy with respect.

If I could've asked Dre one question during that *Behind the Music* taping, it would've been this: In terms of your grudge match with Eazy, did the other guy win?

Let's imagine for a minute that Eazy hadn't died. Would he have ever reconciled with Dre? Would his reputation have ever recovered? We have no way of knowing. What we do know is that Eazy got Dre to capitulate in their feud without ever apologizing to him, publicly or privately. Even when he was near death, Eazy never reconciled with his archenemy. Dre saw Eazy for the last time on March 19, just eighteen days after his diagnosis and seven days before his death. Eazy was already confined to a hospital bed and incapacitated. On *Behind the Music,* Dre said, "It just seemed like everybody knew he was gone."

Part of me wants to believe that Eazy hated Dre so much that he willed himself into near-death catatonia out of sheer pettiness. I know that's not true, but I would've loved to see Eazy's reaction when he heard Dre say on *Behind the Music* that he felt bad that he didn't get to kick it with Eazy before he passed away. I suspect that Eazy's cry of *"BIIITCH!"* is still ringing throughout the celestial kingdom.

The reintegration of Eazy into Dre's narrative—and the use of Eazy's death as a melodramatic plot point in Dre's eventual estrangement from Suge Knight—comes off as self-serving on *Behind the Music.* Nevertheless, Dre was paying tribute to a man whose reputation he successfully destroyed in the years before that man's untimely demise. And this continued for years after Eazy's death. In the ludicrous video for 2011's "I Need a Doctor," Dre even visits Eazy's grave and gives the man also known as Eric Wright his tribute. Twenty years earlier, a Dr. Dre video ending with a scene at Eazy's grave would have surely culminated with Dre pissing on the headstone. But in "I Need a Doctor," Eazy's grave signifies the burdens of Dre's past continuing to weigh on him as he moves forward. Eazy is practically an angel in Dre's iconography now, a stunning reversal from *The Chronic* days.

In life, as in his songs, Eazy was a soldier to the end. He never surrendered in the war against Dre. In a 2013 radio interview, Jerry Heller claimed that Eazy wanted to murder Suge Knight because he blamed Suge for turning Dre against him. Heller talked Eazy out of it, which Heller later regretted. ("I should have let him kill him. I would have done the world a favor," Heller said.) But strictly in terms of grudge holding, what Eazy did to Dre was almost as cold-blooded. Eazy made Dre forgive him.

Grudge holding is not generally considered an attractive trait. For centuries, wise people have advised against it. Confucius once said, "To be wronged is nothing, unless you remember it." (There's a semiterrible Chinese restaurant a mile from my house called Confucius. This quote might've originally derived from a place mat I read there and not from the ancient Chinese philosopher.) In *Jane Eyre*, a book I attempted to finish in the eleventh grade, Charlotte Brontë writes that life is too short "to be spent in nursing animosity or registering wrongs." Then there's Tool's "The Grudge," a deep cut from 2001's spite-inducing *Lateralus*, in which Maynard James Keenan likens a grudge to "a crown of negativity" and an "ultimatum prison cell." Clearly the time I spent listening to Tool instead of reading Brontë paid off.

Being a civilized person (or merely a nondickhead) requires withholding the instinct to catalog all the wrongs committed against you and plot appropriate punishments for every line item. I will fully admit that inside me there's a jilted, perpetually indignant individual obsessed with breaking free and tracking down his enemies like the dogs they are. I call this person Walker, after the character played by Lee Marvin in the classic '60s revenge movie *Point Blank*.

If you haven't seen it: Walker is a thief who is two-timed by his partners and left for dead after a big score. Once Walker recovers, he puts on a sharp suit and goes about tracking down the sons of bitches who screwed him out of the money he's owed—precisely ninety-three thousand dollars. This means taking on a corporatized organized crime syndicate single-handedly.

Point Blank is a great grudge movie because it portrays the ultimate revenge fantasy (all petty people envision having the unshakable rectitude and nihilistic cool of Lee Marvin) while simultaneously showing how pointless revenge fantasies are. Walker is both a monstrous genius and a noble idiot—his anger is totally justified and absolutely self-destructive. This is underscored toward the end of the movie, when Walker finally confronts the head of the syndicate, played by pre–*All in the Family* Carroll O'Connor, who can't believe that Walker has gone to all this trouble for a relatively small amount of money.

"You threaten a financial structure like this for ninety-three thousand dollars?" the proto–Archie Bunker asks. "What do you really want?"

"Somebody's got to pay," says Walker.

Somebody's got to pay. This is the guiding principle of the grudge holder. Something that belongs to me was wrongfully taken, and I want it back. I *need* it back.

I am actively holding two low-level grudges at the moment. I say "low-level" because I currently have no plans to avenge these grudges. I barely even remember them. One involves a college friend (whom we'll call Terry) who dated a girl I was irrationally in love with during my sophomore year. The other grudge involves a professional acquaintance (let's call him Terry, too, as I hate the name Terry) who led me to believe that he could hire me for a job I really wanted, then informed me that another person got it instead in a manner I found to be unchivalrous.

Frankly I'm embarrassed to admit caring even a little bit about either of these grudges. The circumstances of the "wrongs" these individuals committed against me had zero long-term effect on my life. But if I'm being honest, I must admit to being consumed by anger, jealousy, depression, and malice for a long time over these incidents.

You're not allowed to act like Walker in real life. The world frowns on people who handle their business with a Smith & Wesson. So I created a competition between me and my grudgees that existed solely in my mind. Any time I appeared to be doing better than they were, personally or professionally, that was karma correcting the injustice committed against me. Having a satisfying career, marrying my soul mate, and fathering a healthy, beautiful son weren't just hallmarks of a good, lucky life. They were decisive scores in a game only I cared about.

This is what Michael Jordan might call finding the motivation to be great. But at this point in my life it requires way too much energy. Grudges are exhausting. It takes a lot of work to maintain a distorted view of reality. In my mind I was in the right. But if anybody else knew what was going on in my head, I would have looked like a crazy person.

I would have looked like Dave Mustaine.

You might know Dave Mustaine as an outspoken Christian and Obama birther, but since I'm writing about popular music and not writing an Ann Coulter book, I'm going to focus on his brief tenure in Metallica, his controversial firing from that band, the anger-fueled formation of Megadeth, and Megadeth's rise to not-Metallica-level fame. Therefore let's begin with my favorite Mustaine-Metallica nexus point, *Some Kind of Monster*.

As one of the finest rock documentaries ever made, *Some Kind of Monster* is essential viewing for fans of metal, therapy, and behind-the-scenes films about off-peak albums made by legacy bands. In the interest of time, I will limit the discussion of this movie's greatness to just five classic scenes, in ascending order of personal preference:

(5) the scene where Metallica singer James Hetfield admits that he missed his son's first birthday because he was hunting bears in Siberia;

(4) the scene where drummer Lars Ulrich yells "Fuck!" in Hetfield's face—not because Hetfield missed the kid's birthday, just because;

(3) the scene where guitarist Kirk Hammett defends guitar solos (because he's right!);

(2) the scene where Hetfield and Ulrich argue about Hetfield's "stock" guitar parts and Hammett says, "You know what, you guys, why don't we just go in and hammer it

out instead of hammering on each other?" (right again!);
and

(1) the scene where Mustaine confronts Ulrich about Mustaine's being fired from Metallica in 1983, right before the recording of the band's classic debut, *Kill 'Em All*.

The scene happens about forty minutes into the movie. Metallica has commenced work on the album that will become 2003's *St. Anger*, and the process is stalled after Hetfield checks into rehab. The other members are working with a kooky therapist known for shepherding rock bands through trying periods—basically, once your band is too big to break up because the brand is too valuable, this is the guy who will talk you into staying together.

Then some moron decides that it would be a good idea to put Ulrich in a hotel room with Mustaine so that they can rehash Mustaine's canning two decades prior.

The idea (I guess) is that this is supposed to be therapeutic for Ulrich, but Mustaine is the one who gets confessional. Mustaine hijacks the movie as though he were sneaking into somebody else's cab. "I've been waiting for this day for a long time," Mustaine says ominously, and you believe him. He's like Robert De Niro cornering Nick Nolte's family on that houseboat at the end of *Cape Fear*.

Mustaine chastises Ulrich and himself in equal doses, swinging wildly between sounding a little too grandiose ("Do I like being number two? No") and a lot too self-pitying ("People hate me because of you"). Mustaine pontificates with reckless yet endlessly watchable abandon. The best part is when he refers to Ulrich as "my little Danish friend," which somehow comes out sounding like "motherfucker." The whole encounter lasts maybe two minutes, but it has the epic sweep of Ingmar Bergman's *Scenes from a Marriage*. If it were a TV show, I would've been a loyal fan of *Dave Mustaine Tells Off Lars Ulrich* for ten seasons.

Mustaine's termination from Metallica was already the stuff of hesher legend long before *Some Kind of Monster:* Mustaine was, by his own admission, a terrible drunk in the early '80s—loud, abusive, and prone to physical and emotional destruction. Since Metallica spent the entirety of the '80s in a drunken stupor, Mustaine's behavior eventually proved to be an insurmountable problem—cutting off the booze simply wasn't an option. Right before Mustaine was fired, he traveled with Metallica from their home base, in San Francisco, to New York City, where the band's first record label, Megaforce, was located. The band members lived together in a famously squalid rehearsal space. One night Mustaine got screamingly intoxicated, just as he and the rest of Metallica did every night. The following morning, Ulrich and Hetfield presented Mustaine with a bus ticket back to the West Coast.

In his memoir, Mustaine writes that Metallica put him on that lonely bus to post-Metallica oblivion when he was still fucked-up and didn't even give him any traveling money. Mustaine claims he was hungover and hungry, relying on the kindness of strangers for the occasional potato chip. (He specifically mentions potato chips as his sole sustenance.) But he wasn't completely down-and-out: on the floor of the bus he discovered a pamphlet written by California politician Alan Cranston about the dangers of nuclear proliferation. The handbill included the word *megadeath*, a term describing the loss of more than a million lives as a result of nuclear attack. With the removal of that errant second *a*, Megadeth was born.

From then on, "it wasn't enough for Megadeth to do well," Mustaine writes. "I wanted Metallica to fail."

Back to *Some Kind of Monster:* Mustaine claimed later that he was ambushed by the filmmakers. The scene was filmed at the Ritz-Carlton in San Francisco two days after 9/11, and he and Lars were feeling understandably emotional and sentimental. (In his book Mustaine admits that he still harbored hopes of being invited to rejoin Metallica.) When Mustaine saw an early cut of *Some Kind of Monster,* he was incensed and demanded to be taken out of the movie. Mustaine felt *Monster* was "false and manipulative," which is odd, since *Some Kind of Monster* seems like a fair and accurate representation of how Mustaine himself has framed his relationship with Metallica in the years before and after that movie came out.

Nevertheless, Mustaine contended that Metallica had once again stabbed him in the back. Soon after, Mustaine wrote a song, "Something That I'm Not," which doesn't mention Metallica by name but is clearly about Metallica and Mustaine's *Some Kind of Monster* experience. (The lyrics accuse an unnamed subject of being "one big charade," a "fraud," and a "little baby.")

"Something That I'm Not" is included on 2004's *The System Has Failed,* which was not a commercially successful Megadeth record. But by most measures, Mustaine has had a laudable career in music—he's sold in the neighborhood of twenty million albums, he is recognized as one of the primary innovators of thrash metal, and he's still able to tour the world playing his own music for large audiences. Mustaine has been incredibly successful. In his own mind, however, Mustaine is locked in a competition he'll never win. When Megadeth was a legit big-name mainstream rock band—the early-'90s albums *Rust in*

Peace and *Countdown to Extinction* produced several MTV hits—
it happened to coincide with the peak of Metallica's popularity.
When Metallica albums started to suck, in the late '90s, Megadeth albums, inconveniently, started to suck harder.

This is why Mustaine will attempt to reinsert himself into a
Metallica context from time to time. As one of the few people
who still bother to pay attention, I'd like to recount some of the
highlights:

- In 2009, Mustaine protested Metallica's not including
him when they were inducted into the Rock and Roll Hall
of Fame. "To say that I'm not on the record, well, I'd say
that there are 40 million fans with Megadeth and Metallica records in their collections that would say that Dave
is on the Metallica records because my name's on there
[in the songwriting credits]," he told *Metal Hammer.* "But I
guess Lars never really looked past the word 'Ulrich.' He
just stopped there and read it again, over and over and
over."

- In his 2010 autobiography, Mustaine implies that
Metallica stole the "Now I Lay Me Down to Sleep"
prayer part of "Enter Sandman" from "Go to Hell," a
song he recorded for *Bill & Ted's Bogus Journey* and released around the same time. Mustaine does concede,
however, that he did not in fact write the prayer itself.

- In 2012, Mustaine claimed that he was forming a su-
pergroup with Hetfield and Ulrich, prompting Hetfield to
tell a fan magazine, "This is the Dave we kind of wanted
to forget about."

I saw Megadeth in concert at a small club in 2001 and was pleasantly surprised by how great they sounded. Metallica was in shambles at the time, but Mustaine had cobbled together a new band lineup and performed valiantly. However, he wasn't playing a stadium with James and Lars while fans tossed around Kirk Hammett's severed head as though it were a beach ball. I'm guessing that's probably what stuck with Mustaine that night.

My ability to maintain grudges against people who are no longer in my life for offenses I can barely remember bothers me (when I think about it, which is almost never), but not as much as the possibility that there are people out there who hate me for what I've done to them (when I think about it, which is right now).

If I think really hard, I can come up with the names of seventeen individuals who might have reason to speak my name in vain. A few of them come from childhood; the majority are professional acquaintances. I have no idea if this number is conservative in my favor (meaning I'm grossly overestimating the number of people who actively have it in for me) or if I have pissed off way more people than I realize. All the potentially aggrieved people in my life are in my rearview—I thought about reaching out and asking these people if they're still beefing with me, for the sake of research, but then I thought, "Steve, that's a terrible idea. Let's watch *John Wick* again instead."

The advantage of living a regular life (as opposed to performing in a legendary musical act) is that the bulk of the relationships that were pivotal in your life will fade over time. It has been theorized that human beings generate a new set of cells every seven to ten years—the same goes for relationships.

It's rare to be actively engaged in another person's life for more than ten years. To make it past twenty years is truly unusual. You have to live in the same place, or work at the same company, for an uncommonly long time. This has a way of diluting the grudges most of us accumulate. Napping mongrels get to keep on napping, to paraphrase a cliché.

If you're in a band, you don't get to do that. Stupid shit that happened when you were twenty-three still matters. The detritus of letdowns and double-crosses never gets cleared away. *Some Kind of Monster* is the definitive document of this phenomenon—Metallica nearly comes apart because Hetfield and Ulrich can't relate to each other when they're no longer degenerate boozehounds. (The inability to communicate without being drunk is, in my experience, intrinsic to many male friendships.) In bands, the resentments build up until they either kill you or turn you into a self-defeating conspiracy theorist who starts an Alan Cranston–inspired metal band out of spite. Even when you think the sludge has been set aside, it will be redirected in unexpected ways.

Consider Van Halen, for instance.

Van Halen was one of the first rock bands I ever liked. My first Van Halen tape—I only had tapes when I was a tween, because I was a medium-fidelity snob—was *OU812*, which means I was initially into the Sammy Hagar incarnation of Van Halen. I bought *OU812* because I loved "When It's Love," so not only was I into Van Hagar, I was also into Van Hagar's soft, romantic, power-ballad side. I was the Van Hagariest of Van Hagar fans.

After that, I got into two of Van Halen's previous albums, *5150* and *1984*. I knew the hits from *1984*—"Jump," "Panama," and "Hot for Teacher"—so I was fully aware of the majesty of David

Lee Roth. But I did not come to truly understand the superiority of DLR until I delved into *1984*'s deep cuts, which celebrated cool guys ("Top Jimmy"), shapely appendages ("Drop Dead Legs"), and Irish-American rap groups that hadn't formed yet ("House of Pain"). I also played the shit out of "I'll Wait," because I am and forever will be a power-ballad wimp.

Loving Dave did not make me hate Sammy—I also dug *5150*, which I'd argue even now belongs in the upper echelon of VH albums. But most Van Halen fans felt obligated to take sides, and over time it was accepted that Roth was the one true king of Van Halen Nation.

For years there was a drumbeat among true believers that Eddie and Alex should get over their feud with Roth and reunite. When Hagar exited the band in 1996 and Roth appeared with Van Halen at the VMAs to present an award, it seemed like the impossible was really going to happen. Then DLR pulled a DLR and acted like a hyperactive poodle as Beck stood onstage and accepted a Moonman trophy. The Van Halen brothers decided that they couldn't stand to share a stage with their prodigal front man after all and hired Gary Cherone instead. This version of the band subsequently released *Van Halen III* in 1998, which was clearly a smash success for everyone involved.

Flash forward ten years: somehow the incredible happens, and Roth is back with Van Halen. There's a comeback tour in 2007. The band plays seventy-four shows to nearly one million people and grosses $93 million, the most successful tour in the band's history. Four years after the tour concludes, Van Halen releases its first album with Roth in nearly three decades, *A Different Kind of Truth*. And it's actually pretty good! Many of the songs are based on demos dating from the mid-'70s, which seems like the best possible scenario for a new Van Halen album released in the '10s.

Now, if you're a Van Halen fan, you know that I'm leaving out an important detail, and it's what prevents this story from being a redemptive example of how grudges can be disarmed between bandmates. Around the time that the Van Halens reconciled with Roth, they parted ways with their original bassist, Michael Anthony. Anthony's offense was touring with Hagar during one of Van Halen's many inactive periods. Anthony either quit or was fired, depending on whose side you wish to believe, and Eddie's son, Wolfgang, was installed as Van Halen's apparent bassist for life.

My knowledge of what makes Van Halen tick derives entirely from a chapter in Roth's memoir, *Crazy from the Heat*, entitled (fittingly) "What Made Classic Van Halen Tick." According to Diamond Dave, from day one, Van Halen was never rooted in friendship. It was always a war. In a 2013 *BuzzFeed* profile, Roth confirmed that nothing had changed, claiming that he only saw his bandmates shortly before gigs and onstage. Van Halen, like most other long-running rock institutions, was strictly a business. (The exception to the rule is Rush, unless *Beyond the Lighted Stage* is a sham.) I imagine that if Eddie Van Halen would've had two sons and the second kid could sing, DLR would be out of the band along with Anthony. Friendship in rock and roll is transient, but family members tend to stick around for a lifetime.

I've never met or interviewed Michael Anthony, but he always seemed like the least egotistical person in Van Halen by a factor of about ten thousand. He's never appeared to be less than affable. (Chris Farley should've made him a recurring character on *SNL*.) Musically, Anthony's backing vocals were absolutely essential to the Van Halen sound—those high harmonies contribute greatly to that "buzzed on cheap beer on a clear summer night" feeling of classic Van Halen songs. And yet for the dumbest of reasons, his reentry into Van Halen is probably even less likely than Roth's return to the fold was at the height of his dalliances with Steve Vai. A full Van Halen reunion is impossible now, because the Van Halen brothers hate Hagar as ardently as Van Halen's anti–Van Hagar base does, and that hate carried over to their poor ex-bassist. Michael Anthony caught the Van Halen brothers' grudge boomerang. Somebody's got to pay, after all.

CHAPTER 13
Everyone Must Stand Alone

(Madonna vs. Cyndi Lauper and Britney Spears vs.
Christina Aguilera)

FOR THE FIRST six years of my journalism career, I worked for my hometown daily newspaper. I didn't intend for this to happen—for at least five of those years, I was desperate to get out and write for a national publication. I wanted to dance, man! But now I'm grateful for my newspaper roots. For starters, it's so old-timey. Even though I'm only a decade removed from my past in daily dead-tree media, it feels like much longer. It's like I fought in a world war or helped to build the railroads.

I'm sure my son will be confused when I tell him about it. He'll ask, "So the news was printed on paper, once per day, then delivered by hand to readers several hours later, long after the news was still 'new'? And media companies actually made money operating this way? With staffs controlled predominantly by straight white men? Is this real, or is it the dementia talking, Dad?"

Working for a small-town newspaper is what made me a professional. It's one thing to be employed by a glamorous media company in Manhattan, where you get to interview famous people every day—or be close enough to the action as a low-paid twentysomething office drone to get a contact high. That's the cushy life. I spent my early twenties working in the *trenches*, covering stories I had to force myself to care about for the sake of my own sanity.

I was sent to strawberry festivals and catfish races. I wrote about the city's annual boy-choir holiday concert several years in a row. I once covered a mini-tractor pull, which is a competition in which remote-controlled toy tractors pull weights on top of a card table set up in the parking lot of the place where they do regular tractor pulls.

I approached each event as though I were Hemingway contemplating bullfighting. I took fierce pride in my work, because pride was the only thing I had going for me. Otherwise I was stuck in hopeless obscurity.

Sometimes I was able to interview a celebrity. Not a *current* celebrity, mind you, as people such as Jennifer Aniston and Katy Perry typically don't talk to media outlets with circulations topping out at fifty thousand that are located on the outskirts of Green Bay. The people I spoke with were typically blowing through town, either for a one-off concert or as part of a touring theatrical company. I don't want to call them has-beens, so let's just say they were retrofamous.

I was pretty green as a reporter, so I didn't fully appreciate the importance of some of the legends who agreed to do twenty-minute phoners with me. One time I spoke with actress Linda Gray, who was starring as Mrs. Robinson in some second-generation stage version of *The Graduate*. Linda Gray! At the time I barely cared, but later on I realized that in another life Linda Gray played Sue Ellen Ewing, J.R.'s questionably sane and aggressively shoulder-padded SO, on *Dallas,* which my wife and I watched obsessively on DVD one summer many years later.

Linda, if you're reading this, call me. I have so many questions I wish I would've asked. (Question 1: Why in the world did you sleep with Cliff Barnes?!)

The most memorable interview I did during my newspaper days was with Cyndi Lauper. For a person who spent his formative years (ages two to thirteen) living in the '80s, talking to Cyndi Lauper was a little like interviewing the Road Runner or Bozo the Clown. She was a loud, colorful, and cartoonish presence from my childhood who I assumed couldn't possibly exist in real life. And yet there she was, talking to me on the phone. It was truly amazing and completely weird.

Like every retrofamous person I interviewed back then, Lauper wasn't thrilled to be talking to some kid working for a newspaper she had never heard of from a town she couldn't pick out on a map. She was just worse at hiding it. I don't blame her—not everyone can have the charm and courteous professionalism of a Sue Ellen Ewing. I was also really, really bad at interviewing people at the time. In 1984, Cyndi Lauper was one of the world's biggest pop stars. Only the best music journalists—your Kurt Loders, your Martha Quinns—were granted an audience with Cyndi back then. In the early aughts, however, she was stuck with the likes of me. I almost felt sorry for her.

As bad at my job as I was, I knew it was my responsibility to ask questions that the average reader would care about. When it comes to Cyndi Lauper, there's really only one question: What's it like living in the shadow of your MTV-constructed image from the '80s?

I didn't ask the question exactly like that, but I did (tactfully) pose a couple of different variations of it during our interview. I was genuinely curious, then and now. Celebrity is such a strange, indefinable currency. In one sense, Cyndi Lauper never stopped being successful, because her success at its peak was so incredible that it permanently implanted her in the culture. Lauper's debut album, 1983's *She's So Unusual*, sold more than twenty-two million copies worldwide. The LP's signature song, "Girls Just Want to Have Fun," ranks among the four or five most iconic hits of the era. She has at least three other songs ("Time After Time," "She Bop," and "True Colors") that anyone casually familiar with '80s pop can recognize instantly. When I interviewed her in 2001, Lauper was touring with Cher and performing sold-out shows in arenas all over the world. She was still being paid really well to sing songs that are loved by millions.

There's an old *Onion* headline that perfectly captures the way aging postpeak pop stars are commonly perceived: PATHETIC, WASHED-UP ROCK STAR ON FIFTH DECADE OF DOING EXACTLY WHAT HE ALWAYS WANTED. When I interviewed her, Lauper was on her third decade of doing what she always wanted, and yet in the minds of many people, she was viewed as being washed-up because her subsequent albums had a fraction of *She's So Unusual*'s impact.

That's a fucked-up dichotomy, and I was dying to know how Lauper felt about it. However, I imagine *every* reporter wants to ask Lauper about that fucked-up dichotomy. By the time I got to her, she was sick of talking about it.

I remember a lot of long pauses and dissatisfied sighs during our interview. If I were Mike Wallace, I would've used those pauses to my advantage and reverse-spited Cyndi into answering my questions. Instead I felt the hole in the pit of my stomach growing. Was the Road Runner mad at me? After a while, Cyndi and I seemed to find common ground: we both equally yearned for the interview to end.

If anyone is to blame for the perception that Cyndi Lauper failed, it's Madonna. Given that Madonna's career came to dwarf Lauper's by the end of the '80s, it might be hard to remember that they were once pitted against each other by the media. But they were. This can be partly attributed to sexism, as female artists are often measured only against other female artists. But there were legitimate similarities between Cyndi and Madge. They put out their debut albums within three months of each other in 1983. You could not watch MTV at the time for more than fifteen minutes without seeing at least one of them. They both signified the funky hybrid of punk, disco, and hip-hop cultures that distinguished early-'80s New York. They even used some of the same songwriters: the team of Billy Steinberg and Tom Kelly wrote "Like a Virgin" for Madonna and "True Colors" for Lauper. (They also wrote "Eternal Flame," performed by the Bangles; "Alone," made famous by Heart; and "I Touch Myself," a hit for the Divinyls. Few men understood the ladies during the Reagan years better than Steinberg and Kelly.)

Above all, Madonna and Cyndi Lauper were instantly recognizable characters. Madonna was like your friend's sexy older sister who spoke exclusively in double entendres. Lauper was like your friend's wisecracking older sister who self-identified as quirky. They were both larger-than-life yet somehow knowable.

Fair or not, the world of pop music wasn't big enough for both of them, and Madonna was the one who emerged victorious. Students of '80s music have often asked, "Why didn't

Cyndi Lauper have the same longevity as Madonna?" And the answer is always the same: Madonna knew how to evolve, while Cyndi Lauper was quickly fixed as the red-haired, poodle skirt–wearing wrestling fanatic people saw in her videos. Madonna is eternal; Cyndi Lauper is eternally tied to a specific moment in time.

That's the conventional wisdom on Madonna and Cyndi Lauper, which seems pretty cruel to Lauper, though I think it's actually more unfair to Madonna. I would argue that the reason Madonna endured over Lauper (and pretty much every other pop star who emerged in the '80s) is that she had better songs—and more of them—than Lauper or anybody else.

People always forget about the music when talking about Madonna. She has *a lot* of great songs. Sometimes I think she has *all* the great songs, at least when it comes to dance-pop tracks that I want to hear at weddings and in karaoke bars. If you think I'm wrong, try naming all of Madonna's hits without stopping to take a break. You may be surprised by how physically arduous cataloging Madonna's greatness is: "Into the Groove," "Holiday," "Burning Up," "Borderline," "Like a Virgin," "Open Your Heart"—these are just the most obvious numbers from the first two or three years of her career. I'll keep going: "Justify My Love," "Vogue," "Cherish," "Express Yourself," "Secret"—gasping for breath—"Ray of Light," "Frozen," "Music," "Don't Tell Me" ... damn, I think I need to sit down.

Madonna made a lot of great albums, too—1989's *Like a Prayer* is commonly regarded as her best, but I'd put her 1983 debut up against any pop record released during the '80s. People are still trying to remake that record, but they never pull it off. Madonna's run from the early '80s up through the mid-aughts is amazingly consistent for an artist courting mass acceptance and achieving it more often than not. For all the props we give Michael Jackson and Prince, it should be noted that those guys sort of sucked after 1992. They were stuck with Lauper in their '80s periods. But Madonna kept going, kept growing, kept putting out songs that mattered.

Nineties Madonna is some of my favorite Madonna. For a while it was like she decided to be influenced exclusively by "Live to Tell" and become a killer singer of torchy, midlife-crisis ballads such as "Take a Bow" and "This Used to Be My Playground." Then she embraced a kind of cougarfied spiritualism with *Ray of Light*, then dropped the God crap with *Music*. In the new century, Madonna followed up embarrassing "I guess Madonna must be finished" travesties (such as "American Life," which is when she decided to rap) with awesome "I can't believe Madonna is still making me care" comebacks (including "Hung Up," one of the few successful attempts by anybody to remake *Madonna*).

And yet from the beginning of her career, Madonna has been primarily defined not by her music but by her ambition and her ability to present herself in visually interesting and ever-changing guises. These talking points have been repeated in pretty much every magazine profile ever written about her. Even people who profess to be Madonna fans tend to marvel at her wiliness first and her songs second (or third or even fourth or fifth).

"I wasn't really that crazy about her music," feminist writer Jessica Valenti notes in the foreword to *Madonna and Me*, a collection of essays about Madonna by more than three dozen female writers. "It was her—her persona, more accurately—that drew me in. I wasn't necessarily rocking out to her, but I was watching."

I suspect that Valenti's opinion is shared by other pop intellectuals who are more interested in discussing what Madonna means than "rocking out to her." Which is fine, though it does sort of seem like backhanded praise. It's not about enjoying Madonna's music, it's about appreciating her as a constructed image that can be held at arm's length. As for Lauper, she's been relegated to the B side of all this persona talk. If Madonna remained on the pop charts because of "her ability as a pop chameleon" (as Valenti argues), then Lauper must've been stymied by her inability to be anything other than the brassy figure on the cover of *She's So Unusual.*

There is a small but committed cadre of Cyndi Lauper truthers who will always believe that Lauper is more talented than Madonna and therefore more deserving of a Madonna-like career. These people have garnered some support from the critical community, which now regards *She's So Unusual* as one of the decade's best pop records, proving yet again that music for teenagers eventually wins out in the history books. Meanwhile, adult-oriented fiber logs such as Sting's *The Dream of the Blue Turtles* and Don Henley's *Building the Perfect Beast* are stripped of their respectability and forced to die ignoble deaths inside the bargain bins of soon-to-be-shuttered used-CD stores.

The Cyndi truthers believe that Cyndi's refusal to be anything other than herself is what kept her from being Madonna. I resent this argument, because it tricked me into listening to Lauper's other albums, which are significantly less unusual than *She's So Unusual.* But it's indicative of the way Madonna's career has been subsequently deconstructed—the "pop chameleon" aspect of her legacy is emphasized over the "unbeatable pop songs" part. Madonna is regarded as an archetype for pop singers, an example to follow to immortality. If you can change it up like Madonna, maybe you can *be* Madonna.

But you can't be Madonna. She's a freak-of-nature anomaly. Most pop singers would be lucky to even be Cyndi Lauper.

Somebody somewhere at some point decided that the worst thing that a song or artist can be called is dated. "Dated" is so undesirable as a label that you don't even have to explain why it's bad. It's just accepted that good music is "timeless" and bad music is unmistakably rooted in its era.

It's an unquestioned paradigm. However, I don't like unquestioned paradigms. They instantly arouse my skepticism. Who do these paradigms think they are, anyway, dodging questions as they do?

Many years ago, I posited a theory about *Back to the Future* concerning Robert Zemeckis's use of Huey Lewis and the News' "The Power of Love." If you'll recall, *Back to the Future* opens with Marty McFly poking around Doc Brown's laboratory, which appears to be housed inside a nondescript building adjacent to a Burger King. After striking a thunderously loud power chord and destroying Doc's in-house PA system, Marty realizes that he's late for school. So he hops on his skateboard and hitches a ride on the backs of assorted cars and Jeeps. And the song soundtracking these misadventures is "The Power of Love."

Whether you were alive when *Back to the Future* came out or you've been raised to tolerate oldster Gen Xers constantly pushing this ancient time-travel comedy into your consciousness, you will naturally recognize "The Power of Love" as an obvious signifier of 1985. In no other year would a Caucasian man in his late thirties named Huey be presented as a credible figurehead of American youth culture. In 1984, this figurehead would've been Prince. In 1986, it would have been Run-D.M.C. But 1985 was a sweet spot for dorky, aging white men. (See also Phil Collins, Lou Gramm of Foreigner, Mark Knopfler of Dire Straits, Paul Young, the doofuses in REO Speedwagon, the curly-haired man standing next to Grace Slick in Starship, and king honkies Daryl Hall and John Oates.)

As viewers we know that 1985 doubles as "the present" in *Back to the Future.* Marty leaves 1985 to go back to 1955, which is signified in part by the inclusion of period songs such as "Mr. Sandman" and "Earth Angel." If you saw it in 1985, *Back to the Future* seemed like only part period piece. If you watch *Back to the Future* after 1985, however, the movie seems like 100 percent period piece. Zemeckis's 1985 is as archetypal as his 1955 and is signified in part by the inclusion of "The Power of Love."

I don't know if Zemeckis consciously picked "The Power of Love" for his opening sequence because he suspected that the song would come to define the sound (plasticky), production (booming), and emotional tenor (psychotically peppy) of the year his movie is set in for subsequent generations. But "The Power of Love" unquestionably anchors *Back to the Future* in a specific era, which (perhaps accidentally) adds to the effectiveness of the storytelling.

Using songs as shorthand for particular time periods is standard for any film not set in the present. But when I think about the present we're living in this very second, I seriously wonder if contemporary music will be similarly evocative for viewers looking to relive the mid-'10s. Songs simply don't date the way they used to. Think of the way Robert Johnson's small batch of epochal blues recordings have come to color our impressions of the Deep South in the '30s. Or the way Fleetwood Mac's soft-rock confessionals conjure the laid-back LA of the mid-'70s. Or the way the chaotic sound of Public Enemy's early records embodies the feral energy of hip-hop as it took over pop culture in the late '80s. Those records are dated because the way music was recorded has moved on: once-revolutionary technology was inevitably set aside.

But nothing is set aside anymore. Differing styles can coexist because culture has been flattened. *The past never stays in the past.* The Internet has made the average listener much savvier about how to deconstruct every new song into a component set of influences. Everything we hear now is processed as a math equation—artist X is the sum total of Marvin Gaye plus Daft Punk plus the Bush album that Steve Albini recorded divided by Eagle-Eye Cherry.

In 1983, *She's So Unusual* could've been broken down in similar fashion—Lauper was like Lesley Gore multiplied by Lydia Lunch plus one-eighth of Rowdy Roddy Piper. But people didn't listen to music that way back then. They didn't have the technological means to do the necessary research. Instead Lauper was just accepted as new until she started to seem dated.

But what an achievement it is to be dated! So long as people are interested in thinking about 1983, *She's So Unusual* will work as a signifier of its time and place in a way few (if any) contemporary songs will work for our time. In a sense, the Madonna method of consuming and producing culture has become commonplace. Now it's the audience that's expected to constantly deconstruct, synthesize, then dispose of the latest set of bygone references.

If there's one thing we can agree on about the endless marathon that is keeping up with modern culture, it's that being like Madonna is exhausting and not all that fulfilling. Pop stars who try to pull off Madonna's perpetual-reinvention act always wind up learning this lesson the hard way. For instance, look at what attempting to emulate Madonna did to Britney Spears and Christina Aguilera.

Britney and Christina were products of the last truly iconic pop movement before the Internet irrevocably rejiggered the way we perceive culture. I refer to the late-'90s teen-pop boom, which positioned Britney and Christina as Madonna and Cyndi for Millennials. Britney's and Christina's earliest hits, "...Baby One More Time" and "Genie in a Bottle" respectively, are dated in the best possible way. They are magical, monumentally frivolous songs for a magical, monumentally frivolous time. In the late '90s, the economy was blowing up, and the world was relatively peaceful. Bill Clinton was getting blown in the White House, and the majority of Americans didn't care because they were in such a good mood. Life was so awesome that everyday existence felt like it was directed by Michael Bay.

The era's perfectly constructed and wholesome kiddie-pop songs reflect this naive optimism. Britney and Christina were former Mickey Mouse Club moppets who acted slightly naughty but still stayed well within the confines of good clean fun. It was unrepentantly white-bread in a way that pop music never would be again. For kids today, who have grown up in a far more cynical post-9/11 world, 1998 might as well be 1955.

Neither Britney nor Christina wanted to be Cyndi; they both wanted to be Madonna. (Though Christina would've happily taken Mariah Carey or Whitney Houston as a consolation prize.) Britney appeared to have the edge early on—her initial "schoolgirl" incarnation was pure sexual provocation just as surely as Madonna dry-humping the stage in a wedding dress at the 1984 MTV Video Music Awards was. Except that Britney steadfastly denied that she was being provocative. In interviews, she was perplexed by the suggestion that cretinous men in their forties and fifties composed a silent majority of her fan base. Any time a journalist postulated a cultural subtext to her work, Britney rejected it. It was a very un-Madonna move.

Christina was more dutiful about following Madonna's example. Aguilera's next major album, *Stripped*, signaled the beginning of her "Dirrty" phase. Christina was now known as Xtina, a feral, sexually omnivorous hosebeast in assless chaps. Christina was a sweet junior diva, but Xtina was a gladiator in the sex wars.

Aguilera committed to the Xtina guise like a method actor digging into a Tennessee Williams play. She covered herself in tattoos and genital piercings. If you said, "Casual sex," Aguilera said, "Where and when?" Nevertheless, something about Xtina rang false. For starters, she didn't have the songs. *Stripped* is too bloated to work as a suitable bedroom sound track. (Though "Beautiful" almost makes me not hate the song's writer, Linda Perry, for her role in subjecting the world to 4 Non Blondes' "What's Up?")

Christina Aguilera, like Britney Spears, had been bred as a child star. This background imbued every performance with a prodigy's hollow, soulless virtuosity. Madonna managed to make trend-hopping seem organic, perhaps because she was schooled in show business on the mean streets of New York, suffering numerous degradations on her way to the top. Madonna's background fortified her with indestructible resolve. When circumstances aligned and allowed Madonna to have her pop-star moment, she had a sense of self at her core that Spears and Aguilera simply didn't.

This was apparent at the 2003 VMAs, the scene of the infamous kiss between Madonna and Britney Spears. (Oh, and Madonna kissed Christina, too, though nobody remembers that.)

Herein lies the most telling representation of Christina's perpetual second-place status in the Britney vs. Christina rivalry: when you watch the video on YouTube, you can tell that the cameras have been trained to zero in on Britney and Madonna at the precise moment they lock lips. It happened after Britney and Christina both sang a verse of "Like a Virgin," a call back to Madonna's performance on the VMAs five hundred years prior. Then Madonna descended a flight of stairs, looking like an undead Marlene Dietrich who'd been dug up and subjected to rigorous sessions with a personal trainer for six months, singing the just-okay single "Hollywood." Then, blammo, the kiss with Britney.

After that there's a quick cut to Justin Timberlake, who looks pissed and maybe slightly turned on. When the cameras cut back to the stage, Madonna is pulling out of her kiss with Christina. Because nobody cared about Madonna kissing Christina, as we just had our minds blown by Madonna kissing Britney.

After the VMAs, Britney repledged allegiance to Madonna. She claimed, weirdly, that Madonna was her husband from another life and made noise in her inner circle about taking more control of her career, à la the original Mrs. Blond Ambition. But instead of taking control, Britney completely lost it. It got so bad for Britney that *Rolling Stone* ran a cover story in 2008 that referred to her as "an American tragedy." Typically that sort of designation is reserved for disgraced leaders and dead celebrities. Britney was only twenty-six, and the media was already burying her.

What happened? In short: Britney (allegedly) did a lot of drugs. Then she met and married JT's former backup dancer Kevin Federline. Then she had two kids. Then she stopped making music for a few years. Then she was strong-armed by her family into rehab, which she dropped out of after one day. Then she shaved her head and physically attacked the paparazzi, creating a wealth of highly unflattering photos in which she resembled Robert Duvall in *THX 1138*.

I'm leaving some important stuff out. Well, not important, just interesting from a purely prurient perspective. For instance, Britney informed Federline that she was divorcing him via text message, which prompted him to write the following on the wall of a nightclub bathroom: "Fuck a wife, give me my kids, bitch!" Then Federline exited the nightclub and hopped a plane to Stockholm, where he was presented with his Nobel Prize for excellence in douche-baggery.

This is where Britney's story gets downright depressing. There were rumors that Britney fed her kids soda in baby bottles while feeding herself a toxic cocktail of vodka, Red Bull, and NyQuil, known among southern rappers as purple monster. There was also a story about Britney having her very own sex dungeon outfitted with special lotions and spanking paddles. Another thing that happened that's not a rumor is that Britney started dating a guy from the paparazzi pool that happened to be stalking her. According to *Rolling Stone*'s "American Tragedy" story, Britney hopped in the guy's car, put on a pink wig, and took him to a hotel for a late "lunch." (That's the photographer's word, not mine.) It was like when Madonna did her *Sex* book, except Britney let the grossness take over her daily life.

The most fascinating curio from Britney's wilderness period

has to be *Original Doll,* the so-called "lost" album that coincided with Spears's disastrous 2003 Onyx Hotel tour. Spears's camp has long denied *Original Doll*'s existence; Britney herself referred to the mystery album just once, during a bizarre, seemingly impromptu appearance at an LA radio station when she hand-delivered a newly recorded track from the supposed LP called "Mona Lisa."

Mona Lisa was a persona, like Xtina, one that liberated Britney to expose her "true" self. That's the legend that Britney superfans like to believe, anyway. "Mona Lisa" isn't a great song—you can find bootlegs online—but by Britney standards it's bracingly self-aware, mimicking the mock-operatic sweep of Justin Timberlake's "Cry Me a River" while acknowledging in the lyrics that Britney Spears is essentially a broken person.

Supposedly *Original Doll* was to be Britney's confessional record, exposing the Britney That the Industry Doesn't Want You to See. Apparently the Industry won out, because Britney released *In the Zone* instead. The best-known track from *In the Zone* is arguably Britney's best song, "Toxic," but the tune that *Original Doll* conspiracy theorists focus on is the delicate piano ballad "Everytime." Lyrically, "Everytime" was widely interpreted as another response to "Cry Me a River," with Britney apologizing for cheating on JT and inadvertently propelling him to artistic credibility.

"Everytime" is so overwrought that it borders on self-parody (a quality that must've prompted Harmony Korine to include it in his movie *Spring Breakers*). But it's nothing compared with the video, which is Britney's version of "November Rain"—instead of Axl and Stephanie Seymour, we see Britney arguing with a shirtless Stephen Dorff, who (I'm guessing) is intended to be a craggier version of JT. From there we see allusions to domestic abuse and the suffocating crush of fame. Also, it's implied that Britney dies in a bathtub and is reborn as a baby. It's amazing.

Oh, have I forgotten about Christina? Sorry, I have fallen into the same trap as the director of that VMA telecast. After *Stripped*, Christina/Xtina had the "new Madonna" lane all to herself for several years, as Britney took herself out of commission during the mid-aughts. But Christina could never make it work. In 2006, she put out *Back to Basics*, which was her *I'm Breathless*, a questionable move given that she hadn't yet made her *Like a Prayer* or even *Who's That Girl*. (The sound track to *Burlesque* doesn't count.) By 2010's *Bionic*, Christina was experimenting with "a very futuristic, robotic sound and computer-sounding vocals," as she told *Billboard* in 2011. But it just seemed like she was chasing another would-be Madonna, Lady Gaga. A planned support tour was canceled, and her career appeared to be on the downswing.

The aughts were a troubled decade for Britney and Christina specifically and pop generally. As the record industry fell apart in slow motion, the public became fascinated with the hemorrhaging machinery. Singing competitions had been a popular TV genre since *Star Search*, but *American Idol* and its many knockoffs took the format to new heights. An industry kid at heart, Christina Aguilera sustained herself by joining *The Voice*, where she mentored aspiring divas and inspired legions of mini Christinas.

Britney's relationship to the machine was more complicated. In 2008, she was put under the conservatorship of her father (with whom she had previously publicly feuded) and attorney, which gave them control of her assets. On her albums, Britney appeared to be relegated to an uninterested tool for her many superstar producer collaborators. Some of these records (particularly 2007's *Blackout* and 2011's *Femme Fatale*) are enjoyable if you can set aside the discomforting feeling that you're listening to a woman being held captive by her handlers. Otherwise clicking on a Britney track can make you feel like an accessory to kidnapping.

Like Christina, Britney wound up as a judge on a singing show, *The X Factor,* for which she was paid $15 million, the highest payout ever for a celebrity judge on one of these shows. Her big TV salary helped her earn more money in 2012, $58 million, than any other female entertainer. Her next album, 2013's *Britney Jean,* bombed, but she's survived her post-"American Tragedy" moment. I have no idea if that's the same as happiness, but I suppose it could be worse. You keep waiting for Britney to blink once if she's okay or twice if she wants to be rescued. But her eyes are always blank.

Then there's Madonna, who's still the best at approximating the ambition and panache of '80s Madonna. Not everything that Madonna does now is golden—comparing herself to Martin Luther King during the promotional cycle for 2015's *Rebel Heart,* for example, wasn't a great moment. Kissing Drake at Coachella wasn't a great moment, either. I haven't cared much about Madonna's new music since 2006, but she's still a dignified presence, and her Super Bowl halftime show in 2012 is one of the big game's all-time splendiferous spectacles. Madonna is like the polished second draft of Elvis Presley—instead of getting fat and dying off, she got crazy muscular and harder to kill. She might even outlast Keith Richards.

CHAPTER 14
Heritage, Not Hate

(Neil Young vs. Lynyrd Skynyrd)

I SPEND WAY too much time on social media. I also spend way too much time thinking about Neil Young vs. Lynyrd Skynyrd. Naturally these obsessions have converged in my mind. I've come to regard Neil Young vs. Lynyrd Skynyrd as the perfect metaphor for the way communication works online. It is a proto-Twitter feud that unfolded more than thirty years before Twitter was invented. Technology changes, but human nature doesn't.

Before we get to that, please allow me to vent.

The most annoying cliché that new parents endlessly repeat is, "Having a child has made me a more patient and giving person." It's like saying, "Being married has given me the willpower to not solicit hand jobs from strangers." It's humble-bragging about behavior that should be the bare minimum requirement for semidecent human beings. It's also not true. Being a parent doesn't make you more patient; you're either a patient person or you're not. If you're not, being a parent will cause you to climb into your car, drive away, and never come back. For millions of years, billions of parents have opted to not do this. If Neanderthals had abandoned their tiny crazy cave babies by hopping on the nearest mastodon, none of us would be here today. So at best, modern parents are as patient and giving as prehistoric knuckle draggers.

What is true in my experience is that parenthood requires a tactical allotment of your patience reserves. Because this limited supply is used up over the course of an average day of child rearing, little to no patience is left over for other activities. For instance, ever since my son was born, I have been unable to finish a movie that I start watching after 8:00 p.m. without falling asleep for at least ten minutes. I've seen about 83 percent of countless two-hour films. It's like my brain is a highly sensitive laptop computer, and if my mental cursor isn't nudged constantly, I instantly fall into sleep mode.

I used to love watching movies late at night, but this is physically impossible now. It could be a new Coen brothers film starring the reanimated corpse of Warren Oates, *Fast Times at Ridgemont High*–era Phoebe Cates, Morris Day and the Time, and the creepily excitable old guy from those Six Flags commercials, and my brain still wouldn't be engaged enough to remain conscious for the entire movie.

One of the rare exceptions is something I just watched, 2012's "beware of the Internet" film, *Disconnect*. It's possible that you've heard of *Disconnect* if you have ever trawled the depths of HBO NOW in search of noncomedic Jason Bateman vehicles. *Disconnect* is clearly the kind of movie that the filmmakers believed was an important statement while they were making it, and they clearly ended up being wrong. They tried and failed to win multiple Oscars and guide the national discourse.

But *Disconnect* did succeed in keeping me awake, which is why it is on my mind.

Disconnect is sort of like *Crash* for Facebook users. It has a dozen or so characters parceled across three story lines who come together in the final twenty minutes via a wincingly melodramatic plot contrivance that is easily predictable within the film's first twenty minutes. Each story line tackles a separate issue related to the Internet—cyberbullying, identity theft, and porn. (This storytelling approach is known as the Degrassi method.) In one story, Bateman plays an attorney who is constantly talking on his cell phone, which of course means that he's an aloof father about to be lowered a couple of pegs by a family tragedy. His teenage son is a social misfit who composes music and wears his hair in his eyes, which of course means that he's about to kill either his classmates or himself.

In the second story, Paula Patton plays a woman who is not the glamorous ex-wife of Robin Thicke but rather a mother who copes with the grief of losing her son by retreating into the world of online chat rooms. In the third story, a beautiful and unscrupulous TV reporter (Andrea Riseborough) attempts to investigate an underage sex-cam ring and in the process discovers that mainstream journalists can be just as exploitive as pornographers. Or something.

Disconnect is not a good movie. But I was riveted by *Disconnect* nonetheless because it hits on a topic that I think about all the time. The catch-22 of online communication is that we're more connected than ever yet also more alienated. I know that sounds trite, but only because it's intuitively understood by everybody who uses the Internet on a daily basis. The average person is capable of putting out as many words into the world as a media professional is. And this has created a glut of personal expression that's seemingly made it impossible for anyone to get a point across. Everyone is so busy forcing their points of view into the public sphere that taking a moment to listen to another person seems like an indulgence. Instead we're talking to each other in partially received fragments, which are then subsequently decontextualized by aggregators and reinterpreted in new and often misleading ways. Ultimately, a million different misunderstandings end up collectively shaping how we view the world.

An example of this phenomenon is the #CancelColbert movement. In terms of Internet outrages, #CancelColbert is practically the War of 1812. But if you can remember all the way back to the early part of the mid-'10s, you will recall that the official Twitter account for *The Colbert Report* tweeted out a joke about Asian Americans that was intended to satirize Washington Redskins owner Daniel Snyder. In the context of *The Colbert Report,* the gag was a comment *on* racism rather than a racist comment. It still seemed that way on Twitter for most people familiar with Colbert's TV persona. But for a small but vocal group of activists, the tweet just seemed like regular old nonironic racism, and a hashtag was born.

Once it was clear that Colbert was in fact not a bigot, the conversation shifted toward a conversation about white privilege in general. For a variety of reasons, it was decided that Colbert's original intentions were no longer important, for #CancelColbert had initiated a socially redeeming conversation about the woeful lack of diversity in media. In a thoughtful piece for the *New Yorker,* Jay Caspian Kang convincingly argued that no matter what the misunderstandings of the initial protest were, #CancelColbert had facilitated a necessary airing of rarely heard criticisms of white liberal hypocrisy. (It also sparked an equally virulent anti-PC outcry that ostensibly defended Colbert but seemed more concerned with airing the usual "liberal media" grievances.) That #CancelColbert seemed to have nothing to do specifically with Colbert proved that this dialogue transcended a mere misinterpreted tweet.

This sounds perfectly reasonable unless you happen to be the person unwittingly turned into a figurehead for racial insensitivity. #CancelColbert was always going to be at least a little about Colbert, just by virtue of the name. But like all social-media protests, #CancelColbert quickly spiraled off in dozens of unexpected directions. Even Suey Park, the twenty-three-year-old "hashtag activist" who initiated the protest, appeared to be a reluctant participant in this public confrontation. Park had tweeted about Colbert's offending joke while eating dinner; she later told Kang that she was a Colbert fan, adding, "It's not like I enjoy missing *Scandal* to tweet about *The Colbert Report*." Colbert and Park were not really at war; they were stand-ins for vast constituencies on the left and right eager to tear each other apart. If it hadn't been #CancelColbert, it would've been a different argument.

Sometimes a fan can be your most devastating critic. Sometimes the least thoughtful criticism is what ends up resonating in the culture. Sometimes what you actually feel matters less than what your actions signify to the public. Sometimes directly stating your opinion is the worst possible way to be heard. Because it's not about what you said but rather about what people believe (or want to believe) you said.

And sometimes this causes me to dwell on Neil Young vs. Lynyrd Skynyrd.

*　　*　　*

There aren't quite a million misunderstandings that shape the public's perception of Neil Young vs. Lynyrd Skynyrd. (It's more like three.) Here's the gist of the story, which every junior rock historian already knows verbatim: In the early '70s, Neil Young released two songs, "Southern Man" and "Alabama," that caricatured the South the way the end of *Easy Rider* caricatured the South. Lynyrd Skynyrd, a young rock band from Florida that would've been the Rolling Stones had Keith Richards been born in the American South instead of merely snorting a metric ton of Merck cocaine there, responded in 1974 by writing "Sweet Home Alabama," which includes the lines "I hope Neil Young will remember / Southern man don't need him around anyhow."

To borrow a social-media phrase, Lynyrd Skynyrd benefited from punching up. "Sweet Home Alabama" made Skynyrd southern rock's defining band. Before that Skynyrd was considered a satellite group of the reigning kingpins of the genre, the Allman Brothers Band. But the Allmans were never as explicitly provincial as "Sweet Home Alabama" was. The Allmans reacted against the redneck stereotype by becoming the southern version of the Grateful Dead, showing northerners that hippies could exist in the very place where Peter Fonda and Dennis Hopper had been blown to bits. "Sweet Home Alabama," meanwhile, fortified southern pride for southern pride's sake. It was made for *us*, not *them*. It was seen as a direct rebuke of Yankee-imposed marginalization. For this reason, Skynyrd forged a powerfully personal connection with its core fan base.

"Sweet Home Alabama" became Skynyrd's first and only top-ten hit. Three years later, three band members, including the singer and principal songwriter, Ronnie Van Zant, were killed in a plane crash. But Skynyrd was so popular—and classic-rock radio was still playing "Sweet Home Alabama" roughly 10,242 times per day—that what was left of the band reunited ten years later, with Ronnie's brother Johnny taking over front-man duties. Skynyrd proceeded to tour and record for the following three decades. In 2006, the right-wing magazine *National Review* ranked "Sweet Home Alabama" as the fourth-greatest conservative rock song, describing it as "a tribute to the region of America that liberals love to hate, taking a shot at Neil Young's Canadian arrogance along the way."

Now, any junior rock historian will also tell you that "Sweet Home Alabama" is commonly misinterpreted in the following ways:

(1) It's not exactly a serious statement. In a *Los Angeles Times* interview with a baby-faced Cameron Crowe from the mid-'70s, Ronnie Van Zant called the song "more of a joke than anything else."

(2) The song does not endorse Alabama's segregationist governor George Wallace. This is a perfect example of interpreting partially received segments. "In Birmingham they love the governor" appears to support Wallace if you disregard the immediate rejoinders: the backup singers chanting "Boo! Boo! Boo!" and the sardonic Watergate reference in the subsequent line.

(3) Ronnie Van Zant did not dislike Neil Young. He in fact considered himself a Neil Young fan. And Neil Young loved Lynyrd Skynyrd and "Sweet Home Alabama." He said this explicitly on several occasions. Young even

played "Sweet Home Alabama" in concert in tribute to Van Zant shortly after he died.

Anyone who self-identifies as a "smart" fan of Lynyrd Skynyrd will immediately pontificate on number 3 the moment "Sweet Home Alabama" is disparaged as redneck bluster. It is the best-known "little-known" bit of context for the song. The greatest self-aware southern rock band ever, Drive-By Truckers, based their most beloved album, *Southern Rock Opera*, in part on the dichotomy between the perception of the Neil Young vs. Lynyrd Skynyrd rivalry and the reality of it—that Young and Van Zant regarded each other with mutual respect. It was both a metaphor for the Truckers' concept about "the duality of the southern thing" and a skeleton key for a deeper appreciation of Skynyrd's mythology.

In order to get this point across, Drive-By Truckers engaged in some mythmaking of their own. In the song "Ronnie and Neil," Patterson Hood sings that the titular characters "became good friends" and that Neil acted as Ronnie's pallbearer. The former claim is vaguely true; the latter is straight-up fiction. (The part where Hood says that Young wrote "Powderfinger" for Lynyrd Skynyrd, however, is a fact and sort of mind-blowing.) But these misunderstandings add up to a more or less accurate portrait of two artists who were more similar in life than they appear to be in their songs.

The reason the Ronnie-and-Neil relationship is so important to a small segment of Skynyrd's following is that the band underwent a sweeping ideological makeover after Ronnie died and Johnny took over. As a result it's very difficult to talk about the greatness of Lynyrd Skynyrd's music without being quickly tripped up by the band's political baggage. This isn't a problem for Lou Reed fans. Loving *Transformer* is not perceived as tacit support for shooting smack and performing fellatio in public bathrooms. But putting on *Second Helping* at a party will often lead to an uncomfortable conversation about whether you *really* support the Emancipation Proclamation.

Ronnie Van Zant, cowriter of supposedly one of the greatest conservative rock songs ever, was a Democrat who campaigned for Jimmy Carter and argued (in 1975's "Saturday Night Special") that "hand guns are made for killin'" and ought to be disposed of at "the bottom of the sea." It's also worth noting that Johnny Van Zant became a Republican when Ronald Reagan entered the White House—three years after Ronnie died—and it was only under his stewardship that Lynyrd Skynyrd started performing at the Republican National Convention every four years.

In 2009, Johnny's version of Lynyrd Skynyrd finally achieved singularity by releasing an album called *God & Guns*. "God and guns keep us strong / That's what this country was founded on," Johnny sings on the title track. "Well, we might as well give up and run / If we let 'em take our God and guns." It doesn't take a genius to observe that the scary, unseen "them" out to take the guns in this song could very well refer to people like Ronnie Van Zant, a problem Johnny himself seemed to recognize in 2012 when he speculated in a *Washington Times* interview that Ronnie would have become a Republican had he not died young. (I disagree—Ronnie would've pushed for tighter regulation of airplane pilots.)

In a famous episode of his *WTF* podcast, host Marc Maron confronts his guest Dane Cook with an embarrassing story related by a lesser-known comic in which Cook allegedly accused the guy of stealing "his essence." The idea was to portray

Cook as a raging egotist, because the idea of taking a person's "essence" is obviously ridiculous. But people who love what Skynyrd was and loathe what Skynyrd became understand where Dane Cook is coming from, as Johnny Van Zant seemed to straight-up rob Ronnie's essence for his own ends. Once Johnny started singing "Sweet Home Alabama," the song lost all remnants of its former irony. It was reduced to simple-minded cannon fodder for the culture wars. Ronnie Van Zant might as well have been a post-death Republican convert, given that his songs were being used to forward a conservative political agenda.

As much as I want to blame Johnny Van Zant for this, I know I can't hold him completely responsible, because he's not fully in control of what Lynyrd Skynyrd means in the larger culture. At some point he stopped being the creator of Skynyrd's image and started being a product of it.

In 2012, Lynyrd Skynyrd announced that it no longer planned to fly the Confederate flag in concert, a tradition that extended back to the early days of the band. "It became such an issue about race and stuff," guitarist Gary Rossington explained to CNN. Johnny Van Zant echoed Rossington, adding, "If nothing else, we grew up loving the old blues artists and Ray Charles. We just didn't want to be associated with that type of thing."

Skynyrd fans responded by excoriating the band online with vitriolic comments likening them to the Dixie Chicks and referencing the totemistic "Sweet Home Alabama." ("Southern man don't need THEM around anyhow.") And Skynyrd promptly backtracked—Rossington reassured the fan base in a website post that he "only stated my opinion" about the flag being "unfairly used" and that the Stars and Bars truly means "heritage not hate."

YOUR FAVORITE BAND IS KILLING ME

Like the Colbert tweet, "Sweet Home Alabama" was a joke that some people took seriously. When the writer explained his intentions, the focus shifted back to an (incorrect) interpretation that spoke to a marginalized group of individuals. Stephen Colbert and Ronnie Van Zant were more important for accidental reasons than they were on purpose. For Skynyrd's core fans, "Sweet Home Alabama" (and the Confederate flag) represent a prideful resistance to northern scorn and unilateral conformity. That prideful resistance is ultimately more important for those people than Lynyrd Skynyrd's music. Faced with choosing between the flag and Skynyrd, it was decided that Skynyrd could walk. Lynyrd Skynyrd had to either accept this reality or defy it. They chose the former.

In 2006, Neil Young released *Living with War*, a collection of songs addressing the wars in Iraq and Afghanistan and the political climate that facilitated them in the most direct, literal language imaginable. "Let's Impeach the President" is about impeaching George W. Bush. "Lookin' for a Leader" is about Neil Young lookin' for a leader. You catch my drift. Young wrote and recorded the songs quickly in order to maximize their timeliness. The music is purely utilitarian on *Living with War*; Young recycled old Crazy Horse riffs as a delivery system for the words. He even employed a backing choir composed of dozens of amateur singers in order to give *Living with War* the feel of a political rally.

Because *Living with War* was presented as a polemic as much as a record, people tended to like or dislike it based on their feelings about war. Antiwar people were inclined to like it and praise Young for his rhetorical bravery. (Since there's significant overlap between antiwar people and music critics, *Living with War* became one of Young's best-reviewed albums of the twenty-first century.) Pro-war people were inclined to dislike *Living with War* and criticize Young for simplifying complex issues with poorly written songs.

I am an antiwar person, but my opinion of *Living with War* is closer to the pro-war side. I don't question Young's sincerity and wholeheartedly support his right to make a record implying that the president is a war criminal. I happen to agree with a lot of what he says in his songs. I just think that *Living with War*, as an album, belongs in the bottom third of Young's discography. I don't find it the least bit intriguing as art, especially a decade later. As a "bad" Neil Young record, *Living with War* is not half as interesting to revisit as *Trans* or *Everybody's Rockin'*. (Young himself has all but buried *Time Fades Away* because he supposedly doesn't like it, and that album is *amazing*.) There's no subtext to *Living with War;* it's all text, and the text reads like a *Daily Kos* post. A lot of people found Young's anger on *Living with War* to be liberating in 2006. But it's not a "brave" record; Young was parroting what much of his audience was already saying. *Living with War* was his version of *God & Guns*.

"'Southern Man' [and] 'Alabama' are a little misguided," Randy Newman once said of Young's "issue" songs. "It's too easy a target. I don't think he knows enough about it." Young seems to agree with Newman about "Southern Man," telling his biographer Jimmy McDonough, "I don't feel like it's particularly relevant." While "Southern Man" is among Young's best-known songs, he doesn't play it very often. Between 1970 and 2014, he played it 168 times; meanwhile, he played the apolitical "Cinnamon Girl" 669 times.

What Ronnie Van Zant objected to in "Sweet Home Alabama" wasn't just the blanket characterization of southerners as bloodthirsty racists in those Neil Young songs but also the larger cultural and social conventions that allowed an artist of Neil Young's stature to disparage millions of individuals and appear to be noble for doing so. Neil Young and Lynyrd Skynyrd were pandering to different audiences with "Southern Man" and "Sweet Home Alabama"—it's just that Young was pandering to the *right* audience, as far as the media was concerned.

Young supported *Living with War* by reuniting with David Crosby, Stephen Stills, and Graham Nash for the Freedom of Speech tour. Young's relationship with his on-again, off-again bandmates has always been curious and seemingly one-sided. Young is the most talented and respected member of the group; this appears to be accepted even within the confines of the band. Less generous observers view Crosby, Stills, and Nash as Young's deadweight, and that's precisely how Young himself described them in the song "Thrasher," from *Rust Never Sleeps*. Whenever Young drifts back into the group, he tends to keep the other guys at arm's length. During Crosby, Stills, Nash & Young's infamous "doom tour," in 1974—the first stadium-level rock tour to become synonymous with rock-star egotism run amok and *Scarface* levels of coke consumption—Young traveled alone by RV while his fellow musicians lived it up on private jets.

And yet in the 2008 Neil Young–directed concert documentary, *CSNY/Déjà Vu*, it's apparent why Young chose to tour *Living with War* with the group rather than on his own. The film's central theme—more central than the wars Young is protesting—is that *Living with War* revitalized CSNY's reputation as a politically oriented rock group. Presenting "Let's Impeach the President" via the same vehicle that Young used for "Ohio" had greater cultural meaning than if Young had toured the album under his name alone. It elevated Y as much as it elevated C, S, and N. An ABC News reporter whom Young had "embedded" in the tour voices this directly at the end of the film: the point of the tour wasn't to change minds or effect social change, he says, his tone suggesting that to believe otherwise would be naive. It was to merge the group's present with its history.

CSNY's protest-oriented concerts in *Déjà Vu* never seem truly provocative. Rather, they seem like an angrier form of '60s nostalgia. As the film's director, Young doesn't dispute this notion, judging by his choice of interview subjects. For instance, outside a concert at the Red Rocks Amphitheatre, near Denver, a doughy-faced college bro enthuses about finally having a chance to rally against his generation's very own version of Vietnam. (If only wars weren't so derivative. Someday a grunge-rock war will arrive to wipe out the hair-metal wars.)

For protests to appear significant, there needs to be an equally loud and conveniently dumb opposing force. *Déjà Vu* presents the opponent about a third of the way into the movie. During the early stages of the tour, CSNY's audience is depicted as enlightened and levelheaded. Even people who support the war don't react furiously during the concerts' most hectoring moments. This changes when the tour arrives in Atlanta. Suddenly the audience interviews become much more drunken, and every sentence ends with someone screaming "Bullshit!"

One particularly scary man—who, I can only assume, is named Cletus D. Asskicker—glowers into the camera and demands that the senior citizens saying mean things about the president onstage suck his dick. Now, I assume nobody in

CSNY was in actual danger from this dude or anybody else. But still, the hostility is bracing and crudely effective as a storytelling device. As viewers we're meant to watch *Déjà Vu* and admire CSNY for not going the safe route and simply strumming "Teach Your Children" for complacent boomers. If I watch the film and take it at face value, I *do* admire this. But if I examine *Déjà Vu* at all beyond this surface impression, it starts to look like a rigged game.

I don't know that Young intended to depict southerners as brutish, ignorant sumbitches in *Déjà Vu,* just as he had in "Southern Man." But I suspect that the film and the song both came from similar impulses. "Southern Man" was written in anger about the treatment of blacks during the civil rights era. Young wrote it while living in Southern California not long after Los Angeles was ravaged by some of the worst race riots in US history. He could've very well called his antiracism song "California Man," but "Southern Man" was an easier, more potent signifier. People choose the misunderstandings that ring truest, and a person screaming nonsense is scarier when he's doing it with a drawl.

Neil Young and Lynyrd Skynyrd were not really at war; they were stand-ins for vast, ill-defined constituencies on the left and right eager to tear each other apart. Eventually the dialogue they inspired transcended them. In order to not disappear, they had to shout along with their respective sides.

CHAPTER 15

You're Nobody (Till Somebody Kills You)

(Biggie vs. Tupac)

THERE'S ONLY ONE rivalry that I was required by law to write about in this book, and that rivalry is the Notorious B.I.G. vs. Tupac Shakur. (Or, if you happen to live on the coast, Tupac vs. Biggie. Tupac eternally rules the West.) I suspect that many readers will turn immediately to this chapter, as Biggie vs. Tupac is the most obvious example of my thesis. It might also make you want to put this book down immediately and never think about pop rivalries ever again. Contemplating Biggie vs. Tupac tends to make obsessing about pop rivalries seem silly to the point of recklessness. It stops being fun once you realize that taking this stuff too seriously can result in people getting killed.

You could call Biggie vs. Tupac the greatest rivalry in pop history, so long as "greatest" is understood to mean "saddest" and "most tragic." I watched it unfold along with the rest of my generation; in retrospect, Biggie vs. Tupac stands as the logical extreme of the culture's obsession with authenticity in the '90s, even more than Kurt Cobain's suicide. A suicide requires only the act of one person; Biggie vs. Tupac was a conspiracy that will probably never be fully unraveled.

It was predicated almost entirely on misinterpreted statements and misconstrued incidents: here were two hip-hop superstars portrayed in the media as mortal enemies, largely because they were situated on opposing coasts in the nation's largest cities. One was a svelte, conventionally handsome, deeply philosophical Bob Marley figure, and the other was a fat, unconventionally handsome, persuasively suave James Bond–style hedonist. Because they looked the part of rivals, Biggie and Tupac were encouraged to play up their public animosities and reinforce their warring personas. Incredibly, horrifically, inevitably, they both wound up murdered within six months of each other. But they've lived on as bookending archetypes that practically every major rapper has emulated since—Biggie is the methodical fatalist determined to enjoy his empire in spite of mounting paranoia, and Tupac is the free-wheeling messianic figure impulsively (knowingly?) creating his life's work in a limited time frame. These are characters that other artists reboot again and again.

It's impossible to properly explain to a person who wasn't alive at the time how and why this happened. The Internet has made us accustomed to perceiving conflict as both unreal and omnipresent. Flame wars occur now as a matter of course, and they typically end with a barely acknowledged whimper. Biggie vs. Tupac wasn't like that. It was very real and lasting in the most brutal way imaginable.

Nobody will ever take a pop-star rivalry that seriously ever again. Biggie vs. Tupac endures as a line of demarcation that cannot be crossed. This wasn't immediately apparent: the first *Beef* documentary, released in 2003, ends with an ominous overview of the conflict between 50 Cent and Ja Rule, which seemed to be on the verge of a Biggie vs. Tupac–type reckoning. Outside of Eminem, Ja Rule and 50 Cent were probably the biggest rappers on the planet in the early aughts, and there were some minor parallels between their rivalry and that of Biggie and Tupac. Like Tupac, 50 Cent was famous for being shot numerous times and surviving; meanwhile, in *Beef*, 50 chides Ja Rule for *wanting* to be like Tupac while also expressing disbelief that anybody would want to be like Ja Rule.

The 50 Cent–Ja Rule feud did turn violent on a few occasions—50 Cent supposedly clocked Ja Rule in Atlanta in 2000, and soon afterward, Ja Rule's associate Black Child claimed responsibility (and self-defense) for stabbing 50 Cent at a New York recording studio. But for the most part 50 Cent vs. Ja Rule was settled on the charts, and 50 Cent destroyed his antagonist. It got so bad for Ja Rule that he was reduced to proposing a détente moderated by Louis Farrakhan on MTV that was to take place right before the release of his album *Blood in My Eye*. It was part publicity stunt and part capitulation to 50 Cent's enormous popularity in the wake of his 2002 debut LP, *Get Rich or Die Tryin'*. By virtue of his power in the market and the support of fellow superstars such as Eminem, Dr. Dre, and DMX, 50 Cent had neutralized Ja Rule via a bloodless takeover.

For all the hip-hop feuds that followed—enough to justify two other *Beef* films and a TV series—they never approached Biggie vs. Tupac in terms of stature or body count. It's been said that John Belushi's death was a wake-up call for other movie stars enjoying recreational speedballs in the early '80s. I suspect a similar case can be made for Biggie vs. Tupac. It's the ultimate example of "taking it too far": on some level, Biggie vs. Tupac has probably saved countless lives, and not just those of rappers.

Everybody knows that Biggie vs. Tupac ended in gunfire, but the rivalry inadvertently began with gunfire, too. To rehash a well-worn story: In 1994, Tupac was robbed and shot several times in the lobby of Quad Recording Studios, in Manhattan. Shortly after the attack, Biggie released "Who Shot Ya?" as the B side to his single "Big Poppa." Biggie and Sean "Puffy" Combs happened to be recording at Quad when Tupac was shot, and it's long been theorized that they knew about the attack in advance, though Biggie and Puffy made a point of going on MTV to deny it. When Tupac heard "Who Shot Ya?" he interpreted the track as a taunt, even though it had supposedly been recorded before the shooting. (Biggie's insistence on performing the song live after Tupac was shot didn't discourage this interpretation.) "Who Shot Ya?" compelled Tupac to implicate Biggie and the owners of Biggie's record label, Bad Boy—Combs and Andre Harrell—for ordering the hit.

Let's pause for a moment. It's crazy that this issue, at this specific moment, wasn't nipped in the bud. If representatives from Biggie's and Tupac's camps had somehow been able to meet and hash out the beef, it seems possible (if not likely) that things would've turned out differently later on. Biggie vs. Tupac might've been a funny footnote discussed on *I Love the '90s* TV specials. Instead, almost a year later, Tupac became an associate of Suge Knight, who posted $1.4 million in bail in order to spring Tupac from a Florida prison while Tupac's sexual assault case was on appeal.

A former college football player who played two games in the pros as a replacement player for the Los Angeles Rams during the NFL's strike-shortened 1987 season, Knight subsequently entered the music business as a promoter and body-guard for artists such as Bobby Brown. Knight already had a reputation as a hothead—he was arrested twice during a single month in '87, once for hitting his girlfriend and once for shooting a man three times while attempting to steal the man's car. In 1989 Knight formed his own music-publishing company and made his first big score when he secured a percentage of Vanilla Ice's hit "Ice Ice Baby" for his client Mario Johnson, the song's cowriter. (It's part of hip-hop lore that Knight threatened to throw Vanilla Ice off a balcony, though the involved parties deny it.) Two years later, Knight established Death Row Records with ex-N.W.A. member Dr. Dre, vowing that it would become the Motown of the '90s. But Knight never fully left his violent past behind him.

When you start associating with Suge Knight, no matter the circumstances, you have reached the point of no return. Such was the case for Tupac.

Knight had his own beef with Combs. Knight's friend Jake Robles had been fatally shot at a party in Atlanta hosted by Jermaine Dupri, and Knight blamed Puffy. It's not clear to what degree this influenced Tupac, but it certainly didn't improve the situation with Biggie. This was the setup for Knight's infamous provocation of Combs and the East Coast rap elite at the 1995 Source Awards at Madison Square Garden's Paramount Theater, which stoked the flames publicly.

"To all you artists out there who don't wanna be on a record label where the executive producer's all up in the videos, all on the records, dancin', then come to Death Row!" Knight said from the stage, obviously referring to Puffy, in the town where Bad Boy was headquartered. It was practically an official declaration of war.

In his songs, Tupac took repeated shots at Biggie, including the claim in "Hit 'Em Up" that he slept with Biggie's wife, Faith Evans. Some listeners believed Biggie responded in "Long Kiss Goodnight"—the lines "Slugs hit your chest, tapped the spine, flatline / Heard through the grapevine you got fucked four times" seem suspiciously pertinent—but it was never confirmed as an official diss.

The primary reason I didn't want to write about Biggie vs. Tupac is that there is so much we still don't know about how they died or what their true intentions were in going after each other. For instance, it's still unclear whether their murders even resulted from their rivalry. It seems likely that they did, but the murders have never been solved or properly explained. The 2011 book *Murder Rap*, written by former LAPD detective Greg Kading, fingered Combs for commissioning the murders of Shakur and Knight, then accused Knight of paying for Biggie's murder. Both the presumed triggermen were gang members who were later shot to death—Tupac's alleged killer, Orlando Anderson, died outside a Compton record store in 1998, and Biggie's supposed murderer, Wardell "Poochie" Fouse, was killed in 2003 after multiple shots were fired into his back while he rode a motorcycle through Compton. This goes beyond the usual pop-star feud. This is real-life Keyser Söze stuff.

As the murders of Biggie and Tupac drift deeper into history, it's increasingly difficult to talk about them as real, tangible events. The mystery has only deepened; conspiracy theories about cover-ups and crooked cops on both sides of the investigation have made the truth more elusive, if not obscured it completely. It's been theorized that Knight engineered Tupac's death because he was upset that Tupac was about to leave

Death Row. It's been speculated that several LAPD officers—including Rafael Perez, David Mack, and Nino Durden, who were named in a wrongful death lawsuit filed by Biggie's family in 2007 and dismissed from the force three years later—were enlisted by Knight to kill Biggie. In 2002, a Pulitzer Prize–winning reporter for the *Los Angeles Times* named Chuck Philips reported that Biggie visited several Crips gang members in Las Vegas on the night Tupac was shot, essentially overseeing the murder, even insisting that they use his gun. Six years later, Philips was forced to retract an article that advanced a theory about Biggie and Combs having prior knowledge of Tupac's '94 shooting, which had originally sparked the rivalry, when it was revealed that his reporting relied partly on forged FBI documents given to him.

Twenty years later, parsing all this is like trying to prove or disprove that JFK was really killed by Lee Harvey Oswald. Biggie vs. Tupac is so fucked-up it makes thinking like Oliver Stone seem reasonable.

What makes Biggie vs. Tupac a defining pop rivalry isn't so much what actually happened but what we imagine happened. This applies to the media coverage of the rivalry, which arguably made the situation worse by intensifying the burgeoning mythology. But it also derives from the music and the way it was contextualized after both men were gone. Biggie and Tupac capped their careers by releasing brilliant double albums—*Life After Death* for Biggie, *All Eyez on Me* for Tupac—that balance party jams with relentless paranoia. (I suppose you could argue that Shakur's true career capper is *The Don Killuminati: The 7 Day Theory*, which was recorded shortly before he was murdered and released under the stage name Makaveli two months after his death. But I prefer to go with the last

record that Shakur actually signed off on.) It's trite and borderline offensive to suggest that Biggie and Tupac made art
that predicted their own demise: first and foremost, they were
entertainers, and they constructed entertaining personas that
were electric in the context of plush production and magnetic
lyrical swagger. Those albums don't play in the manner of
Nirvana's *MTV Unplugged in New York,* on which Kurt Cobain
basically plays at his own wake four months early. Biggie and
Tupac sound alive—powerfully, vividly, stubbornly—on their
records, regardless of their preoccupation with their own
mortality.

Biggie and Tupac were unlucky in that the fanciful worlds
they brought to life on their records came true in real life. This
typically isn't an occupational hazard for musicians—Marilyn
Manson has been singing about self-destructing on bad drugs
and kinky sex for more than twenty years, yet he's lived to see
middle age and now looks strikingly like Nicolas Cage rolled in
baking flour. Because Biggie and Tupac died in such a violent,
public, and unfathomable manner, it was natural for listeners
to merge the fantasy of their songs with the reality of their star-
crossed lives.

Life After Death ends with a song called "You're Nobody (Til
Somebody Kills You)," a takeoff on the old crooner standard
"You're Nobody till Somebody Loves You." *All Eyez on Me*
concludes with a song with a similarly eerie title, "Heaven
Ain't Hard 2 Find." Neither song is as prescient as it might
seem. The lyrics of "You're Nobody" read like an action-movie
screenplay, vividly describing "gun-testing," "coke-measuring,"
and "spending chips at Manny's," the steak-house chain. It's
true that Biggie spent time in prison before he was famous—
he was pinched in 1991 for dealing crack cocaine in North

Carolina and served nine months. Before that, he was sentenced to five years' probation in 1990 on weapons charges. But Biggie was hardly a kingpin. Very stupid people will hear "You're Nobody" as scary, first-person nihilism, but it's really just a young guy describing some incredibly cool shit he probably saw in a movie once. (Biggie refers to himself as Nicky Tarantino, alluding to Joe Pesci's character from *Casino* and, presumably, Quentin Tarantino.)

The last song on *All Eyez on Me* is romantic in a different way—in "Heaven Ain't Hard 2 Find," Tupac is at his sweetest, asking, "Are you afraid of a thug? / And have you ever made love / With candles and bubbles sipping in your tub?" Does a man who expects to die talk about having sex in bathtubs? Isn't sex in a bathtub the very essence of life, especially when you're twenty-five and on top of the world?

As I write this, Justin Bieber is the most controversial pop star alive. Nobody seems remotely close. It's possible to make a case for Miley Cyrus, but she's a cultural provocateur. Outraging the public is supposed to be what her art is about; taking the bait integrates the listener into her music and iconography, as offended observers are as vital to Cyrus's aesthetic as voluptuous backup dancers or Terry Richardson's skeezy music videos are.

Bieber provokes the public with his personal life. I'm reluctant to delve into Bieber's arrest record, as the statistics will be instantly outdated as soon as this book comes out. Every other week, Bieber is detained for doing something stupid. He drives recklessly and commits acts of vandalism like you and I take out the garbage.

Bieber has entered that rare zone for famous people where

the public expects you to behave outrageously, which therefore empowers you to make even worse decisions. (The king of this zone is Charles Barkley, who could solicit oral sex from a prostitute during TNT's pregame NBA show and receive only mild admonishment from Ernie Johnson.) Bieber once was caught on *multiple* videos using the *n* word, and it not only didn't end his career, it was also forgotten after about a week. If I had to guess what Bieber is doing at this very moment, I would bet that he is smoking weed in the parking lot of a Carl's Jr. If there's a Carl's Jr. in your town, call the police and ask that they do a quick sweep of the premises, just in case.

The consensus view of Bieber is that he is yet another victim of "too much too soon." Becoming a superstar when he was a teenager who resembled a fetus has fixed him in perpetual adolescence. Bieber's world has been set up to cater to his every whim, ensuring that his life will only get worse in ensuing years. Eventually he will succeed in alienating the public, damning him to a long life of irrelevance and the collateral damage of never having had a proper childhood.

If Bieber is headed down a bad road, he's probably not pointed toward the worst destination. No matter how fucked-up he seems to be in terms of his interpersonal development, I doubt that Justin Bieber will die prematurely.

This might sound weird to point out, but pop stars don't die like they used to. In the '60s, '70s, '80s, and '90s, pop stars died all the time. Many of the most popular and important artists of the twentieth century died in their prime: Elvis Presley, Buddy Holly, Otis Redding, Jimi Hendrix, Janis Joplin, Gram Parsons, Nick Drake, Cass Elliot, Jim Croce, Marc Bolan, Bob Marley, and Karen Carpenter all perished at an early age. Many of the most iconic bands had at least one member die before the age of forty: the Beatles, the Rolling Stones, Led Zeppelin, the Who, the Beach Boys, the Doors, the Allman Brothers Band, Lynyrd Skynyrd, AC/DC, the Sex Pistols, Joy Division, and the Minutemen all had significant casualties. During this time, so many famous musicians died from choking on their own vomit that it became one of the best jokes in *This Is Spinal Tap*. For a while it was relatively common for pop stars to be shot to death by people who presumably liked them: John Lennon was murdered by an obsessive fan, and Marvin Gaye was cut down by his own father.

In the early '90s, major pop stars were still dying young at a steady clip. They died in plane crashes (Stevie Ray Vaughan), from overdoses (Johnny Thunders and Def Leppard's Steve Clark), from AIDS (Freddie Mercury), from self-inflicted gunshot wounds (Kurt Cobain), from fan-inflicted gunshot wounds (Selena), and from living extremely gross lifestyles (GG Allin). Then, after the deaths of Biggie and Tupac, something changed. The death rate among iconic musical figures suddenly declined dramatically.

Below is a list of noteworthy pop-star deaths since Biggie vs. Tupac. It is not a list of every pop-star death—I haven't included musicians who died of natural causes at an advanced age (such as Johnny Cash and James Brown) or who passed on in middle age from relatively common ailments (such as Warren Zevon and Levon Helm). I also tried to limit this list to noteworthy deaths—no disrespect to the bassist of Blues Traveler or the guy who designed the awesome soundscapes for the Mars Volta's first record, but I'm only counting legends who died before their time.

Jeff Buckley, 1997, drowning
Michael Hutchence of INXS, 1997, suicide
Aaliyah, 2001, plane crash
Layne Staley of Alice in Chains, 2002, drug overdose
Lisa "Left Eye" Lopes of TLC, 2002, car accident
Jam Master Jay of Run-D.M.C., 2002, murdered
Elliott Smith, 2003, suicide
Dimebag Darrell of Pantera, 2004, murdered
Ol' Dirty Bastard, 2004, drug overdose
J Dilla, 2006, lupus
Jay Reatard, 2010, cocaine toxicity
Amy Winehouse, 2011, alcohol poisoning
Scott Weiland, 2015, drug overdose

Now consider the list of people who haven't died. With the exception of the Beatles, all the artists who put out the bestselling albums of the aughts are still alive: 'NSync, Norah Jones, Eminem, Usher, Linkin Park, Creed, Britney Spears, and Nelly. The same goes for the makers of the bestselling songs: Flo Rida, Lady Gaga, Jason Mraz, Timbaland and OneRepublic, the Black Eyed Peas, Soulja Boy, Coldplay, Taylor Swift, and Katy Perry. None of the major rappers of the modern era—Jay Z, Outkast, Master P, DMX, 50 Cent, Ludacris, Lil Jon, T.I., Kanye West, Lil Wayne, Drake, Kendrick Lamar—have died. All the most popular rock bands—including Radiohead, Green Day, the Foo Fighters, the White Stripes, Muse, Arcade Fire, the Black Keys, Vampire Weekend—have remained intact. Country superstars such as Kenny Chesney, Brad Paisley, Tim McGraw, and Eric Church might sing about drinking whiskey, but none ended up like Hank Williams.

There are four possible explanations for this.

(1) POP STARS ARE HEALTHIER NOW

Out of the thirteen deaths listed above, roughly 38 percent are drug-related. If you attribute suicide to untreated mental illness, that still means just under 50 percent of the list is made up of accidental demises. It seems generally true that pop stars these days are aware of the risks of abusing hard chemicals and will find a way to stop doing it before they are killed. The most obvious example is Ryan Adams. Throughout the aughts, Adams (along with that bozo from the Libertines) was among the most demonstrative consumers of drugs in popular music. Adams occasionally referenced his drug use in his songs, but more often he just appeared to be totally hammered. In another time, he might very well have died. Instead Adams moved to Los Angeles, started hiking, and married Mandy Moore (whom he later divorced in 2015). He'll probably live to be 112 and release 1,012 albums.

(2) POP STARS ARE LUCKIER NOW

Freakish, flat-out fucked-up pop-star deaths occur with less frequency now. R & B singer Johnny Ace mistakenly shot himself in the head with a gun he thought was unloaded in 1954. Chicago guitarist Terry Kath accidentally unloaded a bullet into his skull in 1978. Yardbirds singer Keith Relf was electrocuted by his own guitar in 1976. Acrobatic soul star Jackie Wilson had a heart attack onstage in 1975, went into a coma that lasted nine years, then died in 1984.

Now, Jeff Buckley, Aaliyah, Jam Master Jay, and Dimebag Darrell weren't very lucky. Buckley drowned in a Memphis river. Aaliyah's plane crashed while en route from a music-video shoot. Jam Master Jay was murdered in a recording studio. Dimebag Darrell was unfortunate to have a deranged fan who blamed him for the breakup of Pantera and retaliated by gunning him down while he was onstage in Ohio with his new band, Damageplan. But generally, rubbing a pop star for good luck is a solid policy.

(3) POP STARS ARE UNDER MORE SCRUTINY NOW, WHICH MAKES DYING MORE DIFFICULT

In 2011, Caleb Followill of the semishitty and periodically enjoyable rock band Kings of Leon appeared onstage in Dallas in a visibly intoxicated state. Near the end of the show he said the following: "I'm gonna go backstage, and I'm gonna vomit. [Then] I'm gonna drink a beer, and I'm gonna come out and play three more songs." Then he proceeded to *not* come out, presumably because he got lost somewhere between "I'm gonna vomit" and "I'm gonna play three more songs." Some version of this scenario has played out approximately 1.6 million times in rock-show history. And yet because Followill was caught on video and the incident was subsequently run through the Internet news cycle, tour dates were canceled, and Kings of Leon went on a short hiatus.

Kings of Leon is a cheesy rock band, and the members were caught on tape acting like buffoons. But this incident also illustrates how little patience the public has now for displays of decadence. Being too drunk to perform used to be considered the ultimate in rock-star cool; the mythology of the Replacements is based almost entirely on this idea. But now it's perceived to be pathetic—which it is, but it always was: it just wasn't always thought of that way.

Decadence is only acceptable in hip-hop, though even rappers are no longer allowed to enjoy the drug-taking, groupie-banging lifestyle. On the cover of Drake's 2011 LP, *Take Care,* the Toronto rapper sits at a table in a gold-colored room covered in expensive-looking art. The table is ornamented with an elegant candleholder, and Drake is holding a motherfucking goblet. And Drake looks miserable, because motherfucking goblets now signify a depressing lifestyle.

(4) POP STARS HAVE SUBLIMINALLY ABSORBED THE LESSONS OF BIGGIE VS. TUPAC, WHICH HAS MADE THEM SAFER

Let's circle back to Justin Bieber. He has long claimed to be a Tupac fan. When Bieber appeared on the radio station Hot 97 in 2012, he said he could "spit" Tupac verses at age eight. (Bieber's father, Jeremy, was a fan.) During a trip to South America in 2013 for his *Believe* tour, Bieber Instagrammed graffiti tags he spray-painted on buildings in Bogotá, one of which was "RIP Tupac." As Bieber has gotten older, he has dressed more and more like Tupac, appropriating various Pac-like bandannas and tattoos.

What Bieber hasn't done is participate in a rapidly escalating conflict with another superstar surrounded by a scary entourage. He hasn't courted a violent lifestyle in a serious or authentic manner. He has not introduced Suge Knight into his inner circle. He has dabbled in Tupac's iconography, but he hasn't come close to approaching the void that swallowed Tupac whole. By the time Bieber was memorizing Tupac lyrics, Tupac had already been dead for five years. Tupac has always been a dead person as far as Bieber is concerned. He grew up in a world where a white Canadian could pretend to be Tupac without suffering the consequences of doing so.

Arguing that Tupac's death indirectly spared Justin Bieber's life is vaguely obscene, I know. I just want so badly for Biggie vs. Tupac to mean something. Overanalyzing pop rivalries is enjoyable escapism, because most of them are harmless. But thinking about Biggie vs. Tupac gives me no pleasure. I want to believe that Biggie vs. Tupac made subsequent generations smarter, but even if it did, that doesn't change how pointless it was. I am pushing to find meaning when in fact there can be no meaning at all. Two young men died for no good reason, and their murderers will likely never be brought to justice. There's nothing deep about it. It's as empty as empty can be.

CHAPTER 16
Actual Otter

(Toby Keith vs. the Dixie Chicks)

I BELIEVE IN America. And I believe in "I believe in America." When Bonasera the undertaker stares out from the blackness of Vito Corleone's office at the start of *The Godfather* and gives his speech about how America has made his fortune and allowed him to raise his family in affluence but now he must seek justice outside the legal system, I get what Francis Ford Coppola is trying to convey. This is a man soliciting murder in a back room at a mob wedding. The point of the scene is to undercut platitudes about America with the reality of how the sausage is really made in this country.

I understand the irony. But I also appreciate "I believe in America" at face value. Here is a well-off man who came from nothing asking another well-off man who came from nothing for a favor. What an accomplishment for these guys, to be in a position where they can barter over a killing and then enjoy a private concert by Johnny Fontane. Only in America!

Being an American requires wrestling with a central contradition: we are the best, and we are the worst. We make dreams come true, and many of those dreams turn out to be nightmares. It is impossible to feel just one way about all this. I marvel at and am disgusted by the United States of America on a daily basis. As an American, I hope for us to be better and own the times when we're not. I own it all.

I guess you could call me a patriot, though I prefer to say I'm a long-suffering fan who enjoys the songs everybody knows (democracy, the Bill of Rights, defeating the Nazis) but finds the overall catalog to be maddeningly inconsistent. (The Emancipation Proclamation is one humdinger of a single, but the four hundred years of slavery in the deep cuts is an irredeemable slog.) But fine: if it is easier from a semantic perspective to call me a patriot, I'll own that, too. Being a patriot means that I believe in a version of America that's basically imaginary, but I hope one day it will become real. The America I love derives from John Ford films such as *The Man Who Shot Liberty Valance*—the one in which John Wayne kills Lee Marvin so that Jimmy Stewart can get elected to Congress. Tell me: What's more American than that?

The plot of *The Man Who Shot Liberty Valance* will sound familiar even if you haven't seen the film, because it's an intrinsically American story. At the start of the movie, Jimmy Stewart is badly beaten by Lee Marvin (who plays the film's titular character) during a robbery. Afterward, he is discovered and taken to town by John Wayne. Stewart and Wayne don't like each other—Stewart is a Poindextery man of laws, and John Wayne is John freaking Wayne. Not long after their first encounter, John Wayne calls Jimmy Stewart a tenderfoot, which is code in John Ford movies for "pussy." But the animus doesn't last. Over time, Stewart and Wayne achieve a grudging respect for each other, even though they're vying for the same woman's affections.

The climax of *Liberty Valance* occurs when Stewart finally confronts Marvin in a shoot-out. At first it appears that Stewart kills him, but it's actually John Wayne who hits Liberty Valance square in the chest from a spot in the distance. John Wayne allows the townspeople to believe that Jimmy Stewart is the hero because he recognizes that his town is changing, and it needs tender-footed men like Stewart who can lead them toward a more civilized future. Wayne lets Stewart get the credit and the girl for the good of society. Brute force might've been required in this instance, but the possibility of higher ideals in the future is preserved.

The last time I watched *The Man Who Shot Liberty Valance*, it made me think of what America was like right after 9/11. That was the last time this country's conflicting John Wayne and Jimmy Stewart sensibilities seemed like they might be able to coexist in a kind of harmony. You could somewhat reductively describe Wayne in *Liberty Valance* as a conservative archetype and Stewart as a progressive archetype. Maybe I've been brainwashed by John Ford, but I feel like America is at its best when we can be both those guys at the same time—capable of kicking ass when pushed in a corner but determined to be a little more thoughtful about the world the other 99 percent of the time.

People were so shell-shocked after the World Trade Center collapsed that finding common ground suddenly seemed like a rational idea. Alas, it didn't last long. In real life, John Wayne and Jimmy Stewart never team up for a common cause. Instead they seem to always open fire on each other. And this seriously bums me out, because I have affection for both those dudes.

It's like my affection for both the Dixie Chicks and Toby Keith.

In May of 2002, Toby Keith released a pointed 9/11 anthem, "Courtesy of the Red, White, and Blue (The Angry American)." Depending on your point of view at the time, "The Angry American" was either a righteous expression of feeling pissed off over the deaths of three thousand Americans or an imbecilic call to arms pandering to this country's jingoistic impulses. The music—which attempts to sonically convey the iconography of a bald eagle riding a dirt bike—was beside the point. "The Angry American" could only be loved or hated based on the sentiments of the lyrics. Soon even non–country fans were quoting "The Angry American"—specifically the lyric " 'Cause we'll put a boot in your ass / It's the American way." Everybody agreed that the lyric was accurate—it's just that half the country felt that this truth shouldn't be glorified.

Keith wrote "The Angry American" in just twenty minutes. The song is dedicated to his dad, who died eight months before 9/11. At first he declined to put it on an album and played it only during special concerts for the troops. Keith claimed he recorded "The Angry American" only because Commandant of the Marine Corps James L. Jones said it was his duty to put the tune on wax.

One month after "The Angry American" topped the country singles chart—just in time for the Fourth of July—Natalie Maines of the Dixie Chicks called the song ignorant. Her band's own military-themed single, "Travelin' Soldier," came out not long after, and while it wasn't crafted intentionally as a response to "The Angry American," its lilting, bluegrass-tinged somberness nonetheless seemed like a rebuke to Keith's hot-dog, arena-rock sloganeering. Whereas Keith pushed for America to put its foot in the dastardly backsides of its enemies, the plainspoken narrative of "Travelin' Soldier" soberly calculated the human cost of such bravado. The guy in "Travelin' Soldier" is ultimately killed in Vietnam, but the song was clearly a warning about the tolls of war in the months leading up to the invasion of Iraq.

A few words about Toby Keith before we continue: I used to not be able to stand the guy. But now I've come to view him as a lovable lunkhead. Toby Keith is like a beer commercial with arms and legs. Toby Keith is like the volleyball sequence from *Top Gun* multiplied by the climactic karate-tournament-championship scene from *The Karate Kid*. Toby Keith is essentially the real-life Kenny Powers. My friend Joe calls Toby Keith the Ice Cube of country. Toby Keith owns.

If you hate Toby Keith, I fully understand. But if you like discovering that things you hate might in fact be a lot of fun, I suggest starting your Toby Keith education with *35 Biggest Hits*. (Have I mentioned that Toby has bushels and bushels of goddamn hits?) Then skip ahead to "I Wanna Talk About Me"—this is the one in which Toby raps (!) about his woman talking too much about herself and not enough about *meeee!* (I guess Joe would call it Toby Keith's "Check Yo Self.") The run of bangers after that on *35 Biggest Hits* is unstoppable. There's "Beer for My Horses," in which Toby and Willie Nelson organize a posse, smoke some fools, and then inspire a PETA boycott by getting their four-legged compadres supremely wasted. There's "Whiskey Girl," a harrowing song—disguised as a dumb-guy sex anthem—about loving an alcoholic. There's "American Soldier," which is what I imagine Bruce Springsteen sounds like to people who hate Bruce Springsteen. (I love Bruce

Springsteen more than almost anything, so "American Soldier" sounds to me like a solid *Lucky Town* outtake.)

"The Angry American" is situated amid these tracks on *35 Biggest Hits,* and it squares with them musically and philosophically. "The Angry American" shouldn't be taken any more seriously than the deliriously stupid chestnut on the single's flip side, "Who's Your Daddy?" Toby Keith is no polemicist. (For the record, he once claimed to be a registered Democrat, though he later changed to an independent.) He's a doer, not a thinker.

Keith responded to Maines's comments about "The Angry American" in typical doer-not-a-thinker fashion. Keith said Maines was the ignorant one because she wasn't as prolific a songwriter as he was, and who was she to demean a prolific songwriter? "She said anybody can write 'boot in your ass,' but she didn't," Keith argued. This was irrefutable — "boot in your ass" was strictly Toby Keith's property. *Ya burnt,* Maines.

Keith really stepped up the slams after Maines announced to a London audience in March of 2003 that she was ashamed to be from the same state as President George W. Bush. This caused a terrible shit storm for the Chicks, and Keith gleefully joined the group's growing corps of detractors. After that, when Keith played "The Angry American" live, he projected a Photoshop-altered image of Maines snuggling with Saddam Hussein up on the Jumbotron. Outside New York and Los Angeles, this was the equivalent of driving a monster truck over the Eiffel Tower — in terms of red-state pandering, it was a grand slam.

Maines's retort to Keith was intended to be subtle but instantly backfired. When the Dixie Chicks performed via remote broadcast on the Academy of Country Music Awards in May, Maines wore a T-shirt emblazoned with FUTK. A PR flack claimed it was short for "Friends united in truth and kindness," but everyone knew it was really short for "Fuck you, Toby Keith."

By August Keith publicly declared that he was backing off from the feud, saying that the recent death of a friend's infant daughter made him see the futility of fighting with Maines. But Keith had already emerged as the clear victor from a public-relations standpoint, at least among the people who bought country records. It's true that Maines's antiwar stance endeared her to *Rolling Stone* and other left-leaning media outlets that had previously ignored the Dixie Chicks. But inside the country-music base, Keith had irreparably damaged his rival's credibility.

In the 2006 documentary *Shut Up & Sing*, which follows the Dixie Chicks over the course of three years in the aftermath of what is referred to only as "the incident," a country-music disc jockey from San Antonio named Randy Carroll is asked to explain why so many radio stations dropped the Dixie Chicks so quickly from their playlists after the Dubya protest. Before this scene, the film does a good job of showing how massively popular the Dixie Chicks were over the previous four years, when the albums *Wide Open Spaces*, *Fly*, and *Home* went a combined twenty-eight times platinum. How could the most commercial group in country music go from being everywhere to nowhere, just like that?

Carroll insists that he wasn't upset about the Bush comment but rather was troubled by Maines's attitude toward Toby Keith. To him it signaled a "real contempt for what a whole lot of country-music listeners believe." The rest of *Shut Up & Sing* hardly dispels this perception. The most illuminating parts of the documentary show how far out of touch the Dixie Chicks and their handlers were about the early response to the anti-Bush controversy. The group's English manager even sees the uproar as a good thing initially. "Wouldn't it be great if we could get them, like, burning CDs and banning you from the radio?" he says in one early scene.

Several years later, in a *Rolling Stone* interview, Maines was openly hostile about her country-music past, admitting that she could no longer listen to the Dixie Chicks' second album, *Fly*, because the twang in her voice was so pronounced. "I always thought they accepted us in spite of the fact that we were different," Maines said of the country audience. "It shocked me and kind of grossed me out that people thought I would be a conservative right-winger, that I'd be a redneck."

To understand why the Dixie Chicks might've been perceived against Maines's will as rednecks, it's worth noting the moment in which they rose to superstardom. The Dixie Chicks' success came right after Shania Twain rewrote the rule book for country crossovers with her 1997 album, *Come On Over*, a record that had more in common with Def Leppard than with Dolly Parton. The Dixie Chicks were relatively modest musically, with a sound that harked back to country's sepia-colored past. This push-pull with tradition has existed in country music for decades. In the '70s, insurgents injected hippie culture into Nashville. In the '90s, that outsider element was arena rock. In the twenty-first century, it's hip-hop. Inevitably, the pendulum swings back to acoustic guitars and fiddles, because stalwarts will start complaining about "real country" losing its identity. The Dixie Chicks appealed precisely to those sorts of listeners (while managing to also appeal to the pop-leaning Shania people). Maines might've been liberal in her

personal ideology, but musically, she was one of country's reigning conservatives. Until her politics overwhelmed the music,
anyway.

For the next Dixie Chicks album, *Taking the Long Way,* they
decamped to Malibu to lay down tracks with rock Zen master
Rick Rubin and affable Red Hot Chili Peppers drummer Chad
Smith. It's a good record—like if Fleetwood Mac sacked Lind-
sey and Christine and replaced them with two Stevie clones.
Taking the Long Way sold two and a half million copies and cleaned
up at the Grammys. But most of the tour had to be scuttled because the Dixie Chicks could no longer sell any tickets.

In interviews, the Dixie Chicks made no attempt to reconcile
with estranged fans. Martie Maguire told *Time* that she would
"rather have a smaller following of really cool people who get
it, who will grow with us as we grow and are fans for life, than
people that have us in their five-disc changer with Reba McEntire and Toby Keith." The deliberate distinguishing of "really
cool people" from people who listen to Reba McEntire and
Toby Keith betrayed the way the Dixie Chicks regarded the
country audience. The weariness was understandable, given all
the death threats and diatribes they had endured in the previous three years. But whether by choice or necessity, the Dixie
Chicks had given up a huge following for a cadre of casual
admirers.

Several years later, the Dixie Chicks remained stuck in self-
imposed limbo, and Maines sounded chastened. "I feel like we
are tainted," Maines confessed to *Rolling Stone* in 2013. For now,
Taking the Long Way is the last Dixie Chicks record.

Here's a valuable lesson that's pertinent to the conversation
about pop-music rivalries: your taste in music isn't really all that

important when it comes to defining who you are as a person. It's not *un*important, particularly if the music you love forms a crucial part of how you view yourself. And it's certainly a fun topic to think and argue about. But if studying these rivalries teaches us anything, it's that what matters and what we *believe* matters in life often don't line up. In fact, our stupid beliefs can be the very thing that keeps us from realizing what's really real, which is that people are generally more similar than dissimilar and that we all want basically the same thing, which is for other people to like (or at least understand) us.

For many individuals this will hardly register as wisdom. It will merely be intuitive. But if you have ever proudly described yourself as a music geek, it may sound heretical. "Your taste in music says absolutely *something* about who you are as a person" is a central tenet of music geekdom. This idea was long ago carved in stone, handed down from heaven to Nick Hornby, and disseminated to the masses in *High Fidelity*. Throughout my teens and much of my twenties, I took it as gospel, even as I was confronted with ample evidence that definitively debunked the idea.

As I look back, it's obvious to me now how self-serving this belief is. The music geeks get to define what "good" taste is, as good taste will line up with whatever it is they like. It's not so much about judging others as it is about puffing out your chest. You define yourself against what you assume (sometimes rightly, more often not) other people are like, which is what everybody does when they're young.

This sort of thinking became less common once the Internet made it easy for anyone to pose as a music expert. Definitive knowledge of pretty much any artist and genre can be acquired from *Wikipedia* and Spotify. But you still see it every now and then when the media dismisses an unfashionable artist by perpetuating a stereotypical view of that artist's audience. It seems weird to have to point out that most metalheads are mild-mannered (even nebbishy) folks who have never worshipped Satan and that many One Direction fans (sorry: Directioners) aren't fourteen-year-old hormonal psychotics posting death threats on Facebook against enemies of Harry Styles. It's also bizarre that you have to remind people that not every country-music fan worships Sean Hannity, but even some country fans forget that sometimes.

But those are just generalities. Let's get specific. Let's talk about Lee Atwater.

Lee Atwater is largely forgotten today, but in the '80s and '90s, he was perhaps our nation's most famous and most influential political operative. A pivotal campaign adviser for Ronald Reagan and George H. W. Bush, and a mentor to George W. Bush's top henchman, Karl Rove, Atwater changed the way elections were waged and won. Atwater set a new baseline for ruthless cunning in modern American politics, using wedge issues such as abortion and school prayer to divide the electorate against itself. In the process he preyed upon the prejudices of the public for the personal gain of his candidates. Though he was only forty when he died, in 1991, Atwater's mark on this country can still be seen today, to the dubious benefit of us all.

My fascination with Lee Atwater can probably be traced to that opening scene from *The Godfather*. He personifies how complicated a statement like "I believe in America" can be. He was a self-made man, transcending a humble childhood in South Carolina to become chairman of the Republican Party and America's top power broker. The 2008 documentary *Boo-*

gie Man: The Lee Atwater Story portrays him as a man without strong personal convictions; it's suggested that he could have very well joined the Democratic Party had he not wanted to rebel against the pervasiveness of liberalism in late-'60s youth culture. He wound up joining the Republicans because he felt that the GOP's dearth of young voices could help him advance through the ranks more quickly. He was correct.

Atwater's passion wasn't conservatism, however, it was music. As a white teenager growing up in the South, he played guitar in a rock band called the Upsetters Revue and was good enough to get gigs on his own backing up soul great Percy Sledge. Atwater was especially partial to the blues, and as his political career flourished, he leveraged his connections to meet and even jam with blues legends. In 1990, not long enough after he helped George H. W. Bush win the White House and secured his chairmanship of the Republican Party, Atwater recorded a not wholly terrible blues album, *Red Hot & Blue*, that included guest stars B. B. King, Isaac Hayes, Carla Thomas, and Sam Moore. Atwater was also the architect of Bush's inaugural ceremony, which featured a galaxy of blues and soul luminaries, including Bo Diddley, Eddie Floyd, and William Bell. (The concert was so well regarded among blues fans that it was released on DVD twenty-five years later.) When Atwater was named to the board of trustees at Howard University, he publicly vowed to launch a blues festival at the historically black school.

A 1989 *New York Times* profile describes an encounter with Atwater thusly:

> His guitar was a gift from Ron Wood of the Rolling Stones—a souvenir of Atwater's gala blues celebration at

a Presidential inaugural ball. Drinking beer straight from the pitcher, sweat pouring down his face, Atwater apologizes for going home so early, but the St. Patrick's Day Parade is just seven hours away and he is the grand marshal. His final number is a repeat of his opener: Eddie Taylor's "Bad Boy." "I'm bad, I'm bad," cries the man who masterminded George Bush's 1988 Presidential campaign, "I'm the worst you ever had."

"*Animal House* was not a movie for Lee Atwater," the *Times* profile concludes. "It was autobiography." That's right: this side of Lee Atwater was lewd, crude, and totally rude in the most awesome way imaginable. But the guy who played guitar, dug Jimmy Reed, and drank beer from the pitcher did not make his mark on American life, as the other Atwater did. During the 1988 presidential campaign, *that* Atwater was responsible for engineering the infamous Willie Horton commercial—which not so subtly suggested that Democratic presidential candidate Michael Dukakis was to blame for a black furloughed prisoner's kidnapping and assaulting of a young couple. That Lee Atwater, in a *Life* magazine profile published not long before he died of a brain tumor, was moved to apologize to Dukakis for saying that the Democrat would "make Willie Horton his running mate."

By then Atwater had been widely pilloried for routinely utilizing coded racial language and imagery in campaigns. The inaugural concert was subsequently derided for its cognitive dissonance; Atwater was celebrating black culture after winning the election on the back of scary black-skinned caricature. Atwater's dream of gifting the students of Howard University with a blues festival was also met with incredulous hostility. The student body protested his involvement with the school, and Atwater resigned from the board.

"Spending an extended period of time in his company, one begins to wonder whether there are, in fact, two Lee Atwaters occupying the same body," the *Times* observed. "The first Lee Atwater is every inch a political operative. A visionary, ruthless strategist, Atwater has risen to the top of a cutthroat business by working harder, doing more research, incorporating more sources and, when necessary, cutting more throats than the competition. . . . The second Lee Atwater is a true-blue American archetype: a fun-loving, hell-raising Dixie party animal."

By all accounts, Lee Atwater genuinely loved music played predominantly by black artists. But his music fandom had no discernible impact on his work any more than his well-known affection for Tabasco sauce did. The blues was entertainment for Atwater; when it came time to run campaigns, he put it aside and did whatever was necessary to win. Atwater won because he recognized how easy it is to divide people into opposing camps, whether it's left and right, blue and red, or Team Natalie and Team Toby.

The Dixie Chicks separated from country music in the early aughts for the same reason I avoided the genre completely. When I was still ensconced in my judgmental music-geek phase, the extent of my country-music knowledge consisted solely of plaid-shirt-wearing miserablists such as Jay Farrar and Will Oldham and old-timers such as Johnny Cash and Hank Williams Sr. Any joker who knows nothing about country music can still appear to be moderately informed about the genre by pledging allegiance to Johnny and Hank. It's like the millions of college students who pretend to be reggae fans by purchasing *Legend* by Bob Marley.

This is not to say that I don't really love Johnny and Hank. But back then I ascribed them a moral purity that was beyond all reason. Not only did I believe they were better than the artists who got played on country radio, but I also felt they were more righteous and, above all, more authentic.

Authenticity matters a lot to people when they're young and sort of dumb. I got turned around on the subject years ago when I interviewed the great punk journalist Legs McNeil. I was doing a story on mall-punk goofs Good Charlotte and contacted McNeil in the hope that he would give me a funny quote that dressed them down. But he didn't do that. He did the opposite. McNeil's point was that it isn't his (or my) job to tell people who like something not to like it based on some contrived personal standard. "Punk is whatever fourteen-year-olds say is punk," he said.

He was right—about punk and a lot of other things. Who am I to determine what is and isn't country music? Country music is whatever the country music audience says it is.

If I had bothered to listen to the artists I was broadly dismissing, I would've known that the Dixie Chicks actually did sound a lot like the classic country music I claimed to be standing up for. "Wide Open Spaces," "Cowboy Take Me Away," "Travelin' Soldier"—these are all gorgeous, homemade slices of Americana.

My distaste for Toby Keith was more informed—I covered two of his concerts when I worked for my hometown newspaper in the early aughts. Keith was one of the biggest stars in popular music at the time, but country stars are beholden to small markets like the one where I lived, in northeastern

Wisconsin—a place where country radio wields outsize influence. I attended those shows as a conscientious objector, holding my pen and notepad and using them as a torch and pitchfork to scare off enemy combatants. I was a blue-state liberal living in the midst of red-state territory. It didn't matter that I had grown up there or that I had far more in common with the other concert attendees than I had points of contention. I could not allow myself to like Toby Keith, because in my mind he represented a war and a presidential administration I strenuously opposed.

But here's the thing: Somewhere in the middle of your second Toby Keith concert, you get softened up. You begin to wonder: How different are we, Toby and I? After all, in the weeks and months and even years after 9/11, it seemed as though I spent most of my nights in bars. I watched victims pulled from the wreckage of the World Trade Center while downing pint-size Beam and Cokes and losing to my friend Nate at pool. When we invaded Iraq, I was at a bowling alley, getting wasted on dollar beers. I fancied myself a sensitive, left-wing, antiwar sort of person, but I was living an "I Love This Bar" lifestyle.

I liked the Dixie Chicks and related to Toby Keith, but for years I didn't realize it because my own preconceptions wouldn't let me. But I got over that. I'm better now, and I hope to be better still.

ACKNOWLEDGMENTS

Writing an acknowledgments page for your first book is like sending out wedding invitations: There are people you *have to* include, people you *should* include, and lots of people you *want* to include but can't because how the hell are you going to fit them all inside the same banquet hall? This page is a frustratingly small banquet hall.

This book would not have been possible without my agent, Anthony Mattero, the only person who ever decided to work with me because I'm a Counting Crows fan. (My love of the Adam Duritz songbook usually ends relationships, not starts them.) I'm also eternally grateful to my editor, Malin von Euler-Hogan, for her belief in this project, her hard work in seeing it through, and her tolerance of my criticism of Conan O'Brien and Christina Aguilera.

Writing a book can be very lonely, so kind and patient consiglieres are vital for maintaining sanity. The following people provided invaluable insight and support when I needed it: Chuck Klosterman, Shea Serrano, Dave Holmes, Steve Gorman, Jeff Weiss, Sean Fennessey, Mark Lisanti, Timothy Showalter, Bob Mehr, Ian Cohen, and Mike Powell. My most trusted consultant was the nicest man in rock criticism, Rob

Sheffield, who was always available to read my latest chapter and whose enthusiasm for the book was restorative.

I want to thank the people who have hired me over the years. Ed Berthiaume hooked me up with my first paycheck as a writer, for a review of U2's *Zooropa*, when I was fifteen. Seven years later, he hired me again as a features reporter at the *Post-Crescent*. Josh Modell made my dream come true when he hired me to edit the Milwaukee edition of the *A.V. Club*, and then he promoted me to national music editor. Dan Kois kindly got me in touch with Mark Lisanti, who gave me my first assignment for *Grantland*. Bill Simmons and Dan Fierman later brought me on full-time.

The following albums were essential for inspiring me during the writing of this book: Elton John's *Goodbye Yellow Brick Road* and Kurt Vile's *Wakin on a Pretty Daze*.

Thank you to my power trio of siblings: Paul, Breanna, and Erin. Thank you to my fabulous in-laws: Fred and Mary; Ang, Matt, and Moses; Jonathan and Michelle; and the spouse patrol, Margaret and John. Thank you to my mom for raising me and always being there and teaching me to love the Packers.

I'm lucky to have so many wonderful friends, family members, coworkers, and confidants that have made me the person I am. Many of you are mentioned—though not always named, mostly for your benefit—in this book. I thank you all.

This book, like everything else in my life, is for Val and Hen.

INDEX

ABOUT THE AUTHOR

Steven Hyden has worked as a writer and editor for *Grantland* and the *A. V. Club*, and his writing has appeared in *Rolling Stone, Pitchfork, Slate,* and *Salon*. He lives in Minnesota.